MATTHEW MORAN

D0084072

BUILDING YOUR
I.T. CAREER

A COMPLETE TOOLKIT
FOR A DYNAMIC CAREER
IN ANY ECONOMY

Building Your I.T. Career: A Complete Toolkit for a Dynamic Career in Any Economy

Copyright© 2013 by Matthew Moran

All rights reserved. No part of this book shall be reproduced, stored in a retrieval system, or transmitted by any means, electronic, mechanical, photocopying, recording, or otherwise, without written permission from the publisher. No patent liability is assumed with respect to the use of the information contained herein. Although every precaution has been taken in the preparation of this book, the publisher and author assume no responsibility for errors or omissions. Nor is any liability assumed for damages resulting from the use of the information contained herein.

ISBN-13: 978-0-7897-4943-7
ISBN-10: 0-7897-4943-2

Library of Congress Cataloging-in-Publication data is on file.

Printed in the United States of America

Second Printing: October 2014

Trademarks

All terms mentioned in this book that are known to be trademarks or service marks have been appropriately capitalized. Pearson IT Certification cannot attest to the accuracy of this information. Use of a term in this book should not be regarded as affecting the validity of any trademark or service mark.

)Warning and Disclaimer

Every effort has been made to make this book as complete and as accurate as possible, but no warranty or fitness is implied. The information provided is on an "as is" basis. The author and the publisher shall have neither liability nor responsibility to any person or entity with respect to any loss or damages arising from the information contained in this book.

Bulk Sales

Pearson IT Certification offers excellent discounts on this book when ordered in quantity for bulk purchases or special sales. For more information, please contact

U.S. Corporate and Government Sales
1-800-382-3419
corpsales@pearsontechgroup.com

For sales outside of the U.S., please contact

International Sales
international@pearsoned.com

Associate Publisher
Dave Dusthimer

Executive Editor
Mary Beth Ray

Senior Development Editor
Christopher Cleveland

Managing Editor
Sandra Schroeder

Senior Project Editor
Tonya Simpson

Copy Editor
Keith Cline

Indexer
Erika Millen

Proofreader
Sarah Kearns

Technical Editor
Ed Tittel

Publishing Coordinator
Vanessa Evans

Interior Designer
Studio Galou

Cover Designer
Mark Shirar

Compositor
Studio Galou

Contents at a Glance

Table of Contents

Part II: Filling Your Toolkit

Part IV: More Options to Build Your Career

About the Author

Matthew Moran is a business coach and technology consultant with more than 20 years of experience. He began his career as a data entry clerk at Blue Cross of California (Anthem). Over the next 6 years, he created a variety of database systems and a large automated document assembly system. The success of this system led to several consulting engagements in the healthcare and legal industries.

His consulting focuses on business-centric application development, with a focus on workflow automation. His clients include Northrop Grumman, HealthNet, Power-one, Maracay Homes, Waste Management, Primerica Financial, and others.

He coaches I.T. departments on concept over process, a business-focused methodology for more proactive and solution-oriented technologies. He also coaches entrepreneurs and small businesses on matters of I.T., content strategies, online presence, and social media.

He is a keynote and workshop presenter, speaking to colleges, professional organizations, and I.T. groups. He is also a songwriter and performer, performing solo and with his band.

He lives in Los Angeles, California, with his youngest daughter and their three dogs.

Acknowledgments

I want to thank my editor, Mary Beth, for seeing enough in my articles to track me down and for patiently listening to all my tangential stories during our phone calls. Thank you for second (and third) chances.

A special thanks to Barbara Lynch, my boss, at Blue Cross. Thank you for putting up with my eccentricities and allowing me to create solutions for you for five years. I learned as much during those years as any time in my life.

To everyone at Pearson, Prentice Hall, and Cisco Press—in particular, Chris Cleveland for saying I was a "good writer." All my bravado and pseudoconfidence stripped away, that is something every writer yearns to hear from an editor.

Thank you to my past employers, clients, mentors, and peers—you have been my best professors. I hope to continue to learn from you for many years to come. Kevin and Lori, thank you for believing I have something to say. I'll keep working on that.

Finally, most of all, thank you to the readers, students, and instructors who read the book, sent me e-mails, asked me questions, and encouraged the new edition. Scott, that means you!

We Want to Hear from You!

As the reader of this book, you are our most important critic and commentator. We value your opinion and want to know what we're doing right, what we could do better, what areas you'd like to see us publish in, and any other words of wisdom you're willing to pass our way.

We welcome your comments. You can email or write to let us know what you did or didn't like about this book—as well as what we can do to make our books better.

Please note that we cannot help you with technical problems related to the topic of this book.

When you write, please be sure to include this book's title and author as well as your name and email address. We will carefully review your comments and share them with the author and editors who worked on the book.

Email: feedback@pearsonitcertification.com

Mail: Dave Dusthimer
            Associate Publisher
            Pearson IT Certification
            800 East 96th Street
            Indianapolis, IN 46240 USA

Reader Services

Visit our website and register this book at www.pearsonitcertification/register for convenient access to any updates, downloads, or errata that might be available for this book.

Introduction

In 2002, I started writing some articles for Power Media Group. During that same time, I occasionally posted on the CramSession.com discussion boards—primarily focusing on the career and job discussions.

The response to my articles and to the posts was extremely positive. In June, I posted a question to the discussion board asking whether anyone would be interested in having me compile my prior posts and articles into a "career toolkit." The response was overwhelming and led to this book.

Who Should Read This Book

This is not a "technical" book. Although this book certainly contains techniques and methods, it's really about personal and professional growth. It is directed at IT professionals—both those who are just entering the field (the newbies) and seasoned veterans who want to advance their career.

No certifications are available to guide you on many of the topics covered in this toolkit. To a large degree, they are adopted into a total working skill set that, to many, seems vague or difficult to internalize and put into practice. Pure technical skills, such as configuring a specific brand of router to perform a function or writing a program to achieve a particular end, are often more easily defined. That's why I have framed the book as a toolkit.

I want you to see the techniques as one more set of skills to adopt in your overall career development program. They are skills, just as your particular technical skills that you will use daily over the course of your career. Similar to the way you adopt new technical skills, use the toolkit to help define those soft skills that you must learn and put to use. The result will be a more well-rounded and complete professional skill set.

How to Use the Toolkit

You can read *Building Your I.T. Career* cover to cover, which is the ideal method for someone who is new to the field, or by topic, to fine-tune an already growing career in the field.

Information is spread throughout the book that might interest or help you. Conceptual ideas that run through the book are emphasized in each of the chapters. If you choose to read through specific topics, take time later to revisit some of the other chapters. You will likely find something of interest there, too.

The chapters include a brief introduction to the topic. At the end of each chapter are action points or key ideas. These help to emphasize ideas you have learned in the chapter.

Although it is important to play to your strength, work on those areas that are a challenge or intimidate you. Mastery of a difficult challenge or skill does wonders for your confidence. This confidence further enhances your ability in your areas of strength.

What Is the Toolkit Approach to Career Development?

The toolkit approach to career development is a holistic, proactive, and ownership-based approach to career development. Whereas other books cover the mechanics of preparing your resumé, writing a cover letter, and even interviewing, this book provides the information to help you plan and create a rewarding career over the long term.

This book does not neglect those important topics, but it expands to include them in an overall assessment and plan of action. Armed with this information, you can begin to plan and implement concrete steps into a complete career development plan.

The approach is planned but agile. Because your desires and interests might change during your career, it is important that you are flexible in overall objectives. However, planning and developing key tools and attitudes are necessary for any career. Also, conceptual knowledge should be, wherever feasible, transferred into any new career path.

The toolkit approach positions you as the primary commodity of your career. This means that you need to create a strong sense of the value you provide and your worth to an organization.

For the career technologist, I go even further. You must view and position yourself as a service company. Your employer is in a very real sense your client. You need to think in terms of personal marketing, service level, and client retention.

This is part of the ownership mindset I want to give your career. You should study and understand your career, just as you would a business. You need to understand the various and changing factors that can and will impact your career in both positive and negative ways.

Most of all, you must be able to make changes when necessary. If elements of your career plan are not working, you need to work to understand why and then take corrective action. It is not enough to say that it is the economy or some other exterior factor. Your career must belong to you.

As with any business, negative events will occur. Your overall career plan should include an understanding that such events will happen. Layoffs transpire, companies are sold, and companies go out of business. Your response to these events cannot be shocked resentment. You have been forewarned. Prepare for these events with the tools presented in this book. It will make them far less traumatic when they do occur.

Most of all, have fun! You will hear this theme throughout the book. Every year, people advance along the path to career stardom. Endeavor to be one of them. Don't accept mediocrity as a career objective; demand more of yourself.

Good luck and happy building!

How This Book Is Organized

Although you can read this book cover to cover, it is designed to be flexible and allow you to easily move between chapters and sections of chapters to cover just the material that you need more work with. The book is divided into five parts, each with several related chapters. The intent is that each part and each chapter builds on the previous one. If you do intend to read them all, the order in the book is an excellent sequence to use.

Part I, "Your Career"—The chapters in Part I give an overview of the career development process and introduce you to the toolkit. Part I includes Chapters 1 through 4, covering the following topics:

- **Chapter 1, "The Toolkit Approach to Career Development"**—This chapter serves as an introduction to the contents of the toolkit and what you should expect to learn. It explains the importance of a comprehensive approach to career building and describes how the toolkit can help you adopt such an approach.

- **Chapter 2, "Career Building Defined"**—This chapter covers the concept of career building versus simply getting a string of jobs. It covers essential ideas to place career building in perspective with the hope of providing you with a framework for pursuing your education, the skills you use, and the relationships you develop. Understanding career building can help you grow your career more rapidly and with greater satisfaction.

- **Chapter 3, "Information Technology: A Great Career"**—With the advent of outsourcing, the notable failures of the dot-com debacle, and a general malaise in the industry, this chapter paints a more balanced picture. The premise is that all those events are largely to be expected and must be viewed for the impact on how you approach your career. Rather than focus on those areas of struggle, the idea is to direct you toward areas of opportunity and how to best recognize them.

- **Chapter 4, "Defining Yourself: Attitudes, Aptitudes, and Desires"**—This chapter explains some ways to better understand what drives you. By understanding those things that you believe are important for your career and professional growth, you can better assess the opportunities that come your way.

Part II, "Filling Your Toolkit"—The chapters in this part are more concerned with the development of key skills and ideas that you will use throughout your career. Part II includes Chapters 5 through 10, covering the following topics:

- **Chapter 5, "Self-Assessment"**—This chapter covers a simple set of techniques to help you assess your performance and attitude. The goal is to provide you with ideas to remedy problems prior to performance reviews. In doing so, you increase your job satisfaction and management's perception of your value.

- **Chapter 6, "Attitude"**—This chapter addresses the critical issue of attitude. It is not meant to provide you with positive encouragement but to provide you with concrete steps to help you improve your attitude. The central theme is to create an attitude of value about the work you perform.

- **Chapter 7, "Communication Skills"**—This chapter covers the critical area of written and verbal communications. It explains how these skills impact your career and provides you with resources and ideas for improvement in both areas.

- **Chapter 8, "Technical Skills"**—This chapter addresses the need for excellent technical skills. More important, it removes the anxiety of learning the "next hot technology" by focusing on strategies for more rapidly learning and adopting new technologies through an understanding of their common elements.

- **Chapter 9, "The Cover Letter"**—This chapter explains the role of your cover letter. It offers a formula for building one that will make a positive impact on a potential employer and tells which key elements to include.

- **Chapter 10, "The Resumé"**—The resumé is the mainstay of your professional marketing tools. It serves as your ambassador to the professional world. This chapter explains how to build one that focuses on the value and strengths you bring to an organization. Whether you are new to the IT field or building a more robust resumé, this chapter can help you.

Part III, "Putting Your Toolkit to Use"—The chapters in this part of the book help you put the various skills and tools from the previous section to use. This is the actual groundwork of the career-building process. Chapters 11 through 17 cover the following topics:

- **Chapter 11, "Breaking In to I.T."**—The entry-level dilemma is the idea that you need experience to get experience. This chapter explains how you can gain valuable experience and jump-start your I.T. career. For the more seasoned professional, this chapter offers some tips on how to move into new areas of I.T. or find technology-related opportunities outside the I.T. department.

- **Chapter 12, "Building an Active Contact List"**—This chapter covers the basics of professional networking. Using the adage, "It's not who you know but who knows you and knows what you know," this chapter discusses the importance of continually building a professional network. It also covers key ideas to help you rapidly build a thriving contact list.

- **Chapter 13, "The Job Search"**—This chapter covers techniques that will result in more rapidly finding a job. It covers how jobs are found and how to locate better opportunities.

- **Chapter 14, "The Interview"**—The interview is the moment of truth for most job seekers. It is the moment that you get to better explain your accomplishments, find out if the opportunity is a good fit, and make a direct impact on the potential employer. This chapter gives some concrete tips for what to look for in an interview and how you can have the greatest impact on your potential employer.

- **Chapter 15, "Salary Negotiations and Employment Agreements"**—This chapter explains how to get the most from your current or potential employer. It provides ideas to help you at the start of the interview and as you get to know your employer more. In addition, it helps you create a vision for what constitutes career growth and advancement for you.

- **Chapter 16, "On-the-Job Promotion"**—This chapter covers why on-the-job advancement is your greatest potential source of job growth. It explains how to maximize your current skills and relationships and turn these into advancement opportunities.

- **Chapter 17, "Your Career and Social Media"**—The growth of social media websites and tools deserves special mention. This chapter explains the proper mindset and methodology in utilizing your social media profiles to enhance and not detract from your career development.

Part IV, "More Options to Build Your Career"—This part covers some ideas to help further your career. These ideas are often overlooked or apply to specific situations. Chapters 18 through 20 cover the following topics:

- **Chapter 18, "Telecommuting"**—This chapter explains the benefits and challenges of working from home. It covers ideas to help you and management come to an effective telecommuting relationship.

- **Chapter 19, "Consulting"**—The consultant has the potential to work on the most exciting projects, create a high salary, and gain incredible respect from his peers and clients. This chapter explains key concepts and ideas for those who are interested in the consulting life. In addition, it covers the importance of marketing and the vital need for a sound business mindset.

- **Chapter 20, "Management"**—This chapter explains the skills that are crucial to moving into management. It covers ways to begin using the skills prior to being placed in a management situation and how to assume the role before you assume the position.

Part V, "The Value-Added Toolkit"—The chapters in this part teach some specific value-added skills that you can use throughout the life of your career. These ideas add a dynamic dimension to the career-building process and involve a greater effort and a more comprehensive skill set. Chapters 21 through 28 cover the following topics:

- **Chapter 21, "Making Yourself Indispensable"**—The ideas and techniques in this chapter apply universally to many careers. Specific ideas for the technologist are also covered. This chapter demonstrates ways to become as valuable as possible and how that can translate into career advancement.

- **Chapter 22, "Concept Over Process"**—This chapter covers what is both a mindset and an approach to project development. By focusing on strong conceptual understanding of your employer or client's business, this chapter explains how to build solutions that have incredible value and focus on the solution, not the specific technologies used. In addition, this chapter explains how this mindset and approach help in the adoption and learning of new technologies.

- **Chapter 23, "The Role of Mentoring"**—This chapter explains the need for strong mentors in your life and career. It explains the role that a mentor takes and how you can benefit by serving as a mentor, too.

- **Chapter 24, "Career Coaching"**—Expanding upon the idea of both having and being a mentor, this chapter explores the benefits of a personal career coach. It also discusses how you can take your career knowledge, share it with others, and become a paid career coach.

- **Chapter 25, "Financial Control"**—This chapter explains the need for financial control and its impact on your career. It discusses how financial stress can reduce your effectiveness on the job and how financial struggles reduce your ability to pursue good opportunities. It also provides some tools for controlling your finances.

- **Chapter 26, "A Professional Blog"**—A well-written blog containing valuable knowledge for the reader, is an excellent career development tool. This chapter explores ways you can start blogging and specifically discusses WordPress, a free, feature-rich, blogging and content management tool.

- **Chapter 27, "12 Weeks To Profitable Consulting"**—The chapter takes the information that was started in Chapter 19 and creates a 12-week plan of action you can put into place to begin consulting part time or full time.

- **Chapter 28, "Be Proactive! Be Positive! Add Value! Share Opportunity!"**—More than simply "rah rah, you can do it" platitudes, this chapter offers some perspective to help you navigate both challenging times and times of dynamic career growth.

- **Appendix, "My Reading List"**—This appendix describes some of the books and other reading material I find important, both technical books and more broadly applied books on leadership, creativity, and marketing.

Online Supplements

The first edition of this book shipped with a CD-ROM. However, I continue to add and adjust tools from the CD-ROM as necessary. For that reason, I've established www.ITCareerToolkit.com as a dynamic resource for this book. I will be uploading new tools, blog entries, and providing topics of discussion at the IT Career Toolkit website.

You can find updated versions of tools from the original CD plus many new downloads there.

Developing a Comprehensive Set of Career Tools

For many professionals, particularly those who want to break into or develop their careers in information technology (I.T.), there is a large and growing frustration. Economic changes—in particular, the bursting dot-com bubble and the more recent worldwide economic challenges—have left many struggling. These people have an inkling that opportunities still exist in technology careers, but they are having difficulty taking the next step. *Building Your I.T. Career* has been compiled to bring you, the technology professional, a message that both motivates and educates. This book contains vital information and proven methods that can make a huge impact on your career success.

CHAPTER 1

The Toolkit Approach to Career Development

As someone who has spent many years working in the I.T. field, I place great emphasis on providing actual value. I did the same when starting this project and during its production. In effect, while writing each morning, I asked myself why I was undertaking this project. Why am I, in fact, putting other projects on the back burner to pursue this? I have worked to create a comprehensive and realistic set of tools to help you achieve success in your career-building efforts.

The reason stems from my experience as an I.T. professional, employee, employer, consultant, writer, and self-proclaimed pundit of technical solutions. Over the past several years, I have witnessed a number of promising technology professionals thrive. I have had the pleasure of working on projects with people I consider the best and the brightest in their fields.

I watched with excitement as their careers grew. Just as often, however, I watched as good technologists with excellent skills struggled to advance in their careers.

I'm a people watcher by nature. I find the human aspect of any endeavor of life to be the most exciting. People, as an object of study, are fascinating. I analyze the careers of those whom I would emulate in my own growth and those whose careers have floundered. I have sought to discover patterns in both groups—the successfully growing professionals and those who struggled.

Much of what I have witnessed and analyzed is familiar. Most of the principles of successful career growth relate to "life management" and are not specific to the technology field. From Napoleon Hill to Stephen Covey, the attitudes and skills of success have been studied and extolled. The information is both well known and available; it broadly addresses life and the individual's approach to it.

Don't forget luck! Yes, as much as the die-hard advocates of steering your own course and taking control of your destiny might want to deny it, luck certainly plays a vital part. Chance meetings and unforeseen opportunities can arise and lift an individual through dramatic professional growth from time to time.

Certainly, some individuals experience more luck than others throughout their lives; however, all career builders do, at some point, experience luck. With this as the case, my goal is to prepare you to take advantage of that eventual lucky situation. Author Denis Waitley stated that *LUCK* is an acronym for *Laboring Under Correct Knowledge*. I believe this is true. In relation to career building, this means striving to build your career with the best information and tools available. In this way, when a lucky situation presents itself, you are best prepared to capitalize on it.

That is the objective of this project and book. Simply put, this book provides you with the tools necessary to create opportunity and take advantage of those opportunities that arise.

What you, the reader, will discover is that you already know most of this, or you at least will find the information sensible in its simplicity. This book has no secret formulas, no catch phrases to lift you out of professional obscurity, no single technique to separate you from the masses of other professional career builders, and no special skills to master. The information is easy to understand and can be adopted, with more or less proficiency, by anyone.

However, a word of caution: Although the information I convey is simple to understand and master, its application is anything but. *Simple* does not necessarily equate to easy. Applying what you learn requires work and practice. More important, as with anything of long-term consequence and value, it requires diligence.

At the opposite ends of this spectrum are two types of individuals:

- The individuals who, when building and applying their toolkit, meet with success immediately. Their career is launched with relative ease by being at the right place at the right time. For these people, the danger is an abandonment of the toolkit approach.

- The individuals who, when applying the information and skills from the toolkit, do not experience the success they would like in a time frame that suits them. Perhaps they see or hear of others who meet with immediate and tangible benefits or career growth without applying a special approach. They also might abandon the toolkit approach.

For both types of individuals, my admonition is to stay focused on the long-term objective of building a well-rounded career. As you will see emphasized throughout the rest of this book, your career is not synonymous with landing a job, no matter how good. Your career is made up of a series of decisions over a long period of time. Therefore, immediate success or short-term frustration is of minor importance.

I have coached with predictable results the careers of several individuals. I have watched as relatively simple methods, philosophies, and hard work have resulted in dramatic career success and the success of the projects for which they were charged. I discovered over this time that, although I enjoy defining and implementing high-tech solutions, I garner even greater satisfaction in watching the career growth of those with whom I work.

I have presented and written several pieces directed at technology professionals, particularly with assisting them at furthering their careers in some tangible way. Many of them asked me to write this information down. Several suggested I formalize my ideas into a book.

This book is the embodiment of that work.

Over the past several years, I have watched many technologists flounder in the area of career development. Some of these men and women I know to be extremely effective in their utilization of technology. For a number of reasons, however, their careers have faltered. Some even chose to leave the field and find work in other professions. Sometimes I felt this was truly a loss, both for the individual and for the industry.

This notion was emphasized during a recent conversation I had with a programmer I know. I worked with him several times over the past 7 years. He is both diligent and technically proficient, but he spent the past 3 years struggling in his career.

He recently told me he was pursuing another line of work. His desire was to remain in I.T., but he was burnt out and dejected. As we discussed his recent challenges, it was apparent that his approach to career development in general, and his perception of his role as a technologist in particular, was ineffective. I am convinced that he can have a rewarding, growing career in I.T. if that is his desire, but it will require the adoption of new ideas—ideas that he largely ignored during the past I.T. boom but that I cover in this book.

It is not my goal to convince people to remain in an industry or career for which they do not possess drive or passion. Instead, I hope to create both hope and a plan that matches the drive and passion they already have.

The I.T. field and individual technologists suffered through a correction in the early 2000s. This correction, the causes of which are defined more clearly in Chapter 2, "Career Building Defined," stifled the I.T. industry and individual growth. Since then, a series of financial upheavals, ebbs, and flows has caused additional uncertainty. Industries and individuals suffer, often needlessly, through corrections and financial turmoil. However, regardless of economic climate or industry correction, both boom times and financial challenges present opportunities for the savvy professional to grow his or her career.

The I.T. field is maturing. As it does so, the normal growing pains will make themselves known. For the astute professional, however, even times of correction and challenge provide opportunity.

The opportunities in I.T. will still be abundant, but they will be more refined and specific in their reach. This requires I.T. professionals to be equally refined and specific in their approach to building a technology career. I.T. professionals must know where to look for opportunity, what it looks like, and what steps to take to maximize their potential in taking advantage of the opportunity.

Justifying the Need for an I.T. Toolkit

I have analyzed my career and those of my peers, some of whom have met success and others who have not. In addition, I have read articles, previewed career fairs, and discussed the topic with I.T. employers and employees alike. Over time, I developed a set of techniques and ideologies geared to assist technologists in wading safely through the myriad options and questions they have regarding career choices. I codified these options and questions and placed them into this toolkit.

To understand why a toolkit is important, consider the following situations.

Recently, a client asked about my choice of a particular technology to complete a task. The client had been informed that a more powerful technology was available. I likened the client's concern to an analogy I use often when addressing such a question.

I asked which of two tools was more powerful: a jackhammer or a standard handheld hammer. Certainly, the jackhammer is the more powerful of the two, which the client acknowledged. I then asked whether the client would use a jackhammer when hanging a picture. The client, of course, could see where I was going with this.

A more powerful technology is not necessarily the most appropriate or superior technology for a given application.

In the same way, many technologists, even those who have met with some degree of success, rely on either pure technical skills or on the certifications and degrees that they have acquired. As you probably already know (and will read more about), technical skills, certifications, and degrees are effective tools; however, they do not make up a full-featured toolkit.

In another example, an auto mechanic would be considered foolish if he carried only a screwdriver and 12-mm wrench. In the same way, the career builder would be imprudent if he relied only on a couple of career-building tools. *Building Your I.T. Career*, although geared toward technologists, is a package that can easily be adapted to other industries.

I titled this book a *toolkit* to convey the idea of a complete package of information and techniques that a person can use over the life of his career.

Many of the ideas and techniques put in place here can be used, without modification, in other professions. Although some sections within this book are specifically technology related, even these contain concepts that are transferable in their application.

My hope is that you can apply the information in this book toward your career in I.T.. Why? Because I believe that for the person who loves working with technology and enjoys the challenge of rapid change and constant learning, no career choice offers so much.

Whether you have been looking to enter the field of technology or have been working in the field for some time, this toolkit can benefit you. Look past the doom and gloom that permeates the discussion boards and ignore momentarily the naysayers claiming saturation in the field.

The I.T. boom is continuing. Employers will continue to look at candidates walking through their door. The need for comprehensive skills is great. Your ability to master a comprehensive skill set (to fill your toolkit) will determine your ability to take advantage of the coming opportunities.

This toolkit will make that goal a reality.

Actions & Ideas

1. Quickly assess your career up to this point.

2. Are you excited about your future prospects? Why? Why not?

3. Have you have taken actions that have hindered advancement? Write these down.

4. Upon reading this chapter, do you get a sense of excitement about your career? Why? Why not?

5. Have you relied too much on one skill or talent at the exclusion of others?

6. What is your greatest strength?

7. What is your greatest weakness?

EXPAND YOUR TOOLKIT

Remember to visit the book's website at http://www.ITCareerToolkit.com for supplemental and ongoing advice, tips, and data relevant to this chapter.

What Is a Career, and How Do You Build One?

The planning and execution of an ongoing career development strategy is something that most professionals largely ignore. Although everyone would agree that planning is an important element in reaching an objective, for many, career development often appears random and haphazard.

This chapter explains why career building is vital. The toolkit approach to career building helps you step away from your current job or work situation and lets you define broadly applied goals, skills, and tasks to move your professional life forward. In addition, it attempts to strip away your fear of making an "incorrect" career choice by helping you develop an understanding of a long-term career perspective versus a job-to-job analysis of success and failure.

CHAPTER 2

Career Building Defined

There are misconceptions about what constitutes a career. For many, a career is simply a string of successive jobs—typically within the same industry or vocational area. I want to challenge this idea and offer a broader definition. My definition, when embraced, opens you to greater flexibility and control over your career. If understood, this definition removes some of the anxiety associated with those times in which you are not working or advancing in the way or with the speed that you expect.

I define a *career* in the following fashion:

> A career is the ongoing development of skills, attitudes, and relationships that lead you into and through various professional positions and objectives.

What this means is that your career occurs both when you are working and when you are not. You are always involved in your career and its development. This understanding is important (and should be motivating) because you can begin to find value in those activities that occur outside of your job or when you are not working. This helps you realize opportunities to advance skills and relationships that can bring value to your career regardless of the position you hold now or will hold in the future. Hopefully, it prompts you to be more aware and become more proactive in your overall career development.

You will notice throughout this book that I refer to *career building*. I want the idea of building a career to be ingrained into your mind. Careers and buildings are similar in that they do not normally happen by accident. I use an analogy of a builder whom you have hired to add a room to your house.

If the rhetorical builder were to arrive at your house with a bunch of wood, paint, and stucco but no plans, you would justifiably be concerned. If he walked up to the side of your house and began nailing boards together in some haphazard fashion, you would be certain the project was doomed.

Now, it might be that this builder is so accomplished that his innate skills provide him with everything he needs to complete the project without planning. It could work out that what is produced works in harmony with everything else on the house. But I don't think you would count on that.

And yet, with careers, we often do just that. We take one job after another in a particular field (perhaps), but with no plan on what our career should look like when we are finished. It has been my experience that individuals plan their vacations more carefully than they do their careers. But unless you are one of the wealthy elite, you likely will spend much more time working in your career than you will taking vacations.

Many believe that this type of planning is too rigid. Some technologists claim it is impossible for them to know which area of technology they want pursue or what direction they want to take their careers without some experimentation. Don't worry, I'm not suggesting that you not experiment and try different roles or technologies. In fact, I advocate quite the opposite.

Of all people, I am at heart spontaneous. I fully understand the dilemma of the question, "What do you want to be when you grow up?" I was always amazed when children answered the question with complete assurance of their life's ambition. I, however, still claim I don't know what I want to be when I grow up.

I am not implying that your objective in technology necessary be tied to some ultimate unchanging goal. Nor am I against quickly adopting a new course of action. In fact, with the rapid and constant changes in technology, this is one of the benefits of the field. The fact that technology opens the door and allows for change to new skills and avenues for your career makes it exciting and fun.

In fact, let's go back to the example of the builder. For those who have watched or taken part in a building project, you know that changing plans are a constant. Builders get weeks into a project only to have the owner or architect suddenly introduce new plans and features. Add a window here, a door here, and so on. The builder must adopt the new elements into his existing structure and make it look as though it was always part of the plan. Sometimes the builder even has to tear down some of what was built to move forward.

You can do the same with your career. New technologies, opportunities, and desires force you to continually reevaluate your career direction. You must be flexible and adaptable. Fortunately, the constant change of technology allows for this.

My goal is to leave you with some skills that transcend the changes in technology. You can use the skills outlined here whether your career takes you from programmer to analyst to manager to consultant or to business owner. In fact, the adoption of these skills will make such transitions much easier and less stressful.

The Danger of a Tool-Driven Mindset

Knowing that transferable skills can help you quickly advance in any field should reduce the stress associated with such changes. Many professionals I've spoken to express a fear that their field of technology will one day be phased out. They worry that the skills they have built and counted on will become obsolete, forcing them to learn new skills and setting their career back to entry level.

There is a sense that this could occur. If a technology professional is locked into a stagnant or dying technology, refusing to learn newer tools, he will find himself in a precarious position. This, however, is due largely to a mindset that I refer to as the *tool-driven mindset*. You can understand it best by looking back at the builder.

If a builder were to show up for a project with only a hammer and a screwdriver, claiming he was a "hammer and screwdriver builder," you would probably question his sanity. The tools do not define the worker. And yet, how many times do you hear programmers, for example, claim that they are a particular type of programmer?

"I'm a VB programmer." "I'm a C# programmer." "I'm a .NET programmer." These phrases and other similar ones are indications of a tool-driven mindset. I address this idea briefly in Chapter 3, "Information Technology: A Great Career." Later in Chapter 22, "Concept Over Process," I discuss how to change from being process driven to concept driven, which is critical to the growing career.

You must view your career with an overall plan. Such a plan might involve methods more than actual results—particularly at the beginning of your career. You might include a period of fact finding and soul searching in your career plan. In fact, I recommend it.

Over the course of your career, continue this type of assessment. One challenge that veterans of any field face is the sudden realization that their interests have suddenly shifted. Because of their belief that they are too far into their career to change, however, they plod along with little passion. This ends up becoming a self-defeating and demoralizing approach because the employees' performance decreases with their interest and desire.

Good career coaches understand that careers can be repurposed in much shorter time than the average employee believes. This is particularly true if you find an area that really interests you.

Doing so ensures that you bring your best to the job. You will have a much greater interest in the developments in your industry, and you will have much greater job performance.

Better performance, in general, leads to better value. The employee who provides better value in turn receives higher compensation.

Make sure, as your career progresses, that you assess your overall enjoyment and interest. This does not mean that you should immediately drop a given career direction because you read about a job you believe you would like more.

Although I believe you have to make concrete career decisions, you would do well to carefully assess whether something that interests you is a career or a hobby and whether it is likely to keep your interest for an extended period of time.

Also, if you find something that you have great interest for, is there a transitional career route that lets you leverage the bulk of your developed skills?

A Job Is Not a Career

Understand that no single job or career choice defines or predicts ultimate failure or success. If viewed properly, even those career choices that don't work out bring value to your overall career success. The more you learn about yourself—your aptitudes and desires—the greater your chance for satisfaction over the life of your career.

Having methods that help you transfer existing experience and knowledge into new areas, and an understanding of the tools to help you rapidly develop both expertise and contacts in the field, will provide you with the freedom to change your plans. You will feel comfortable knowing that if you decide to alter your career path after 10 years in one direction, those 10 years have not been lost.

Even if you decide suddenly to leave network engineering and move into multimedia presentation, the skills provided in the toolkit and the perspective offered will make the transition possible.

As stated earlier, no job makes a career, and no job breaks a career.

Perspectives on Career Development: Careers Are Nonlinear

One of the more damaging and career-stifling ideas is that careers are linear in nature. That is, you progress neatly from job to job, with incremental increases in pay, responsibility, and title, until you reach a theoretical apex.

Careers are far less structured. In a few cases, someone's career might take on a linear feel or appearance. However, for the huge majority, careers are more free form. They have tangible substance, in the form of a plan and long-term objectives; however, they necessarily take twists and turns along the way.

It is important to understand that this is the case for a few reasons:

- To reduce your anxiety when something *unexpected* happens. For some, unexpected career changes often produce a feeling of being left behind or of having been removed from their career path. Here are two things to consider:

    a. You are always in your career. Even when you are out of work, you are in your career.

    b. As stated earlier, no job makes a career, and no job breaks a career.

    Often, these detours allow the development of critical skills or key relationships that you would not have been exposed to otherwise.

- Understanding that careers are nonlinear allows you to make job/career change decisions more easily. You can look at an opportunity with a less biased view. Your assessment of opportunity can be squarely considered based on the opportunity—not based on a mythical career path.

Perspectives on Career Development: A Working Plan Makes Tedious or Unrewarding Jobs Bearable

This is a critical idea. If you have a plan and are enacting it, your ability to survive and even strive in more tedious jobs is greatly increased. Imagine working in a fast-food restaurant as a clerk. (This is easy for me because I did exactly that in my youth.) If you knew you had to work there for 2 years, how would you perform, and what would your psyche be?

Now imagine that you are informed that if you can learn key skills at this job, at the end of 2 years, you will be paid $5 million. How would you perform then? How would it impact your attitude and your ability to extract career-enhancing jobs even while at that job?

A plan that is being acted upon makes the tedious or less desirable job more than bearable. This perspective will have you actively looking for ways to improve yourself in preparation for your total career.

Conclusion

Take the time to develop your toolkit. View it as a total package that is part of a complete career. Take the time to assess where you are with each facet of the toolkit. What are your areas of deficiency? What are your strengths?

Let this understanding drive the choices you make to help you become a well-rounded professional. It will give you the confidence of knowing you are firmly in control of your career and that you can grow in your career with any changes that occur in the technology industry.

Actions & Ideas

1. Before reading this chapter, did you tie career growth to pay with your most recent job?

2. What is your idea about this now?

3. What does the word or idea *career* mean to you?

4. Write down your ideal career. (Be realistic.) What is the most important skill you need to develop to achieve it?

5. Do you have a less than ideal job now, or have you had one in the recent past?

6. Based on this chapter, what was your perspective of that job, and how could it have been improved?

7. How did you or could you have drawn positive skills or ideas from that job?

EXPAND YOUR TOOLKIT

Remember to visit the book's website at http://www.ITCareerToolkit.com for supplemental and ongoing advice, tips, and data relevant to this chapter.

The Right Time to Build a Career in I.T. Is Now!

Whether you are new to technology or have been in the field for some time, the recent financial malaise, like the dot-com bubble of several years ago, might have left you scrambling for answers.

What happened?

Is information technology (I.T.) a good career choice?

Is the industry in decline, or do opportunities still exist?

Rest assured that I.T. is and will remain one of the most dynamic and rewarding careers available. In fact, the recent changes in the industry are cause for celebration—forcing the industry to better define its objectives and allowing true innovators and professionals to create dynamic career growth.

CHAPTER 3

Information Technology:
A Great Career

Information technology (I.T.), once a hotbed of easy employment and rapid advancement, has become an enigma of sorts. To be sure, the need for skilled I.T. workers remains high. Companies are still building information infrastructures, applications, and web technologies. But thousands of I.T. workers seem to be caught in a vortex of declining salaries, career indecision, and a more difficult job market.

Reports seem to say that thousands of I.T. jobs remain unfilled, yet job postings remain unanswered, resumés sent in response to newspaper ads are unrequited, and day by day, we become jaded to the opportunity that just a short time ago seemed so commanding.

In addition, a dilemma largely unknown in the mid to late 1990s has reared its ugly head: experience requirements. During the technology boom of the late 1990s, when the convergence of the Internet as a business medium and the most robust economic growth of the past 50 years caused an unprecedented demand for technology workers, experience became an unrealistic expectation.

The need for technology workers far outstripped the physical bodies who worked in the industry. This gave rise to entire new industries hoping to cash in on the I.T. skills gap. Boot camp training, CD-based curriculum, and web-based training tools promised to provide the skills needed to build a career in I.T. And for some, it worked—at least for a time.

However, the dot-com revolution gave way to a more tempered and realistic approach to the adoption of new technology. Dramatic technology project failures and the loss of millions of dollars preceded a correction in the I.T. job market. More important, companies changed their requirements regarding technology professionals.

Having a degree or certification has quickly become secondary to your experience.

The term *paper-certified,* meaning an individual who has technical certifications but little hands-on or practical experience, has entered the employer's vocabulary. In fact, certifications, once highly demanded, have given rise to skeptical analysis. An "Oh, you're certified; I won't hold it against you!" attitude has risen among prospective employers who were either directly burned or have heard the horror stories of CCNAs who could not perform the most rudimentary tasks and MCSEs who could not bring up a server or correctly install and support the most basic of business applications. The same holds true for certifications in project management and other areas.

Where before the certified professional received daily calls from headhunters, busy stealing talent from one company to place at another, the phone remains silent, and many technology workers are faced with shrinking salaries and no longer receive calls touting the latest opportunity. The face of I.T. career advancement has taken on a distinct squeamish pallor.

All of this gives rise to a compelling question:

Is I.T. still a good career choice?

The answer: A resounding *yes.*

The first thing to understand is that I.T. is neither a new field nor a declining field. In fact, it remains one of the greatest career choices both in demand and opportunity. The fact remains that the need for I.T. talent continues to grow, and a good number of technology jobs remain unfilled.

Few fields offer the wide variety of career paths, opportunities for promotion, and sheer enjoyment from fun and challenging work. And, if past experience is an indication of future potential, it's only going to get better.

However, the "correction" experienced over the past few years is simply a normal reaction in a maturing industry, bringing it closer in line with other professions and careers. The idea that someone leaving school with a technology certification should earn 30 percent to 40 percent more than his peers in another nontechnical industry is unrealistic. And yet, this is the complaint. I hear of people complaining that they cannot find work in the $50K to $70K a year range after gaining their certifications. Of course they can't!

I realize that radio advertisements still dangle the "big money" carrot, claiming that after you take their courses and have your certifications, you can earn $50, $60, $70 thousand, or more, right out of school. Yes, and if you take this little pill, you will lose all your extra weight and develop the body of your dreams without exercise while eating everything you want.

As a budding I.T. professional, you need to have a realistic idea of the market. More important, you must understand the steps necessary to advance your career as rapidly as possible. The entry-level dilemma of experience needed to gain the experience needed is simple to solve. However, your career moves after you are in the field will have a much greater impact on both the speed and level to which you rise in your profession.

I.T. is and will remain an incredible opportunity for the career-minded professional. It has historically offered, and will continue to offer, rewards more readily than many other careers. More important, it is a *production/results-based* career. That is to say, in the final analysis, career advancement depends largely on production rather than on tenure and formal education.

That should be cause for excitement. What that means is that your career potential in I.T. falls largely on your shoulders. You are in control. Few other careers offer as much opportunity for results-based advancement as I.T.. In fact, the trend is moving down this path right now. This is why, on discussion boards and in conversations, the talk has shifted from how to pass the next exam in your current certification track to how to acquire needed experience. More precisely, how do you get the necessary experience in a catch-22 situation?

I regularly hear complaints about the difficultly of breaking into the field. "I need experience to get the job, but the entry-level position requires more experience than anyone in an entry-level position would have." Although in actuality this might be true in some cases, it is important to understand the employer's perspective. Rest assured that, in most cases, a prospective employer is not posting a position with the idea that no one can fill it. The employer is typically in need of a skill set. More important, he is in need of a solution. Most companies would not take on the effort of posting, collecting, and reviewing resumés, and conducting interviews with dozens of candidates or more, if they were not interested in eventually filling that position.

Employers are looking for someone to do something. It is your job to convince employers that you are the person who can do that needed something, and that they should pay you a decent wage to do so.

The chapters in Part II, "Filling Your Toolkit," discuss how to do this with resumés, interviews, and other things.

Why I.T. Is a Great Career

With a job market apparently teeming with people but suffering from scant opportunities, it would appear that I.T. has seen its day as a great career. I hear from technologists who have paid thousands for certifications and spent months looking for their first opportunity. Many are now second-guessing their decision to become technologists. The promise of unrestricted growth, high pay, and opportunities has given way to a somber realization—they cannot find a job.

Perhaps the preceding description fits you. Perhaps you entered I.T., excited about the prospects of attaining success in a lucrative field, and one that has the byproduct of respect, too. But now you worry that you have made the wrong choice—that you've been had. If that is the case, I want to give you some hope.

I do not believe that the career prospects from I.T. are dead. In fact, I believe that the current status of the market makes sense in the context of the past boom, and it is cause for guarded optimism, if not outright celebration.

Why? Because I.T. remains an incredible career for the same reasons I started down that path in the 1980s. The primary reasons are these:

- Options
- Performance-based advancement
- Opportunities for continuous learning
- Pay and perks

I address each of these in the sections that follow.

Options

Options. That one word might be a defining reason why I.T. is so compelling as a career choice. It is a vast field. In fact, it is segmenting daily into new and growing areas of specialty, including the following:

- Multimedia
- Network operations
- Application development
- Web technologies

- System analysis

- Database administration

- Security analysis

This segmentation is a great predictor of opportunity. Companies are looking for expertise in a number of areas. Each area represents the need for talent, whether you are an in-house expert or whether you work for a company that provides these valuable services. In each case, a person, a job, must be created to fill that particular need.

Because all these varied areas fall under the I.T. umbrella, career moves are more easily made, providing movement from one area of expertise to another while maintaining the consistency of being an I.T. professional. It creates an artificial sense of job continuum while allowing you to move, in fact, from field to field without having to rebreak the entry-level barrier.

That's exciting! If you are a technologist who has expertise in an outdated technology, you can parlay your conceptual knowledge with your actual years of experience into new career directions without starting over.

This is why I counsel programmers, for example, to frame their careers in relation to their broadest skill set. I explain that they should not say they are a *Cobol programmer* or a *VB programmer.* This has the effect of placing them in the undesirable position of having to be completely retrained in newer, more prevalent languages. Instead, I want them both in conversation and mentally (in their own psyche) to refer to themselves simply as *programmers.* The language of choice is simply a tool they currently use.

In this way, when programmers learn a new language or even begin their study of that language, they are simply continuing to advance their career as a seasoned programmer who uses .NET or VB as a tool.

I.T. provides choices unknown in other industries. More exciting, however, are the prospects and qualifications for advancement.

Performance-Based Advancement

I.T. certainly provides its practitioners with choices. It is neither industry nor geographically limited. This means that your expertise is not tied to where you live or the type of company you work for. Every company out there, from large multinational conglomerates to the mom-and-pop bakeries down the street, uses computers in one way or another. Yes, this is exciting, but the qualifications for advancement are even more so.

I.T. as a career offers a unique opportunity for what I call *performance-based advancement*. What this means is that you are not limited by a specialized degree, as, for example, a doctor or attorney is. After you are in the door, your success is largely gauged based on the perception and actual practice of the users of your product.

This is great news! If you are confident in your ability to produce effective solutions with the technology at your disposal, you can quickly separate yourself from the rank and file. Technology, when properly applied, has a dramatic effect on how successfully people work.

Because of the incredible positive impact technology can make within a company, your effectiveness at developing solutions has the potential to propel your career. When you, as a technology professional, make a solid contribution to your company, it is noticed.

It quickly becomes apparent that you are a producer. Technology affords this notice much more readily than virtually any other industry. Understanding this phenomenon is a key to rapidly developing a successful career. Learn to identify the areas of need in your company and proactively develop solutions using technology, and you will reap the rewards.

Opportunities for Continuous Learning

I am impatient and easily distracted. I admit it. Before entering the I.T. field, I bounced from job to job. I drove a plumbing truck, managed a bookstore, worked for a bank, sold copiers, and had assorted other jobs. Keeping my attention has always been a challenge. What is new seems to shine and catch my eye, while the mundane and repetitive quickly lose my interest.

Looking back over many years as an I.T. professional, I recognize that a technology career was a savior of sorts. I.T. is in a constant and rapid state of change. It forces professionals to remain in a state of constant learning and provides new and exciting avenues for growth and career direction.

Many careers have continuing education requirements involving an hour or two a year to stay current. In contrast, technology's continuing education requirements are daily.

In fact, this should be a factor in your decision to stay in the field. Although performance-based advancement might be a wonderful product of the field, if you do not want to be under the constant pressure to learn new technologies, study the upcoming trends, and watch other sectors of the industry, you will quickly reach a point of burnout.

To remain at the top of your game, you must include time for reading new literature, the quantity of which can be huge. Of course, there are creative ways to manage this.

When running my own company, I discovered that the number of weekly technology journals and magazines was amazing. We could receive three to five magazines on any given day. Often, we would receive one for each person in the company. Most sat unread and became huge quantities of recycling at the end of the week.

We all wanted to read the magazines. But the fact was that most of the content was not pertinent to our careers or current company projects. We did not, however, want to miss the mention of a product or methodology we could adopt personally or as a company.

Our solution was to assign different magazines to different people in the company. Each person's job was to peruse his magazine looking for those nuggets of wisdom that needed to be shared with the rest of the company. If someone found an article that included information that the rest of the group might find interesting, he copied and distributed it.

I still employ this tactic today with other peers in the contracting and independent consulting fields. I simply make the request that if they read something they feel I might have an interest in, they should pass it along. Sure, sometimes I receive duplicates of items I've already read, but in most cases, they are passing me articles I either overlooked or forgot about.

This think-tank approach can greatly help you with the tasks of staying up-to-date on evolving technologies and trends. In addition, it forces professional correspondence with your peers which, as discussed in Chapter 12, "Building an Active Contact List," is critical to accelerating your career growth.

Pay and Perks

Although the recent job market includes a trend toward lower pay for technology professionals in general, I want to emphasize the positive outlook for pay in the industry.

Once again, you must first understand the unrealistic pay previously offered to the rank and file technologist during the late 1990s. Of course, as the correction is made, the pay offered to entry-level technologists will drop greatly. You should expect this.

In most cases, the dropping pay scale is primarily focused on what I consider "widget" technology. These are technology jobs that involve repetitive clerical-type tasks. An example of this is a local-area network (LAN) administrator who maintains desktops and adds users to the network.

This type of job has never required extensive training or experience. It is not synonymous with network engineering, system architecture and planning, and more important, aligning I.T. projects with the business model and goals.

These are entry-level types of positions. They are where you start your career, not the apex of your career. If you view them as such, you will be much less concerned about reports of lower pay.

The fact remains that technology professionals fare much better than those in other industries when you compare education and experience.

For example, consider someone entering medicine. This person spends 9 to 12 years in school, at considerable expense, and then puts in a few more years as an intern before he can achieve the financial rewards associated with the career.

If you are a technology professional and have put in a good 10 to 15 years of career development, chances are you will be earning a decent salary, too. If you expect to be earning the big money 1 to 5 years after entering the field, however, you have set yourself up for disappointment.

Technology professionals are those who have worked to perfect their craft, add value to their companies, and put in place the various tools at their disposal to advance their careers. For them, the pay and perks will always be available. If you are willing to put time and planning into your career development, you can also earn good money.

These reasons make I.T. one of the greatest career choices you can make. Current market conditions notwithstanding, you can advance more quickly, in more areas, without the burden of performing the same stale tasks day after day, week after week, and year after year.

Take that as an affirmation. If the idea of constantly learning new technologies and tackling business challenges appeals to you, I.T. might be a great career choice.

What About Outsourcing?

Outsourcing is, without a doubt, the single-most cited reason for malaise in the I.T. sector. Articles about lost jobs, disenfranchised workers, and the demise of an industry abound.

But will all I.T. jobs be outsourced? Is there a place for the I.T. worker in an outsourced/offshored economy? Can the astute technology professional develop skills that will make him both employable and not easily displaced with a low-cost replacement overseas?

The fact is that all jobs will not be outsourced. In fact, the current government forecasts through the next 10 years still place technology jobs as having the greatest growth and higher average pay.

Although I will not minimize the impact that outsourcing has had on some, the bulk of technologists have remained employed and are fairly well compensated. Normal economic cycles have played as much a part in the industry malaise as outsourcing.

I am a huge believer in the agile/free-agent-driven workforce written about in books like *Free Agent Nation,* by Daniel Pink, and *Winning the Talent Wars,* by Bruce Tulgan. I have found their message pertinent in both my own professional life and that of other technology professionals who strive for advancement.

When speaking of outsourcing, I am speaking more precisely of offshoring, or the practice of hiring workers in other countries due primarily to economics. *Local outsourcing* also exists—the movement of business departments and functions out of an organization and over to an organization with competencies in that area.

Outsourcing of the offshore variety is what worries and angers many technology professionals. The problem, as they see it, is that there is an uneven playing field. To a large degree, they are right.

There are moral and economic challenges when a company sends work to an underdeveloped country without the same standards and restrictions regarding environmental protection and working conditions.

With that said, however, notable failures in corporate offshoring are also prevalent. It is my belief that many of the more analytic and business-centric functions of I.T. will create nearly insurmountable challenges for outsourced projects. These will turn into opportunities for the astute, local technology professional.

Outsourcing Is About Value, Not Costs

Many companies do not see a significant value in keeping jobs in the country. They find it difficult to quantify talent of their in-house technology workers.

If you are going to pay a premium for talent and get little perceived or realized value in return, why not send the work overseas? Companies sometimes find that their in-house staffs are not providing value. By sending the jobs overseas, they still receive little value, but the bottom line is protected.

The objective for technology professionals is to better define their value. This is a common theme throughout this book. Value to the business is what makes technology appealing, not the rote tasks associated with technology maintenance or even implementation.

Such tasks have to occur and are critical, but they are not quite as critical in the overall scheme of things. Executive management is looking for ways to drive profits. For many companies, technology is a necessary evil and has little strategic value. If your company has this perspective, your job will always be less secure. Your ability to create value will become your greatest source of job security.

If you are a technology professional, or you aspire to be one, you need to quickly see where you stand in the value chain of your organization. Initially, while you develop your skills, you will be pretty low on that chain. However, the quicker you adopt a value-driven mindset, the quicker you will find your career advancing.

Companies outsource primarily when the I.T. function in question is perceived as more of a cost than a strategic value. If you are a producer, it is less likely that a company will want to let you go. Even if particular functions are outsourced, highly productive employees stand a much better chance of being placed in another role within the organization.

You might also find that your company outsources to create a second shift—effectively increasing the length of its workday without paying a premium for overtime or after-hours talent. Once again, your ability to provide a greater strategic value should be the silver bullet of security that you strive to attain.

This is less about working harder, per se. It involves your ability to see smarter, more effective ways to perform your tasks. In addition, it involves becoming better at determining company needs and then delivering value-rich solutions. This has always been the case. Outsourcing has merely accented the need to adopt this strategy.

The Jobs That Won't Be Outsourced

Although outsourcing is highly publicized, it is much more prevalent in larger corporations. Most jobs, however (80 percent or more), fall into the small-business category. The small-business category is composed of companies that have between 10 and 500 employees. Most of these companies maintain small I.T. departments, where the overlap of talent and business knowledge is critical.

These small organizations provide the greatest opportunity. Because of their size, you might be required to provide training one day, infrastructure support the next day, and simple programming assistance the following day. In addition, due to the smaller size, you will be required to be more aware of company projects and plans. You will be forced into a more strategic role. This has great career benefits.

You should also consider jobs that have geographic significance. Managing outsourced projects, working to train and support technology staff at smaller organizations, onsite integration of technology, and others provide clues as to which jobs will remain within your country. In summary, you will find that more strategic roles and those requiring communication with staff and management tend to remain within the country.

Later, should you plan to take your skills into a larger organization, the more comprehensive skills will help you. You will, quite simply, provide more value.

Conclusion

After reading this chapter, you can see that careers in information technology still offer tremendous opportunity. However, it is critical that you position yourself as a value-add to your organization. It is not enough to be technically proficient; you must master the entire skill set.

It is also important that you compare your career and future potential in light of other professions and the time needed to build a similarly profitable career. Do not buy into the "get 20 weeks of training and you'll be at the earning's pinnacle" mentality. This will lead to discouragement and bitterness.

View your technology career in the same way you would any career—for its long-term potential and personal satisfaction

Actions & Ideas

1. Create your vision of value: What makes you valuable?

2. Identify fears that you have with tackling an I.T. career. Then think of two actions to compensate each fear or anxiety. Action—with directed focus—is great at dispelling anxiety.

3. Of those reasons why I.T. is a great career, which appeal to you? Rank them and think about why. Do you see your reasoning changing in the next 5 to 10 years?

EXPAND YOUR TOOLKIT

Remember to visit the book's website at http://www.ITCareerToolkit.com for supplemental and ongoing advice, tips, and data relevant to this chapter.

Defining What You Do By Defining What You Are

Although many are excited about the prospect of a career in information technology (I.T.), many embark on such a career for the wrong reasons. Using income as a primary objective, while ignoring your ability to maintain the level of performance required in the hi-tech sector, can lead to burnout and frustration.

However, income is a powerful motivator and should not be ignored when determining career direction.

Creating a comprehensive picture of your skills and desires allows you to more quickly make career decisions that emphasize those factors, in turn increasing your enjoyment and performance on the job.

CHAPTER 4

Defining Yourself: Aptitudes and Desires

You've probably heard this question your entire life: What do you want to be when you grow up? For some, the answer was/is simple. In elementary school, I heard kids talking about wanting to be a doctor, a surgeon, a construction worker, and so on. Even though they tended to modify their answers over time, they had answers ready.

I never really had an answer. I struggled, thinking through possible career choices—something I wanted to do over the course of my life—and came up empty. My entrance into a career in technology somewhat reflected this.

Even though I have been programming since the age of 13, I never considered technology a career choice (even into early adulthood). While in school, I focused on courses I enjoyed: English, philosophy, earth science, and so on. I believed that I would enter teaching one day.

As I moved from job to job, adopting new skills, my "life's work" was forever elusive.

Eventually, a large insurance company hired me as a data entry clerk. The job was offered more because of my typing ability than any true computer skills I had. However, I soon found myself offering computer-related assistance to the department. When a staff programmer left on vacation and management needed some ad hoc reports, I muddled through the tasks, providing them the information they needed. Nine months later, I was across the street, in a new department, working as a junior database administrator.

I mention this to emphasize a point made earlier. No career move is without benefit, and if you actively review your aptitudes and desires, a career choice will start to become evident.

This is especially true in the computer industry and technology professions. People often approach me asking my advice about entering the technology field. "Should I learn programming?" or "Should I go to school for network security?"

These people are, unfortunately, letting the proverbial cart drive the horse. My answer is typically the same in all cases, "Sure, if you like it."

What they are really asking is whether they can make a decent living as a technologist. However, I am more concerned with their long-term prospects and whether the career choice is a good one for them. I have already made it apparent that I believe the I.T. industry is a great place to build a career.

Ideally, you can make a lot of money as an attorney; however, if you absolutely hate the field and the prospect of working in that industry, the money is secondary. Job burnout is caused by pursuing a career—any career—without regard as to how it makes you feel. You are going to be in a career for a long time, so you might as well like it.

While working for a large law firm, I had the opportunity to work with some of the highest paid attorneys in the country. Many of these attorneys were making more than a million dollars a year. During one project, a managing partner looked at me and said, "I wish I was doing what you're doing."

He had been a programmer in school and thoroughly enjoyed it. Now he was a well-compensated attorney who disliked the field but was caught in a gilded cage of sorts. I, of course, commented that I would trade some of my fun for some of his money. But the fact remains that performing work you dislike, even when you're well compensated, is usually miserable.

And yet, people continually look at their careers from the standpoint of money first, desire second.

I am a realist, too. I understand that someone's desire might be to be a professional baseball player. However, that person's aptitudes simply do not provide the opportunity. I am not advocating an irresponsible perspective whereby you pursue a dead-end profession with no opportunity simply because you like it. If you are realistic, these types of desires are best relegated to hobbies and pastimes.

The same can be said for technology careers. Be honest and realistic with your particular aptitudes. If you have a hard time understanding control constructs and the logic associated and required for programming, your desire might not be enough to overcome that barrier. Matching your desires with your abilities and aptitude is critical for career growth and long-term career enjoyment.

All is not lost. The person who likes technology but has a love for baseball can still create a truly enjoyable career. With proper positioning and a dedication to networking, that person could work for a sports-centered organization while providing technical solutions. I have seen this type of thing done with great success for the individual. It is a molding of professional aptitude with an area of extreme interest, to create passion in a day-to-day career.

It is not my intention to downplay the need to find a career that provides good compensation. In fact, you will find that pay is of primary importance when determining what your options should be.

Considerations in Your Career Choice

This section covers some considerations you need to factor in as you build your career. They are not listed in any particular order—certainly not in an order of importance. What is important to me might not be important to you. In addition, what is critical at this juncture of your career might be much less significant in the future.

The sections that follow provide general guidelines and topics of internal assessment.

Factors to Help Decide Your Career Path: Needs

What must a job provide you? In many cases, people view this strictly in the form of monetary compensation. I want to look at the topic more comprehensively, though. Certainly, money must play a part (unless, of course, you have inherited a family fortune). For the majority of us who have not been so lucky, the following needs will be framed as both physical and psychological:

- Pay
- Insurance
- Training
- Commute
- Working conditions (people, culture, environment, hours)
- Future growth potential

Pay

After all my talk de-emphasizing the importance of pay, I've placed it first on the list. First, remember my disclaimer: The list is not organized in any particular order. Also, pay is no small issue. Pay is significant, but it shouldn't overshadow your love of what you do.

Pay and associated material compensation such as vacation, auto expense, insurance, and training (although the latter two are considered in a separate section) are critical. You must be able to eat and live. In addition, there is a psychological benefit to being well compensated.

However, at different stages of your career, pay should have more or less importance. Too often, people—especially young professionals—place so much emphasis on pay that they overlook great opportunities. **Pursuing the short-term dollar places you at risk of missing opportunities for long-term payback.**

When I counsel technologists on their careers and when I have hired technologists, they often refer to the "average" salary for their field. Salary surveys become the guiding factor in helping them make decisions on which job they want to take.

This is a dangerous practice. Typically, I counsel them to throw away the salary surveys. I simply ask them, "Are you planning to be an average professional?" Normally, the answer is no. "Then, why do you care about the average salary?"

Looking at the average pay in a given field, although perhaps informing you of the salary range, creates an artificial ceiling on potential earnings. I have never been one to strive for average. I don't recommend you do that either. You certainly deserve compensation for your work, but remember that we are looking at a more holistic approach to your overall career.

Note	While I was with the large insurance company, I worked in a user department. I did not work in the traditional I.T. organization. From the standpoint of the work I produced and the skills I brought to the table, I was paid poorly.
	However, I was the sole technologist for the department. I selected the tools to use, provided hardware and software support, performed almost all the network administration tasks, and was free to work outside of my job description.
	The experience gained during that time has been instrumental in my career growth. The year I left the life insurance company, my salary *quadrupled*. Yes, quadrupled. I suppose I could have left the job I was in for one where I made an additional $5,000 more per year. This would have been more in line with the *average*, but it might have cost me thousands in opportunity and experience.

Pay is a principal factor, but you must weigh it properly against future potential and the experience offered.

Insurance

Although insurance should ideally be viewed as part of the material compensation, along with pay, I dedicate this small section to its discussion because of its importance.

Caution	Disclaimer: I am not serving as a financial advisor, and you must determine your insurance needs based on careful analysis and your own comfort level. This topic requires consideration of your individual circumstances. I recommend speaking to a qualified professional on this matter.

At different times in your life, insurance is more or less critical. I believe you should always have insurance and must look for opportunities that provide it or at least pay you enough to buy your own. However, the level of insurance for someone who has a family is different than for someone who is single.

If you have or are starting a family, for example, health insurance should be comprehensive and not include high co-pays or prescription drug payments. Insurance might become a primary factor in deciding which opportunities to take. A single emergency can be financially devastating if you are inadequately insured.

However, if you are a healthy single, you might need only major medical coverage—insurance that starts paying after you have paid a larger out-of-pocket deductible. Monthly premiums on this type of insurance are typically far less expensive. If you visit the doctor infrequently, coverage is less expensive over time. You are basically "betting" that you will remain healthy. Insurance needs change over the course of your lifetime. You should factor them into any career decision you make.

Training

For the technology professional, this question is a career constant: "What have you done for me lately?" The pressure to perform is exacerbated by frequent changes in the tools of the trade. Your ability to stay up to date on key skills greatly enhances your overall value and provides continuous opportunities for professional advancement.

With this being the case, a company's commitment (or lack thereof) to continuing education must be factored into the total compensation program. With certification courses running thousands of dollars and management seminars costing even more, training in the proper area is like money in the bank.

When I say in the proper area, I mean from both a pragmatic (the technologies I'll be using immediately) standpoint and from an industry trend (technologies that will be used in the future) standpoint. For example, you might be required to learn an outdated technology because it is necessary for the job at hand. Although the technology is highly pragmatic, it has little future worth. Or you might have the opportunity to learn technology that is not being used by the company in the hopes of a future adoption of that technology.

In addition, soft-skills training is invaluable. Skills such as time management, communication (both written and verbal), and leadership are critical to your overall career growth. In fact, these skills will go further to provide long-term career stability and growth than your technical talent. These are the skills you need as you move from being a staff technologist toward management.

The easiest way to find out about your potential employer's commitment to continuing education is to ask during the interview cycle. Remember, the interview is a time for you to find out about the employer as well. The type of training you will receive may be an important factor in where you choose to work.

> **Note** I often tell technologists that understanding business communications and business concepts is more critical than their technical skills. As an employer, if I had my choice between someone who was highly proficient technically but lacked an understanding of business concepts and communication skills versus the opposite—someone who was highly proficient in business concepts and communications but lacked some of the technical know-how, I would hire the latter. Technical skills are rapidly obsolete unless coupled with good conceptual business knowledge. (See Part IV, "More Options to Build Your Career.)

Commute and Travel Time

Commute and travel are worthy considerations when making a career choice. Their impact on your quality of life can be dramatic. I have seen some whose commutes consume nearly 4 hours of their life every day.

Time is our most valuable commodity. When you consider a position, factor your commute and associated on-the-job travel into the equation. For instance, a job that pays you $25 per hour is quickly devalued if your commute averages more than 2 hours per day. With commute time factored in, you lose $5 an hour, reducing your actual earnings to $20 per hour.

You must also factor in wear and tear on your vehicle or any rapid-transit fees that apply. This further reduces your actual compensation. I have watched individuals make career moves that include a higher salary but actually produce lower total compensation when these other factors are considered.

I am not indicating that you should never take a position that requires a commute. I only recommend that you consider its impact on quality of life and total compensation.

I have effectively kept my commute to less than an hour each day for most of my career. I would rather move closer to my company than commute. I did, however, once take a position that required a 2-hour commute. When considering all the other factors, it was a sacrifice I willingly made. Part of what made it feasible was the fact that the employer paid for train and subway fare. I used the time on the train to catch up on reading.

Travel is loosely associated with commute. A position that requires extensive travel time can be devastating to your personal life if you are not careful. The rigors and demands of living out of a suitcase and logging considerable airport time are quite stressful.

For a time, these job demands might be fun, even glamorous, but you have to consider their overall impact. Although I have enjoyed those business trips I have taken, I cannot imagine spending weeks at a time away from family and friends.

You must also factor in what that travel time means to your overall compensation. Even if you are not working, your time away in a hotel is still being sacrificed. Invariably, being away on travel leads to longer working days in many cases. There is simply little else to do in an unfamiliar city.

Once again, I am not indicating that you turn down a job that requires travel. You need to gauge the impact to your life and overall career plan.

Jobs that include travel do have some benefits. My sister travels professionally. She actually assesses various destinations and travel programs for her company's clients. Although she would honestly tell you about the rigors of constant travel, she has also had the opportunity to visit exotic locations and stay at world-class resorts.

Working Conditions (People, Culture, Environment, Hours)

When considering potential career choices, you would be wise to assess the overall working conditions at the company in question. Several factors make up working conditions.

The people you work with and the overall attitude and feel of a company (the culture) play a central role in your satisfaction and enjoyment of a particular opportunity. If the culture is stoic and conservative and you are not, you might find that personality conflicts occur. The adverse might also be true.

I am cautious here. I don't want you to preclude an opportunity just because your personality or style might be different from the company as a whole. The variation you provide might be (should be) a great addition to the culture's diversity.

Still, you would do well to understand the personality of the company and how that might impact you. I have been in organizations that I considered stodgy. They lacked creativity, imagination, and any concept of levity. Even as a consultant, I turn down such clients and the potential revenue. I know that eventually my nature is going to create a culture clash somewhere.

Your ability to feel as though you share goals and interest with the team is a big factor in career satisfaction.

The physical environment also plays a factor in your overall career enjoyment. I once worked in a building with almost no windows. I found it stifling to have no view of the outside world. I didn't necessarily need to have a window desk, but the ability to have more than a clock's input as to time of day proved crucial for me.

Is the environment clean, inviting, and well maintained? I bring this up for two reasons. First, a poorly maintained work environment can be depressing and sap energy. This, in turn, can lead to poor performance and dissatisfaction.

More important, the physical environment might indicate business management's or ownership's care for its employees. If employees are working in subpar conditions, advancement might be similarly subpar.

You have to evaluate this for yourself, however. Perhaps the business is just starting out or saving money for future expansion. This might be an excellent place to work—effectively hitching your career to their upcoming growth.

The hours you are expected to work are also critical. There are always times when additional hours are required for project completion. In I.T., this is particularly true. If you find that long hours are considered the norm and that advancement is tied largely to your working those hours, consider how this might impact your life.

I have four children. They take part in various activities and sports. Every season, I try to coach one or two of my children's sporting activities. I would not work for an employer who had unreasonable expectations for the time I spend at work.

That said, you need to have a realistic expectation in this area. Sometimes, particularly early in your career, long hours are necessary. As you develop your skills and tools, you exert additional effort and spend additional time to do so. It is when the lengthy hours become part of your life that problems and conflict can occur.

Future Growth Potential

Often, long-term gain is sacrificed when the future growth potential of a given position is overlooked. At some companies, technical talent is strictly relegated to each person's particular job function. Network administrators perform only network administrative tasks, and programmers work only on their particular programs. Cross-training and exposure to new technologies are extremely limited.

From a career-growth standpoint, this can be limiting and can also lead to job burnout and boredom. If you entered technology because you desired exposure to the many facets it offers, such a situation will frustrate you.

As we evaluate a prospective employer's offer, pay so often dominates our evaluation that we overlook the opportunities provided in ancillary areas. A smaller company, or a position in a non-I.T. role where I.T. skills must be diverse, can provide opportunities that are seldom available in larger, more established I.T. shops.

Particularly, when you are new to the field, carefully consider what you hope to glean from your job experience. If you simply want something to put food on the table for that year, pay will be the deciding factor. If instead you want to develop a broad skill set, with exposure to as many different technologies as possible, you might sacrifice in pay.

I am certainly not saying you cannot get both. When you constantly expose yourself to new technologies and take on diverse projects, you become more valuable to the company you are with and more valuable in the job market. Although most people have their specialties, a specialist who also develops many general skills is a unique commodity; when this person is discovered, he can command a larger salary.

Your commodity as a technology professional is *solutions*. For companies, this means creating tools that help increase revenue or reduce costs (either directly or through increased efficiency or better information). To be effective at creating such solutions, you must understand the broadest range of technologies and the company products or services, how they bring these into the market, and the departmental support and interaction within the company. A company that provides cross-training and cross-project opportunities can help you learn to create these solutions.

Factors to Help Decide Your Career Path: Desires

Although you must meet core needs, don't overlook your desires. Once again, in your long-term plan, your desires are vital for keeping you motivated to pursue career growth. It is hard to stay at peak performance when you are doing something you dislike.

I caution you, however, not to use this as license to pass on great opportunities because of some uncomfortable or difficult facet. The happiest workers are those who are generally happy in any circumstance. I want to emphasize happy or content, not satisfied. Happiness and professional contentment can exist without satisfaction. Be content in your job, but be intent on growth.

For example, if you want to become a programmer, but the only technology-related position involves simple report writing and administrative functions for some period, don't become frustrated and quit. If, while performing these functions, the company you are with treats you well, compensates you fairly, and is not overtly attempting to thwart your attempts to advance, consider staying.

It might be that the job you want is simply not there for you—yet. Are you consistently performing your job so well as to have your employer take notice? If not, you might still have some skills to master.

Sometimes you need to be diligent and demonstrate the self-discipline to work independently (at home, after hours) on the new skills you want to acquire. If you relegate this responsibility to your employer, you will not only be frustrated, but you will limit your potential growth and earnings. Part of what makes technology an exciting career is the new skills you get to learn, but this is your responsibility, not your employer's.

Also, have you talked to your employer about your career desires? There is a damaging notion among employees who believe that an employer should recognize their desire to move up or change jobs and proactively present the option. In a fantasy world where deadlines, their own career concerns, other employees, and day-to-day operations do not exist, this might happen.

It is better to have a candid discussion with your boss early. Let him know where you would like to be professionally and why. Employers would rather find in-house talent—a known commodity—instead of going through the expense and time attempting to hire from outside the company.

Take stock of your career desires. You should have both short-term and long-term desires to motivate you and direct your decisions.

Factors to Help Decide Your Career Path: Skills

This one can be a killer for young technologists. Why? Because they often overestimate their skills. In many cases, they rank themselves as more talented or knowledgeable than they actually are. This can lead to bitterness because they perceive their entry-level role and compensation as beneath them.

Your skills will, of course, play a part in your overall career plan, both short term and long term. You must have a realistic perception of what you bring to the table. If not, you will overlook those from whom you can learn, and you will not be motivated to find optimizations and enhancements to your current skill set.

I often tell my clients when addressing a new technology project that I am going to get advice from the "smart people" in the field. I say this tongue-in-cheek, but in a real sense, I understand the limitations to my knowledge. My willingness to acknowledge and understand these limitations provides continuous opportunities for learning.

Even those things that I believe I have mastered are subject to the evaluation of my peers. With technical knowledge, someone always knows a little optimization or tweak that you have overlooked. In addition, new tools are developed for existing technologies on a daily basis. Your willingness to gather information and advice from your peers keeps you up to date on such developments.

On the other side of the spectrum, don't underestimate your ability to acquire new skills while on the job. If you take a position that places you well within your skill set, there's little hope for advancement. However, if you take a position that involves skills that are far beyond your actual talent, you are inviting failure.

It is best to find a position where your current talent can make an immediate and positive impact, but the need for new technology is available to motivate and stretch you to advance your skills.

Beware: Analysis Paralysis

A note of caution: I've given you several factors to consider when making career decisions. Certainly take these into account. However, don't overanalyze these factors in a way that freezes you. I know too many people who play so many what-if scenarios in their head that they never make a choice.

Or if they do, they spend the next several years second guessing the wisdom of their decision. I've mentioned it before and will do so again: No job makes or breaks a career. All jobs, even those that result in negative situations, add value. They give you skills and experience that you will use to make better career choices in the future.

Conclusion

When taking a job or leaving a job, you have many factors to consider. More important, there are factors to consider when choosing a career path. You need to find a realistic combination between those items I discuss in this chapter and any other intangibles that you find important.

Information technology offers myriad possibilities, from the highly creative to the highly analytical. As you progress through various opportunities, try to determine the factors that best motivate you and mesh well with your innate abilities. These will provide you both opportunity and enjoyment.

Actions & Ideas

1. Create a list of needs and wants.

2. Use the Weekly Cash-Flow Planning spreadsheet from this book's accompanying website to create a budget so that you can have a base understanding of your material needs.

EXPAND YOUR TOOLKIT

Remember to visit the book's website at http://www.ITCareerToolkit.com for supplemental and ongoing advice, tips, and data relevant to this chapter.

Looking in the Mirror

To take the most effective control over your career, self-assessment is vital. It is foolhardy and professionally disastrous to wait until your official performance review before making modifications and mid-review corrections.

Even if you are self-employed, the tools and methods of self-assessment, as conveyed later in this chapter, can provide an excellent way for you to identify weaknesses and strengths.

Armed with this information, you can develop a plan of action to further develop your strengths and correct your weaknesses.

CHAPTER 5

Self-Assessment

Self-assessment or self-evaluation, when done properly, can greatly benefit your career. It allows you to frequently assess your performance with all other areas of your toolkit. This can be an assessment of your core skills, your attitude on the job, your communication skills, your teamwork, or any other facet of performance that your job might entail.

The Power of Self-Assessment

Self-assessment is particularly effective because you can do it between official job reviews. This allows you to make corrections without management's prompting. If you have done your groundwork, and you correctly view your job as a partnership between you and management, you will have a good idea of what your boss is going to review you on.

If you are honest, you probably know what your boss will focus on during his assessment. A few times when counseling technologists on their careers, I heard about a poor performance review, with the employee complaining that he did not know what his boss was looking for.

I have to tell it to you straight. For all the times I've heard this, I am convinced that it is rarely the case. What makes a good worker is not mysterious:

- Mastery of the skills needed to perform the base functions of the job

- The ability to effectively plan and communicate the work to be done

- The capacity to work effectively with management and coworkers

Outside of these key ideas, little elaboration is required.

The Dangers of Self-Assessment

Self-assessment is dangerous—vital, but dangerous. Typically, you are either too hard on yourself or far too lenient. This is critical to note.

If you are too hard in your self-assessment, you will lack motivation because of hopelessness. If you are too lenient, you will lack motivation to pursue further training and growth.

The balance requires that you always view your contribution from a long-term perspective. Growth is not measured in comparison to other employees but in comparison to your own past performance. For example, I do not assess a programmer's growth in comparison to another programmer but in relation to where he was 6 months ago as a developer.

Sometimes assessing where you are from where you've come does not apply. For instance, if you are insubordinate or inappropriate in actions or word, you cannot make a gradual change. Such cases require a dramatic about-face and the willingness to deal with the consequences as they come.

Self-assessment only works when you are willing to be honest with yourself—not in some masochistic, here-is-everything-I've-done-wrong, take-no-credit–for-anything type of way. When done properly, self-assessment is extremely powerful and motivating. Why? Because it allows you to give yourself kudos for what you have done well, and it allows you to create a game plan (corrective action) for what you have not.

Part of this honesty requires evaluating your attitude toward your work. Do you expect excellence, or is mediocrity satisfactory? Before you answer too quickly, think about your expectation for tomorrow's tasks. Are you expecting to provide real value? Do you even think in those terms—the value you provide to the organizations you serve?

I can remember approaching my boss at Blue Cross and performing an impromptu self-assessment in the hallway. I covered where I thought I was doing well and where I thought I needed to improve. I then asked whether my assessment sounded accurate. She thought about it and nodded. I explained that my goal was to work specifically on one particular weakness before our next official review.

That simple conversation paid dividends in many ways. First and most important, I saw that I was in tune with my boss in regard to my performance. I was able to walk away with the liberating knowledge of where I stood. That was better than finding out "suddenly" that I was not meeting management's expectations in some area. Besides, it is easier on the ego to point out your own shortcomings rather than have someone else do it for you.

In addition, this impromptu self-assessment served as notice to my boss that I understood my performance. This freed management from having to approach me with a plan of corrective action for areas of poor performance. Being a self-starter in this area immediately separates you from the majority of your peers.

As a manager, if I have an employee who knows what he has to improve on, I do not have to micromanage that correction. I need only to make available the resources needed, and the employee (theoretically) can take care of the rest.

In addition, sharing your self-assessment allows your manager to provide some input prior to a raise-contingent meeting. Your manager might disagree with your assessment, feeling you are doing well in an area that you feel deficient in, and suggest another area to work on. It might be that you need work on both areas, but the meeting allows you to see where management is focusing and adjust your personal growth accordingly.

Another benefit of my impromptu meeting was my realization that I needed to work on time management. After discussing this, outside of a performance review, my boss sent me to a time management seminar. This was significant because the seminar was sponsored by the company, for management only. My boss pulled a few strings to cover the cost of the full-day seminar and the associated planner.

She did this, I am convinced, because I was accurate in my self-assessment, and I approached her, not in a defensive manner, but with a request for assistance in improving in this area.

Management is not interested in seeing employees fail or "keeping them down." In the huge majority of cases, employees' success elevates their managers, and they know it.

Four Questions of Self-Assessment

How can you effectively perform a self-assessment? Numerous resources are available to help you with this. Books dealing with personal growth abound. You can take your pick of which titles to read. Include several in your library. However, as a jump-start, I provide you with the four magic questions of self-assessment.

I must warn you, however, that the questions presented here were initially given to me as an employer. They were imparted to me as a way to determine whether I should fire an employee. I restructured them to be viewed from the employee's perspective. I figured that if the questions were valuable to me, as an employer, they would be equally effective for employees to assess their impact in the company.

The Origin of the Four Questions

As the owner of a small software integration company, I was faced—fortunately, rarely—with an employee who did not have the skills needed and showed no desire to acquire them, or an employee who had the skills but showed no interest in using them.

I am a nice guy, and the last thing I want to do is leave someone without his livelihood. Rest assured that most employers are in the same boat. Most have no desire to see anyone fail because it is both costly to business and is an emotional drain.

However, during one such time—when I had an employee who could not or would not produce—the following information was given to me to assist in creating a more objective evaluation of talent and contribution.

The four questions were provided to me strictly from an employer's perspective and were framed as "Four Questions to Help You Decide If an Employee Should Be Fired." The questions were given to me during a breakfast meeting with Richard Thayer of Thermax/CDT. (A special gratitude to Mr. Thayer for opening this dialogue after many years.)

Read through each of the questions and see how it covers the key elements of skills, attitude, and team perspective in your career effectiveness.

Make a mental note of which questions give you the greatest cause for concern. Take one question at a time and determine an associated corrective action that will make that aspect of your career more solid.

Continue to perform this assessment over the life of your career. You will discover, at times, that different questions stand out and require corrective action. The great part about the questions is that they neatly provide direction for personal and professional development.

I use these four questions daily when assessing my performance. I still do this as a consultant and as a writer. I simply change *employer* to *client* or *editor*.

Question 1: Do I Make My Employer's Job Much Easier or Much More Difficult?

Some employees, although skilled, do not contribute enough to make up for their detrimental action. You must remember that you have been hired to take on particular tasks. You are being paid to make work "go away" in one sense. Few things are as frustrating to an employer as an employee who creates work, making management's and other employees' jobs more difficult.

You might perform your job well, but through your attitude or unwillingness to step outside of your job, you end up making another person's job more difficult.

As you go through your week, understand the relationship that your work has on other employees and management. Being busy and working hard are not enough. Don't confuse action with production.

You should, if promotion and growth are the goals, always be looking for ways to make your work more efficient for yourself and for those you come in contact with. If you see a way to streamline a task that makes less work for the next person, propose it to management.

Question 2: If I Gave Notice Today, Would My Employer Have an Instant Sense of Relief or Dread?

This is a great one! Ask yourself the question. Think about it for a while. If you can honestly say that your employer would dread your departure and have a difficult time replacing such an exemplary employee, you are on the right track.

If, however, because of personal conflict, poor performance, poor attitude, and so on, you realize that your departure would be cause for celebration, you had better determine corrective action, and fast!

Question 3: Do I Perform My Job Better Than My Employer Could Perform My Job If He/She Needed To?

Remember that you are seldom hired to perform the job that your employer performs. You are hired to perform certain key tasks that a business or department needs. Overlap is certainly desirable through cross-training, but the fact remains that if you can master your specific job functions and perform these better than all others, your value is increased.

If you are simply another repeated skill set, you will likely be subject to the next economic downturn or "force reduction."

Question 4: If Asked How I Can Improve in My Job, Do I Cite External Factors—People and Resources—or Do I Take Responsibility?

From an employer's perspective, few things are as frustrating as an employee who, when given a performance review, cites everything but himself as a barrier to his performance.

Instead, this employee speaks about how Joe in accounting doesn't complete forms properly, how his desk is uncomfortable, how his computer is too slow, and on and on. These things can certainly be factors, but employers are usually aware of problems with other resources or employees.

The fact is, in the huge majority of cases, areas of improvement in a performance review regard personal productivity. They are things that you control. It might be that Joe in accounting doesn't complete his paperwork correctly, but be careful about citing this as a reason for your own performance problems.

This is perhaps the single most critical element of your self-assessment—ensuring that you focus your areas of improvement squarely on yourself. Although it is appropriate to be honest if certain resources are inadequate for the job, do not let them dominate your self-assessment. Remember: The focus of your self-assessment is caught up in that first word: *self.*

By keeping the focus on yourself, you set yourself up as a leader. If you are willing to take responsibility for yourself, you are one step away from being able to take responsibility for others.

Conclusion: Making It Personal

Using the four questions, make a list of skills and attitudes to work on. Then go to your bookstore or library and find resources to help you take corrective action.

Or, better yet, approach your boss with your self-assessment. Find out what resources he recommends. As I've said, this helps you stand out as a leader and, you might be surprised, your manager probably has some good ideas to assist you.

Self-assessment is primarily a personal responsibility. It is not meant specifically to help you directly with a performance review. The role of self-assessment is more for ongoing career correction, regardless of whether your company has a formal review system.

Self-assessment is something that you should do regularly. The four questions are just one tool that can help you effectively view yourself as your employer views you. In career development, that is always the most critical viewpoint.

Actions & Ideas

1. Take a moment today to go through the four questions. Be honest. If you want extra space to write your answers, you can print out the Self-Assessment form that is included on the website accompanying this book.

2. Question 4 talks about personal responsibility and factors that you can control. What are three items you control that could be improved to help your overall performance and value?

3. Look at the coming year. Knowing when you might have performance reviews, set up a time to perform a formal self-assessment at least 2 months prior to your next review. Ask a trusted peer or mentor to review your assessment.

EXPAND YOUR TOOLKIT

Remember to visit the book's website at http://www.ITCareerToolkit.com for supplemental and ongoing advice, tips, and data relevant to this chapter.

An Effective Plan of Action Drives Perspective

Attitude is largely affected by circumstance and perspective. For many technology professionals, a jaded and negative perspective of the potential that is available in the industry contributes to poor career choices and, more critically, poor performance.

This is combated and cured by having a plan of action, a long-term perspective, and emulating those who have and continue to achieve success.

CHAPTER 6

Attitude

Attitude is a tool in that it provides inroads and can become a factor in your performance on a given job or project. Attitude cannot replace performance, but it can impact it just like the sports team that makes a big play and turns the momentum of a game around.

Your attitude can help you master and adopt new skills more easily.

The perception that your peers and superiors have of you is also driven by your attitude. If you can convey confidence during difficult projects and then deliver, your attitude will become a central factor in their confidence in you.

The Effect of Attitude on Your Career

The impact that attitude has on career growth and opportunity is significant. Attitude provides the internal fortitude to deal with disappointments and setbacks and conveys a confidence that is most certainly a necessary component of overall success.

This chapter discusses a few facets of attitude, identifying the idea behind a positive mental attitude, and your attitude toward the I.T. industry, your employer, and your coworkers. This chapter also looks at the attitudes of personal value and ownership and how they impact your performance and potential for growth.

Positive Mental Attitude

Throngs of books line the shelves. From business to self-help to parenting, the idea of positive mental attitude (PMA) permeates our culture. Everyone has an angle on how to improve your PMA and how it benefits you and the people around you.

These people are correct. Certainly, PMA is critical to advancing in life. Lack of motivation breeds a lack of energy, which, in turn, creates a lack of action. Lack of action is a seal of doom on career advancement. This is particularly true in a performance-based career such as information technology (I.T.).

PMA Is Not a Panacea

PMA is not a panacea. It does not, in and of itself, produce anything. In fact, although I certainly do not knock those who write, promote, and sell PMA books and seminars, I am also a pragmatist. Without a go-forward plan, the rah-rah high that is achieved at many such seminars is lost within weeks or even days because of a lack of direction.

Few things are as unmotivating as being hyped to action and having no place to put that energy. You leave an event, excited about your life prospects, but you suddenly discover that you have no plan of action. The effect is a slow disillusionment with your previous excitement.

PMA and a Plan

The goal of this book is to foster the PMA needed to create action, coupled with a plan that has achievable steps in a particular area. I have covered why I.T. is a great career. In coming chapters, I provide tools and a plan of action to put those tools to use.

In this chapter, you will discover attitudes that lend themselves to success. The concrete plan of action you follow both to create your toolkit and to put it to use will bolster this attitude, providing an outlet of action for the energy.

This is the type of PMA I enjoy. I call it "PMA with a plan." It provides a means to achieving the objectives and goals that created the PMA to begin with. It becomes a self-perpetuating energy. You will find, as you move through the creation of your toolkit, that concrete steps do more to foster a positive attitude than any high-powered coaching can.

Beware: Two Pitfalls of Attitude

For the job seeker/career move, attitude is not everything, but its role must not be diminished. Certainly, it can provide a leg up on the competition. However, it cannot overcome unrealistic expectations or huge skill deficits.

Unrealistic Expectations

Unrealistic expectations typically come in the form of salary requirements and ideas on how quickly one should advance in a role. Myriad certification and training advertisements have done little to control this. Radio and print advertisement routinely tote the message of "high salary" in no time, after completing your certification program.

Although this might have been true in the talent-hungry 1990s, a backlash I call "certification cynicism" has infected the hiring attitudes among many companies. Newbies, those who entered the industry during the technology talent gold rush, have discovered that companies are paying little credence to their certifications and placing the emphasis on proven experience.

It is not that I dissuade anyone from going after a degree or certification to bolster career chances. Believe me, both are positive. What I want to dissuade is the expectation by the prospective employee that degrees and certifications create opportunities in and of themselves.

Skill Deficits

Your attitude can open a lot of doors. If yours is properly placed, it can serve you well in overcoming any skills deficit that you might have. Although companies are hesitant to hire unproven talent, a consistent application of positive work ethic and a willingness to take on new projects without *immediate gratification*—the expectation of a bonus or pay raise for each new skill developed—can open doors that were previously barred shut. When an employer discovers someone who is willing to, in fact, request new projects, he will respond. If that employee can proactively develop new solutions while enhancing his skills, management *will* reward him.

The Role of Attitude

Barring the two challenges of unrealistic expectations and skill deficits, attitude becomes of primary importance in building your career. What attitudes do you need to develop? The sections that follow discuss these and provide some insight on how you can put them to use in both career advancement and in the job search.

What You Think of Your Employer

Your perspective toward your employer and your ability to understand his perspective goes a long way toward creating a work environment that is enjoyable and productive.

It amazes me how willing people are to work for someone they disdain. They act as though a job is both a right and a prison. And their employer becomes an object of a bitter attitude. This ultimately serves no one.

I ask—no, I admonish—you to take a good, hard look at your attitude toward your employer. In many cases, I've found that employees have two damaging perspectives when it comes to their employer.

The "Us Versus Them" Mentality

This is a killer. Few things are as damaging as a perspective that places you and management or business ownership on different teams.

If you find that your peers spend considerable time bad-mouthing or complaining about management, I caution you to select a better peer group. That might sound harsh, but if you have peers who cultivate an "us versus them" mentality in speech and action, you are limiting your career advancement potential.

First, you will create a barrier between good management and yourself. You will not seek management's company and certainly will not attempt to emulate management. Why? Management is the enemy.

Second, you will be known for your membership in that negative peer group. You will emulate the group's attitude. It ultimately kills the desire to rise into management. A negative peer group exerts a tremendous amount of pressure, and the effects can prove disastrous to a career.

Management Got There by Luck or Schmoozing, Alone

The general assumption here is that managers don't have the skills for their job. Perhaps you really are in a situation in which that is true. But I caution you. In most cases, managers have performed to achieve their success. Most managers have produced consistently to be recognized for their achievements and have attained success through hard work.

Often, the perspective is created by misunderstanding your employer's or manager's role. Understand that you are meant to provide skills that augment the company, not necessarily duplicate those already in existence.

Often, an employee possesses some skill that is unique in the company. The danger is that having that unique skill can foster an attitude of superiority. This is extremely common with technologists. They view their specific talent as "the talent" that the company needs. This perspective creates a general disdain for those who do not have this talent. Often, this attitude becomes directed toward a boss or management.

This is a career killer. You must remember that no matter how unique, every talent is replaceable. Ultimately, if the trouble that you bring to a company exceeds your value, you will be replaced.

To gain the most from your employment in the areas of simple enjoyment and opportunity, you must view it as an agreement between you and your employer. Each of you brings something of value to the agreement.

Your employer brings work and a steady paycheck. He assumes risk in running and financing a business. He needs to have specific tasks performed, and these tasks require specific skills.

You bring those skills or the ability to master those skills. You bring a desire to excel at what you do. You bring to your employer the solutions to the company's business challenges.

To understand the nature of this agreement, you must be able to see the employer's perspective of the relationship. You must also be able to see where you fit in the organization and the value that you really bring. Having this understanding can help you better assess the opportunities that exist and determine whether the agreement is a good one for both you and the employer.

Your Coworkers

The attitude that you carry into your job is largely impacted by what you think about your coworkers. If you feel that you are part of a team working to achieve a common success, you will arrive at work motivated to achieve. You will feel comfortable with the knowledge that your "back is covered" as you enter the fray of technical work.

If you think that your peers do not care about you or the tasks at hand, however, you will lack motivation.

I would like to tell you that I am going to provide methods to make your coworkers like you or that I can give them a desire to achieve. Unfortunately, those don't apply here. In fact, I cannot impact your coworkers one iota, and you can't either. What it ultimately comes down to is you and your attitude toward your coworkers.

This is all you can control. You are the one reading this book and showing an interest in your success. This already separates you from others in one regard. A desire to succeed requires a commitment to personal growth. This book is a step in that direction.

Although you and I cannot impact your coworkers directly, I guarantee that your attitude toward your work, your peers, and the company and its management *can*.

Don't be naive. Keep your great attitude and be perceptive as to what is going on. Remember: You are working on correcting your attitude and trying to make a positive impact through that. You can't turn onions into apples, but you can recognize that you have onions and grill them to put on your steak.

Humble Arrogance: The Attitude of Personal Value

All of us, without exception, bring some type of skill to the table. Often, the job seeker and employer look only at the hard skills. This is particularly true in I.T.; however, an assessment and understanding of how you can benefit your employer is vital to feeding your attitude.

The attitude of personal value is an internal realization of the awareness that you bring something to the table. Perhaps in the early part of your career it is the willingness to learn, to put in the time and effort to develop new talents and refine existing ones. Later, it might be the actual hard skills you bring to the table. Ultimately, it will become your ability to lead others and transfer both conceptual and hard knowledge to your staff.

If you do not believe that you have something to offer, some value that you bring your prospective employer, your attitude will most certainly suffer. Inevitably, you will view the time and effort you trade your employer for pay as a type of stealing. Although you might not verbalize it in this fashion, you will carry this attitude, and it will place you in a vulnerable position.

You will live in a type of fear that your lack of value will be discovered. This will remove any ability that you have to bargain for higher pay and opportunity. It will kill your incentive.

You must find which skills you bring to the table and cultivate and promote them. You must also work to develop skills that will serve you well as your career progresses.

This humble arrogance is really misstated, but I want the juxtaposition of the phrase to stand out in your mind. Having a strong understanding of your worth, but without the attitude that comes from overstating its value, can help you carry yourself with confidence in any position. I am not looking to create techno prima donnas who believe they stand above their peers in some type of career aristocracy; however, I do want you to believe that you have skills and ideas that bring value. I want you to believe that you can master those skills you currently do not possess. And I want you to feel confident in your ability to develop any talents that are necessary to bring value to your job. In doing so, you forward your own career.

Ownership

The attitude of ownership is another vital component to your career growth. You must take responsibility for the tasks assigned to you and more. Having managed a number of people, one of the most damaging attitudes I've seen is the idea that a job description defines clear borders of responsibility.

I've listened with disbelief when an employee responds, "That's not my job," when assigned with a task. In many cases, the employee does not express this sentiment to management but instead complains to coworkers and peers. It is something I've never understood. I hope that this phrase never enters your mind.

Your ability to tackle varied and multiple tasks is the proving ground for your talent and a wonderful opportunity for growth. The idea that your job description must include any tasks assigned is foreign to those who understand dynamic career growth. Accelerated career advancement is about separating yourself from those who do "enough" by expanding both your production and your effectiveness. You cannot afford to wait until you are promoted to begin taking on the tasks of your next position. Start doing them now.

In addition, the willingness to roll up your sleeves and get dirty shows your willingness to see projects through and help out wherever possible. Management appreciates this. As your career advances, you will, too. As a business owner, I used to have employees who would "catch" me cleaning the sink at the office or taking out the trash. Occasionally, they commented that I shouldn't be doing that.

However, if all my employees were busy on project work and I had a moment, the task was there and had to be done. I don't consider this a martyr type of attitude, just a pragmatic reality. You should try to carry the same "get it done" approach.

While at Blue Cross of California, much of my career advancement rested with the fact that I sought out projects that exceeded both my current skill set and my responsibilities. I sought out a mentor who was either directly involved in the project or elsewhere in the company who could provide me the input, training, and direction to succeed in the new area.

Caution	In some cases, your peers might ostracize you. Some view their job from a victim's perspective. It is critical that you do not allow this to infect your perspective. When you tackle tasks that are necessary to take you beyond your current job, you will inevitably make others, who are unwilling or unable to do the same, nervous.
	Prepare yourself for this. The fact is that most of us have the ability to feel envy. When someone gets "luckier" than us in his career, we must fight the urge to harbor bitterness. And we must understand when people harbor such feelings toward us.

There is a difference between having an attitude of ownership and being in a situation where unrealistic expectations and unachievable goals are set for you. I am not suggesting that you take on every task in your department. There are limits to your time and your talent.

If you find that your company is consistently assigning you projects and tasks that fall outside of your expertise and negatively impact your current workload, you must take action. For better or for worse, there are only two reasonable responses to this situation:

- **Address it directly with management**—Explain the situation and assess your manager's response. Either he will agree and alter the expectations, or he will not. If your manager does not agree or you see no change in your workload or his expectations, I would start looking for a job elsewhere.

- **Start looking for a new job**—Remaining at a job where management is unrealistic and the chances of your success and internal promotion are greatly inhibited is a recipe for failure. Most organizations and most managers are interested in the success of their employees. Seek out companies and management with a mindset that is more conducive to your growth, goals, and promotion.

The Myth of the Self-Made Man

Many of our attitude problems, particularly in our peer or management relationships, are fostered by the myth of the self-made man. When we achieve some type of success, it is our human nature to be willing to take full credit. And yet, if we are honest, we will admit that we were helped along to some degree.

No one operates, learns, or achieves on an island. It might be that you had a mentor, a person who has provided some direction in your life and career. Or perhaps your mentor was found in books or articles. Perhaps your solid upbringing has provided you with an attitude that allows you to attempt and fail enough times to attempt again and then succeed.

Whatever it is, if you search hard enough, you will find that you are not self-made. Someone—typically many such someones—along the way provided input that helped prepare you.

This understanding can assist you in maintaining a proper perspective when you are faced with peers who are envious of your success or, worse yet, when you feel that envy as you watch others succeed. Knowing that you received assistance to get ahead and that your peers also received assistance helps keep you from becoming arrogant or becoming intimidated. Both of those attitudes are damaging to your career.

Attitude Checks

Put yourself in a state of continuous and corrective attitude checks. This requires a realistic self-assessment of the thoughts you are having. During recent speaking engagements, I instructed the participants to swallow their pride to achieve their goals and dreams.

Find role models who will not allow you to feel self-pity or bitterness. Incorporate a get-over-it attitude that involves developing corrective action instead of internal mental struggle. One forces you inward and away from success, whereas the other provides a plan. Remember: Action feeds positive mental attitude.

Conclusion

I was careful to point out in this chapter that a positive mental attitude (PMA) without a plan of action leads to frustration. Do not underestimate your PMA's effect, however. Regardless of work environment, coworkers, and challenging bosses—all of which you will experience—you are responsible for your attitude. Your attitude will be a separating factor in how you work and, more important, how you are perceived at work.

If you start correcting your own attitude problems and continually work to bring an attitude of value to your work, soon you will find that attitude self-fulfilling. You will begin to expect opportunities and you will see them. You will personally expect value out of yourself and you will get it. Your peers and management will view you as a critical and healthy part of the team.

All of this will lead, in time, to a more rewarding career.

Actions & Ideas

1. Take a personal inventory of your attitude. When you think of work, your coworkers, and your company, what is your first thought? If the first thought is negative, beware: You might be the problem.

2. Get input from someone whom you trust (a mentor) to be honest with you. Ask this person what his perception of your attitude is. Don't make excuses for the answer he gives you. Take it to heart and consider how you might correct it.

3. Create a written plan of action. Keep it close at hand and refer to it often. It should include overall career objectives and short-term goals.

4. Concentrate on a single facet of your plan. Success in one small area, whether expanding your professional network of contacts or improving a single aspect of your toolkit, goes a long way in improving your attitude and making your other goals seem achievable.

5. Numerous self-help books are on the market. Pick one and read it. Turn to the "Reading List" in the appendix or visit http://ITCareerToolkit.com for some recommended reading.

EXPAND YOUR TOOLKIT

Remember to visit the book's website at http://www.ITCareerToolkit.com for supplemental and ongoing advice, tips, and data relevant to this chapter.

Communication Breakdown

Technology professionals have a long history of deficiency in communication skills, which has fostered jokes and parodies.

Tragically, however, this might be the single most important aspect of effective career development. Poor communication skills result in misunderstandings, project failures, and ultimately, career stagnation.

The development of good communication skills is rarely given appropriate time and effort. The technology professional is typically consumed with learning technology-based skills, not the ill-defined and misunderstood soft skills.

CHAPTER 7

Communication Skills

Communication skills are some of the most essential to dynamic career growth. Unfortunately, they are the most overlooked. When I speak of communication skills, I cover broadly the gamut of possible communications. These include the following:

- **Verbal**—This includes presentation skills, meeting skills, and effective conversation.

- **Written**—This includes memos, reports, letters, and e-mail correspondence.

Communication falls into those often-nebulous soft skills. The soft skills are prized beyond all others, yet their definition and teaching are often elusive. In the world of information technology (I.T.), this one skill set might be the golden nugget that can support incredible career growth.

Communication skills are seldom mastered, however, falling prey to a schedule that is filled with technical training and a library of books geared toward staying at the top of your field—from a technological perspective. Those things that are ill-defined seldom make it to the top of our list, and this is the case with the technologist and communication skills.

Perhaps a definition of what these skills are and how they work for you is in order. If you clearly understand the nature of a given skill and how its mastery directly impacts your ability to grow in your career, it is more likely that you will work to conquer that skill.

Defining Communication Skills

Communication skills are one of those transcendent skills that follow you from job to job and from technology to technology. Once learned, these skills seldom become obsolete. In fact, a well-written letter from 100 years ago would, minus irrelevant or outdated references, sound much like a well-written letter today.

This should be great cause for excitement. The fact is, when you master communication skills, you will use them throughout your lifetime. In an industry where technical talent is quickly made obsolete, it is nice to identify important skills that maintain their value.

The Benefit of Communication Skills: An Effective Communicator Is Viewed as More Intelligent

Consider two technologists of equal abilities. Both present their ideas or project summaries to management. One is an extremely poor communicator. He does not understand social mores, does not carefully select words for impact, and speaks in techno-jargon.

The other is well spoken. He's not extravagant, but he has practiced speaking slowly and carefully. He selects words that paint a picture of his proposed solution without using techno-jargon. He appears fairly comfortable, not fidgeting or unaware of his posture and hands. Even if nervous, he follows a clear line of thinking because he has learned to organize his thoughts into a presentation format.

Who, of the two, do you think management will view as smarter? It might well be that the first person is the brighter of the two. However, his inability to communicate effectively will far overshadow any brilliance he might have. The second person, in contrast, will appear as though his project is well thought out. He will appear more in control.

Management will put its trust in a better communicator nearly every time.

The impact that this has on your career cannot be overstated. I am not advocating that every person learn how to give presentations to hundreds of people. Nor do I expect every person out there to write manuals or books.

However, you must understand some basic communication dos and don'ts.

Written Communications

This is a simple primer on written communications. Numerous books are available on writing for business and writing in general. I'll offer a piece of advice here: Writing for business is really not that different from any good writing.

When it comes to a manual for effective writing, there is only one I need to recommend. *The Elements of Style* by Strunk and White is considered the standard in the field. It covers basic writing rules and usage that, if adhered to, produce excellent results. Although many other books exist, I begin and end my recommendation here.

With that said, the sections that follow provide some guidelines to effective written communications.

General Guidelines

General guidelines for all forms of written communication include the following:

- **Be brief**—It's not about volume. The goal is well-understood and relevant content.

- **Make your point first, and then back it up**—Those who write infrequently often begin by filling in details in an attempt to take the reader through their thought process. Don't! Instead, make the point and then fill in any necessary information. You will find in many cases that the point itself is sufficient.

- **Watch punctuation**—A question is a question. Commas separate thoughts. It simply looks more professional and more intelligent to punctuate your work properly.

- **Break up your ideas**—Use paragraphs to separate ideas. In the freeform world of e-mail, this rule is often abused. Long, unbroken paragraphs are difficult to read. In addition, use spacing between ideas to create a logical break for the reader.

The Letter

Few pieces of written correspondence have the impact of a well-written business letter.

Properly address your letter. If you are unsure of the addressee, call the company or call the person who is receiving the correspondence.

Use the person's name in the letter. This demonstrates your ongoing recognition of that person.

Create a logical flow in your letter. Use the tips for structure that are described in the section "The Well-Crafted Page" later in this chapter. This can help you organize your letter's ideas.

Keep your intended recipient in mind as you write. Have a clear understanding of what this person is most interested in. Don't include tangential information that dilutes the primary message.

Make a clear call to action or request. You are writing the letter to give information, request something, or spur some type of response. Make sure you let the person know what you expect as a result of your letter. Don't be vague.

E-Mail

I have always found it surprising that individuals who normally write well-conceived and organized communications (letters or memos) throw all that out when it comes to e-mail.

This disregard takes the form of sloppy punctuation, lack of organization, a general disregard for capitalization, and other problems. For some reason, many believe that e-mail communications do not have to adhere to the normal rules that guide any of their other correspondence.

If that has been your approach, change it. With few exceptions, e-mail should follow most of the same guidelines used in other written correspondence. Just because it starts in electronic format does not mean it stays there.

Also, it is likely that your e-mail will be passed along to someone else—perhaps someone you do not know. Those scattered thoughts and run-on sentences might be some other individual's only exposure to you. Believe me, poor grammar in an e-mail can have an impact.

If your e-mail is a short clip of information, use the same guidelines as you would when creating a memo. If it is a longer correspondence, it should read—and be written—like a letter.

I understand that there are exceptions. A quick yes/no type of clipped response can be appropriate. However, communications of any substance should not take on the roguish and unstructured format often present in e-mail correspondence.

The Well-Crafted Paragraph

If you have never been much of a writer, I am going to give you a basic formula for a well-crafted paragraph. Understand that I deviate from this formula often. It is a format to provide a guideline to help organize your writing. After you have learned this and practiced it well, you can depart from this form, too.

Your standard paragraphs should have four to seven sentences. The introductory sentence introduces the main idea or topic. Two to five sentences form the body and should explain the idea introduced in sentence one. The final sentence concludes your thought by reiterating the original topic and the ideas presented in the body.

Example:

> Career building is a long-term activity. It requires formulating a plan that involves coordinating skills and desires. After you've formed the plan, you can modify it based on your circumstances. However, a big-picture mindset is required to ensure that changes in the plan are not based on reactions or compulsive behavior. Keeping such a perspective greatly enhances career development and opportunities.

I'll admit it: The paragraph isn't great. But it does have a natural starting and ending point. The last sentence effectively summarizes the information presented. You would do well to follow this structure and pattern.

But what about the rest of your document? You now have a formula for writing a paragraph, but maybe you still can't put together a document.

The Well-Crafted Page

Fortunately, the formula for writing an effective paragraph can be used quite nicely to write a longer piece, too. In fact, the formula works well to organize thoughts in general.

When writing a longer piece, such as a memo, use the following formula:

- **Paragraph one**—Introduces the main idea or ideas to be conveyed in the memo.

- **Paragraphs two through four**—Provide content for the ideas to be conveyed. Each paragraph, of course, still follows the simple guideline outlined earlier.

- **Conclusion paragraph**—Summarizes the ideas presented and wraps up the document by issuing a decision or call to action on the ideas presented.

I am not advocating that all business correspondence should be 25 sentences long (5 paragraphs × 5 sentences each). The formula simply provides guidelines for those who are unfamiliar or unpracticed in writing.

> **Note**   For those who have children, this same formula produces easy-to-read essays and book reports and provides children with a concrete direction to use when writing.

Your writing will improve with use. And as it does, you will feel comfortable enough to move away from the formulas presented here. However, I still find myself following these same guidelines when words or ideas are hard to come by. They are highly effective.

Online Presence/Social Media

The world of social media provides a glut of opportunities for individuals to write and respond instantly to a large group of people. I cover this more completely in Chapter 17, "Your Career and Social Media," but it is worth mentioning here.

Blogging, Facebook, LinkedIn, Pinterest, Foursquare, and so on. With new opportunities to publish your thoughts and ideas popping up seemingly every day, you really want to understand the upside and downside potential of these new mediums.

The immediacy of social media allows you to quickly respond to trends and information as it comes in. The downside is that it is very easy to respond rashly or without tact when emotions become involved. In addition, because of the way that social media is shared, such errors in judgment can quickly be spread by those in your network.

I maintain a general positive and forward-thinking tone. Rather than attack an idea, I pose ideas. And to take that a step further, I maintain the following mantra for my online presence:

Be proactive! Be positive! Add value! Share opportunity!

Remember, your strongest network of opportunity consists of your friends and acquaintances. This obviously extends into your social network. Use these tools wisely.

Verbal Communication

Of the two primary means of communication covered in this chapter, basic writing is the simplest to master. Verbal communication is much more difficult. The reasons are obvious:

- **Verbal communication is live**—There is little chance for mistake and revision. You cannot move or edit the spoken word.

- **Public speaking of any type is ranked by many Americans as a fear greater than death**—Many are, in fact, more afraid of being asked to give a public presentation than they are of dying. This is remarkable but true. And the fear manifests itself in ways that are damaging to a career.

However, verbal communication is much more than public speaking. Certainly, that is an aspect that should be addressed. Ultimately, if you really want to see your perceived value at a company skyrocket, become effective at giving presentations. The simple truth is that an audience defers a great amount of respect to the person at the podium.

Before entering the public speaking arena, this section covers the more mundane, everyday verbal communications.

Conversation

It might sound trite that I've included a section on conversation. However, for all of us, this is the most used form of verbal communication. Conversation is as natural to us as breathing. We've been doing it since we were toddlers. But in business, we cannot overlook certain guidelines for conversation.

The following are not rigid rules but general guidelines I've found to be effective:

- **Never joke at another's expense**—This seems natural, but I have witnessed some extremely poor judgment calls on this one. Your relationship with an individual might warrant an extremely relaxed attitude. However, you do not necessarily know the relationship that person has with others in the group. If you must express humor, self-effacing humor is best. You are seldom considered insensitive for making a joke at your own expense.

- **Use a person's name in conversation**—People like few things more than hearing their name. In conversation, speaking someone's name shows that you recognize him. Be careful on this one, though; if you have just met an individual, you should refer to him or her as as Mr. or Ms. Last Name until he or she gives you permission to do otherwise.

- **Look people in the eye**—Don't become the "all-seeing" eye of Sauron. Don't stare or make someone uncomfortable, but it's rude to look away or act distracted—even if you are.

- **Ask for input**—In general conversation, you become a bore and appear arrogant if the other person cannot express his ideas or opinions.

- **Stick to the primary point**—This is more critical for meetings. You can waste a considerable amount of time pursuing topics that yield little or no positive result. This is particularly true in group meetings. If information that you need to make a decision is unavailable, don't continue discussing the various theoretical possibilities. Instead, assign investigation/research to one or two individuals with a time frame for reporting back to the group.

This last point is a particularly important one. I attended one meeting in which the color of a flyer was discussed and debated for almost 30 minutes. Eventually, I asked two members to make a decision out of the meeting and let everyone know via e-mail.

Time is critical in business, and your effective use of time greatly enhances your ability to move your career along.

Presentations and Training

The sections that follow describe some key points regarding effective presentations. In addition, some excellent resources available for the prospective speaker are as follows:

- **Toastmasters International** (www.toastmasters.com)—Toastmasters is an international organization of clubs that meet (typically weekly or monthly) to provide a safe learning environment for presentation skills. Attendees are provided instruction and the opportunity to prepare presentations, receive feedback, and even practice ad hoc, on-the-fly presentations. Most major cities contain clubs.

- **National Speaker's Association** (www.nsaspeaker.org)—The National Speaker's Association is geared toward the professional speaker; however, it has local chapters that often have "candidate" or other less-formal instructional groups. Many of their members also provide coaching to nonprofessional speakers.

- *Public Speaking for Dummies* **by Malcolm Kushner**—This book covers fundamental guidelines for preparing a presentation. Kushner gives advice for the occasional presenter on keeping your audience's attention, overcoming stage fright, and ways that speaking can enhance your career.

- **AskOxford.com** (www.askoxford.com/betterwriting/osa/ givingpresentations/)—The AskOxford website has a nice tutorial on preparing and giving a presentation.

- **Community college courses**—If you struggle greatly in this area, consider taking a course on public speaking at a local community college. One thing is for sure: Practice is the single greatest way to overcome fear of speaking and to help you learn how to create more compelling and interesting presentations.

Don't Wait Until You Are Asked to Speak to Learn This Vital Skill

At some point in your career, if you are moving forward and aggressively seeking opportunities, you will be asked to give a presentation. If you wait to prepare until you are asked to speak, you will severely hinder your ability to shine during this pivotal moment.

The opportunity to speak can be a groundbreaking moment for your career. As I've mentioned previously, a great amount of respect is given to those who speak in front of an audience. If you do it well, your credibility with those in attendance will grow tremendously.

If you have never trained as a speaker, I recommend taking a speech communication course at a local college or, better yet, join Toastmasters. Toastmasters (www.toastmasters.org) is an organization that provides training and practice speaking opportunities. Most groups meet either every week or every other week.

The ability to speak will help you present yourself better in interviews, group meetings, and even with individual presentations.

Cover No More Than Three to Five Main Points

As a rule, I break my presentations (regardless of length) into three tangible points. I might ultimately cover more information in the form of subtopics and tangential points; however, members of the audience usually remember information better if you anchor it on a few key points.

Focusing on a few key points helps you, the speaker, stay focused. This is critical. The world of technology has so much information that, at times, we strive to get all the information to those who are interested. The drawback is that we end up losing a good portion of the audience. Information takes time to digest, and too much of it makes the presentation appear disorganized.

Work from an Outline, Not a Script

It is distracting to watch a speaker read his presentation directly off of a paper. I start thinking that I could read the presentation myself—I don't need something read to me. Instead, create an outline of the topics to be covered. You can write a script, but plan to use the script only in practice. When giving the presentation, use the outline.

This allows you to look up during the presentation and creates more synergy between you and the audience. Even if you lose your place and have to refer back to the outline, the audience will enjoy your presence more if you are making eye contact.

Maintain Eye Contact with Your Audience

Expanding on the preceding point, make sure to maintain direct eye contact with your audience. If this proves difficult for you, just look over the room starting from your left, and as you are speaking, scan to the right. By doing this, you ensure that you do not leave out any portion of the audience. Making eye contact keeps the audience *interested* in you and your presentation.

Of course, countless other techniques can help you speak more effectively. However, practice is the best solution. You will mess up a few times during presentations. And although some people seem completely natural in front of a group, the fact is that they have probably given numerous presentations to get them to that point.

I cannot overstate the value of public speaking. That skill and the ability to effectively run a meeting will place you at the forefront of projects. The exposure will ensure that your name is at the top of the list of respected professionals at your company and even within your field.

A Brief Note on Listening

This chapter focuses on your ability to communicate with others effectively. However, the ability to listen effectively is also a big part of communication skills. Although I do not cover this skill, it is one that will greatly impact your ability to succeed.

Understanding what management or your client is saying and translating that to effective technology is critical. Too often, technologists tend to listen with a preconceived notion of how the problem should be solved, without actually listening to the need or desire. This can lead to misdirected projects that, although effective, do not address the primary concern.

Conclusion

Communication is a total-package skill. Using the techniques addressed in this chapter can greatly increase your value to nearly every company you might work for and provide a transcendent skill regardless of changes in technology.

Actions & Ideas

1. Are you afraid of giving presentations? If your first thought is "I could never do that," put this skill at the top of your list of skills to develop.

2. Consider attending a local Toastmasters meeting. Visit www.toastmasters.org to find a club near you. If that is not possible, consider taking a class on public speaking or presentation at a local community college or university.

3. When writing letters or work summaries, use the five-paragraph structure discussed in this chapter. Even if it's not required, write a weekly summary of work in this format. Practice is the best method for improving your writing. Let a peer or supervisor assess your work.

4. Make an effort to write e-mail with a logical beginning, middle, and end point. Use an indent or an extra space between paragraphs to break them up.

5. Pick up *The Elements of Style* by Strunk and White. This book is indispensable for improving your writing.

EXPAND YOUR TOOLKIT

Remember to visit the book's website at http://www.ITCareerToolkit.com for supplemental and ongoing advice, tips, and data relevant to this chapter.

The Search for the Next Hot Technology

Inevitably, the most pressing question heard from technology professionals is this: What is the next big thing?

The pressure of ensuring your relevance in a career that seems to be in a constant state of change can be daunting. To reduce this pressure, you must develop skills of transcendent value.

However, key concepts are available to assist the technologists in both identifying and learning the next big thing, greatly reducing the stress. This chapter identifies some strategies to help you quickly adopt new technology.

CHAPTER 8

Technical Skills

Your ability to produce great technical solutions is critical. The brick and mortar types of skills gleaned from study and application of books are ones you will spend the majority of your time developing and using. However, in one sense, I feel the need to deemphasize them.

In fact, as you read this chapter, you might sense that I am taking something valuable away from you. You might feel some anxiety and even anger. I'll make this promise to you: If you track with me in this chapter, you will find that I make a fair trade.

If you have hinged your career solely on your technical abilities, then yes, I will be taking something away. In its place, I will leave a solid understanding of the importance of technology talent. In fact, I will leave you with an understanding of how to more quickly adopt and learn new technical skills.

Your Technology Skills

Most technologists know the importance of technical skills. These skills represent the starting point for a career in technology and are, logically, the first tool mastered. Unfortunately, they often become the last tool mastered, too. For many technology professionals, tech skills become their only focus. They are the single peg on which they hang their career hat.

Technologists often overlook entirely the critical elements of professional networking, communication skills, and understanding business concepts. This ultimately leaves them with a toolkit that is incomplete and hinders their ability to complete the project of building their career.

When I speak to technologists about this, most admit to a nagging sense of missing something. They typically point to some technical skill that they feel they are lacking. And for this reason, they are in a headlong race to increase their intellectual capital through continued learning.

The Role of Learning

Don't get me wrong. I am not against continually improving your technical skills. Technical skills are the heart of what you do. They produce the results that earn you a paycheck. They are vital and will play a huge role in your overall career development strategy.

However, in my experience, the straight technical skills are seldom the problem in technology careers. Most technologists have some skills. They have, in fact, garnered talent and can put it to work.

Their career development, however, has become lopsided. They are similar to the bodybuilder who spends hours in the gym developing his biceps and shoulders. After years of work, his arms are models of muscular perfection. But as you step back, you notice spindly legs that hardly seem able to hold up the rest of his frame. The technologist who works entirely on his technical skills while ignoring the rest of the package is similarly atrophied.

The Fear of Obsolescence

"It changes so fast. I've got to stay up on it."

That phrase, above all others, captures the essence of the problem. The rapid rate of change in technology forces technologists to continually study and learn. In fact, in prior chapters, I point to this as one of the most desirable elements in technology: the need for continuous learning.

However, this need for continuous learning can quickly become a burden if you fear that you are on the verge of losing your technical edge and moving into obsolescence. The learning process starts to become viewed as "treading water" professionally speaking—keeping you from drowning, rather than adding value.

This drive to continuously add to your technical skill set and predict and learn the next wave of technology supersedes the acquisition of the soft skills mentioned in other chapters. Although most technologists admit to the importance of soft skills, they think that there is simply too much learning on their plate—they can take on only so much. Soft skills development is sacrificed because of this.

Another Perspective: Transcendent Skills

This concept of the value and need for ongoing technical skills development is driven by a misunderstanding of what is truly valuable. Recently on an employment discussion forum, a technologist was bemoaning this fact.

He was asking for input on what skills had the longest useful life. The concern was that the constant grind of learning and trying to figure out what skills were the next *hot ones* on the horizon was burning him out. What skills, he wondered, would yield a value for more than two years? Many others shared this concern.

There are two things to note here:

- Soft skills are transcendent.

- Most technology skills are similarly transcendent.

The first point might be well understood, if not adopted. Yes, soft skills provide ongoing bang for the buck after you learn them. Communication skills, although needing practice to remain sharp, do not change with technology. The medium of communication might change, but not the ability to communicate.

But what about the second idea? Aren't pure technology skills quickly made obsolete? How can they be transcendent? Just ask all the Cobol programmers of the 1970s and early 1980s. They will be the first to tell you that their skills became obsolete because they didn't update them.

Reducing the Parts

Part of the problem is in how technologists categorize skills. I used to explain to my development staff that you are not a particular type of programmer. You are not defined by the tool but by what you produce.

In truth, most technologies share common elements, with the differences largely being semantic and logistic. But the core implementation of one technology is, in fact, quite similar with that of another related technology.

Here are some examples: With the emergence of PC-based computing, many mainframe professionals failed to recognize the power and growth of PC networks. Later, Novell engineers were left behind upon the emerging market dominance of Windows NT. They thought that they didn't have the time to learn Windows NT while supporting and developing their current NetWare environments. Today, technologists still often adhere to a "my pet technology or die" sort of mindset.

However, technologists who understand that the differences between various systems are not so great, quickly add the new systems into their skill set. They understand that whether it is NetWare, NT, Banyan Vines, Linux, OS X, Windows 7, any flavor of Windows Server, or some other network operating system, notable similarities make the technology philosophically similar.

In their core utilization, the network operating systems mentioned are still simply methods for the storage, retrieval, or integration of data and applications. In each, you had users, groups of users, protocols, and connectivity.

I am purposely oversimplifying the idea to make the point. The fact is that many technologists who were more conceptual in their approach made the transition with little or no training. They understand how to study and adopt new technology quickly and without panic, as described in the section that follows.

Tips to Speed Up the Learning Process

Although these tips might be geared toward the technology profession, many are simply methods used to speed learning in any medium. As a father whose children were home-schooled for many years, I teach my children the same concepts.

Start with Concepts
This is perhaps the most important piece of information I will give you in the technical skills game. The ability to quickly adopt and understand new technologies will be enhanced if you start with their concepts. In technology, that is what the technology is trying to achieve, or its core function. This is in contrast to a technology's specific methods or functions.

Many technologists are obsessed with knowing every command and tool at their disposal, but their grasp of when and how to apply them is often poorly defined. Unfortunately, when those screens and menus change, they feel as if they are relearning the steps to complete the tasks.

In the past, I have been chastised by some friends who specialize in midrange systems. They did not like that I referred to an iSeries as the same thing as a PC running Windows 7 or 8 or Linux. They would moan when I made the comparison. I get the same reaction today from any technology pro who knows and supports his "pet" technology, but they are missing the point.

I understand that certain systems and operating systems far outclass others in performance and specific utilization. I understand that some systems run thousands of users, and that is something that a PC certainly cannot do.

But I am not speaking in terms of how the platform performs, only in terms of what it is doing conceptually. I point out that both platforms have CPU, memory, disk space, operating systems, applications, and I/O. The name of the game is to get the data in and the data out as effectively as the system will allow.

The differences are academic.

This might sound simplistic, but it has allowed me, in my career, to take on projects using systems to which I had almost no previous exposure. I would look at the conceptual understanding of what we were trying to achieve and then learn the semantic particulars of the new system in question.

Start with the concept—the why—and the process will closely follow.

Don't Study What You Know

As technology changes or new tools are developed, don't spend time studying elements that are common to well-known technologies. For example, if you have a strong understanding of user administration, groups, and shares on a network, it's not necessary for you to study these topics in depth during the release of a new network operating system.

The fact is, most of the concepts that you knew before have changed little, if at all. A cursory view of a book exposes items that are new or different. You must then determine if these items are truly new in concept and approach or simply in logistical placement.

You need to understand new concepts well. These are the items that you should spend time learning. Slightly altered tasks or methods don't require much study time, so don't waste your time with them. As long as you know that these things are available, if they have little conceptual difference to what you already know, simply knowing the differences is enough.

Don't Worry About Catching the Latest Trend

Because of the emphasis on the *how* over the *why* of technology, many technologists become process driven. Because of this conceptual misdirection, they perceive their value as tied to their knowledge of the step-by-step tasks to be performed. This, in turn, leads to a fear of spending time learning the "wrong" thing.

The idea is that if the technologists spend time learning the wrong thing, the right thing will pass them by and they will have missed the chance to learn the hot technology of the day. This, in turn, will negatively impact their career.

However, if you adopt a concept-driven approach to learning technology, this fear will be reduced. Instead, learn to identify the key concepts that are offered in any given technology. This conceptual understanding will leave you feeling much less stressed about the process—the how to—because it will become apparent that it is more of the same thing.

This is why understanding the role of technology is more critical than understanding any given technology. Particular technology is just the tool for achieving a particular job. The technology is not the result; the solution is the result—or at least it should be.

Note	During the initial years of the dot-com revolution, my company used to have a phrase:
	"E does not equal S."
	Simply put, it meant that E does not equal a solution. The heavy emphasis on companies providing products and services that were only valuable because they were preceded with an E in the name was, as we used to say, "E-foolish."

In truth, if you understand the role of technology and technology concepts, you can quickly change gears and adopt the "hot" tool.

Focus on Solutions, Not Technology

This goes hand in hand with understanding the role of technology. The fear of being left out of the latest technology is built on the misunderstanding of what companies want. If you are effective at solving business challenges with technology, your career will flourish.

Management will be less likely to focus on the tools currently at your disposal if your track record is one where, regardless of technology used, you provide a solution.

I worked for a large law firm that had an incredible I.T. manager. He was focused on solutions, not the tools to achieve them. When a project (read challenge) arose, our first task was to create a vision for its solution, not necessarily formally, but in discussions.

"How would you solve this?" was the question. As answers and ideas were tossed around the group, a vision for what the solution looked like would appear. He then assigned it to one of us to find the best tool for the job.

When doing so, we always started with the known tools because they were easier to adopt. However, if newer tools offered enough performance or simplicity to warrant, we adopted them.

There was never a question of whether you had actually used the tool. The focus was on whether the solution was well conceived.

Focus on solutions, not on the technology to achieve them.

Conclusion

You must maintain technology skills. However, placing technical skills before understanding of concepts will hinder your ability to learn and adopt new technologies. The how-to of technology is much easier to adopt when you understand the concepts.

Actions & Ideas

1. Do you find yourself worrying about the next hot technology? If so, look at your current technical skill and review an older technology that is similar. Take note of how terms and some functionality have changed but core concepts have remained the same.

2. As you look at career advancement, do you think that your greatest strengths are hard technology skills or conceptual problem-solving skills? What would you like your greatest strength to be? After you've identified it, create a plan or ascertain where you could develop those desired strengths.

3. If you are working on a current technology challenge, create an idea of how the solution would look, regardless of the technology. Come up with a somewhat different solution or architecture and compare the two.

4. Identify areas where you do well with a conceptual approach versus those areas in which you are largely process driven in your thinking.

EXPAND YOUR TOOLKIT

Remember to visit the book's website at http://www.ITCareerToolkit.com for supplemental and ongoing advice, tips, and data relevant to this chapter.

The Human Side of Career Development

Your personality, your likes and dislikes, and your views and opinions will become apparent when you're working for a company. The makeup of a company—its culture—represents an important factor in your ability to have an enjoyable time and an effective career experience.

Your cover letter should represent, to some extent, your personality. It allows both you and your perspective employer to have a clear understanding of each other.

The cover letter, more than your resumé, is a chance to convey the type of employee that you will be. It is one part information and one part marketing.

CHAPTER 9

The Cover Letter

Whereas your resumé serves as an ambassador to potential employers, your cover letter serves as a vital introduction to both your resumé and you as a person. Your resumé is a summary of skills and talents, a list of facts that provides little insight as to your personality, attitude, or likes and dislikes. Your cover letter, however, should introduce you and your resumé in a way that conveys more about you, the person.

This chapter explains the role of your cover letter. You learn how to create one that is both effective and exciting and discover the key elements to be conveyed.

The Purpose of Your Cover Letter

Your cover letter is meant to augment your resumé. It should not simply restate what your resumé already states. In fact, if crafted properly, your cover letter should provide a reason for the prospective employer to look more closely at and regard with more credibility your resumé.

In your cover letter, you are attempting to demonstrate how the skills and experience in your resumé are part of a larger, more complete picture. Not only do you have value and skill, but you also have a professional attitude that will benefit this company. In effect, your cover letter serves as a bridge between your resumé and a specific opportunity.

Your cover letter also provides a place for you to do a little bragging. You might remember the adage "If you don't toot your own horn, nobody will." This is certainly true, but you must handle it with tact.

Some might disagree, but I am a big believer in self-promotion. Proclaiming your successes can work to convey a sense of pride in what you do. Although you do not want to appear arrogant or conceited, confidence in your ability to achieve can go a long way toward helping a potential employer become comfortable with you.

Every time an employer hires someone, he is taking a chance. During the hiring process, from the initial contact with your cover letter and resumé, and through the interviews, you must work to make the employer believe that giving you a job is a good idea. The employer will not get to that point unless he is confident that you can do the job.

Your own confidence helps the employer gain confidence. Imagine a prospective employee being asked why hiring him would be better than hiring the next guy. If you are the prospective employee in this case, it would serve you well to have an answer that exudes confidence.

Remember the first tool in your toolkit: the attitude that you have something valuable to offer. Your cover letter is the first place where you get to use that tool.

Three Vital Ingredients in Your Cover Letter

The cover letter has three vital ingredients:

- Gratitude for the opportunity

- A significant accomplishment

- Your interest in becoming a producer

You will find in Part III of this book, "Putting Your Toolkit to Use," that I believe in constructing as generic a letter as possible. As you meet people during your job search, you can provide customized elements. However, these three ingredients should be conveyed in each letter.

Gratitude for the Opportunity

Although you come to your job search with an attitude that says "I have something valuable," the fact remains that the employer is taking time to give you an audience. Even if that means simply reading your cover letter and looking over your resumé, you should remember that the employer's attention requires many other tasks.

Your cover letter should be succinct. Whenever possible, keep it to one page.

Although I have seen some good letters that break the one-page rule, you do so at your own risk. It's time-consuming to read lengthy cover letters. A single-page letter is adequate for conveying the most important ideas about you as a potential employee.

A Significant Accomplishment

Here is the section of the cover letter where you get to brag a little bit. This section might be difficult for some people to write. As a culture, we are taught to be humble. During the job search, however, you need to provide your prospective employer with reasons why you are the right person for the job. You must be willing to promote yourself and your accomplishments. You can rest assured that someone else looking for the job will be promoting his accomplishments.

The significant accomplishment is not a pass/fail type of item. For some, the accomplishment might be management of a multimillion-dollar project. For others, it might be the completion of a particular task. This section of the cover letter should reflect an accomplishment that represents the level of competency you have achieved. It should also convey some idea of your ability to succeed in your desired role with that particular organization.

I have met some new technologists who have a difficult time with this one. They believe, in error, that the accomplishment must always be technical in nature. However, I know many employers who would be happy with someone extolling the fact that they never missed class or that they passed all their courses for the past 2 years.

Employers respond to confidence. Your willingness to consider something that you've done significant enough to mention on your cover letter will go a long way by itself. As your experience grows, so, too, will the level of accomplishment.

Your Interest in Becoming a Producer

For many people whom I counsel, the single-most damaging mistake they make is not asking for what they want. They go through life frustrated, waiting for their employer to recognize what they want to do and then help them get there.

The same is true in your cover letter. You should clearly identify what you would like and how you are going to help that happen. In your cover letter, you should identify what you would like to do. This section can replace the objective on your resumé.

For example:

It is my plan to work for a company locally in both a support and network engineering role. I would love to speak with you further about how I might be able to assist your company in this capacity. I will follow up with you in 2 to 5 days. However, if you have any questions you would like me to answer, please feel free to call the number I've listed.

Note two things here:

1. You were specific in letting the employer know your intentions.

2. You want a job with this particular company.

Number 2 is important. You have informed the employer that you will be following up in a few days. This is critical. Many job seekers have relegated themselves to a wait-and-see type of mentality. They get their resumé out the door and then watch helplessly for their phones to ring. The mental anguish with this approach can be devastating.

I advocate a much more direct approach. Although I don't want to appear pushy, I do want the employer to know that I am on a timetable to make a decision about my job. It's not wise to make contact with a company and then simply wait.

You must understand that people run companies and people make mistakes. People get busy. They forget. In a perfect world, the company could make contact with all potential employees to let them know the status of their resumé and the job in question. However, in the real world, the employees who are charged with reviewing your resumé might have dozens, if not hundreds, of resumés on their desk. Add to this their own primary job responsibilities, and it is unlikely that a call is forthcoming.

A more direct and proactive approach is more effective for another reason: It gives you a better sense of what is happening at a company. You might find that although the primary job was filled, the employer is looking for someone to fill a similar position. You would be surprised at how many times a different job, similar to the first, opens up, but the company starts its employee search from scratch.

Your follow-up calls to the company should be designed to acquire the following important information:

- Has a decision been made?

- Is there a time frame for the decision?

- Are other, similar jobs open now, or will there be in the future?

- If you're not selected for an interview, can the employer give you specific advice on improving your chances elsewhere or for that company in the future?

Conclusion

The cover letter is the human side of your marketing collateral. When you are unable to be there in person to shake someone's hand while you give them your resumé, your cover letter is your best first impression. Make your cover letter professional, yet human. Your cover letter should convey a sense of who you are.

It is best to be real here. You don't want to convey an image of stoic professionalism if you are a bubbly and gregarious personality (and vice versa). You're better off not being hired for a position where your personality will create conflict or will not mesh well with the company culture.

Note	If the problem with your personality or attitude is you, you had better adjust it quickly. Most companies can and do hire a broad spectrum of individual personalities, but virtually none can afford an abrasive and difficult person.

Actions & Ideas

1. Create an outline for a generic cover letter.

   a. What is your most significant accomplishment?

   b. What role would you like with the company?

2. Review some of the sample cover letters included with this book's accompanying material online.

3. Write a cover letter and have a mentor or honest peer review it. Let this person know that you want feedback on whether your letter will generate interest in you as a person and in your resumé.

4. If you have recently or will be sending your cover letter to some companies, make sure you include a specific date for following up with those companies.

EXPAND YOUR TOOLKIT

Remember to visit the book's website at http://www.ITCareerToolkit.com for supplemental and ongoing advice, tips, and data relevant to this chapter.

Your Career Ambassador

When you give someone a message to convey to someone else, your hope is that the message is understood.

In many cases, your resumé is the first message that you give to a prospective employer. It is vital that the message is clear and effective, represents your abilities, and helps the reader understand who you are.

CHAPTER 10

The Resumé

Of all the tools placed in your toolkit, the resumé is perhaps the one that gets the most focus and initial use. I won't go so far as to say that it is *the* most important. Remember: The goal of this book is to help you build a career, not necessarily get interviews or even get a job. However, I will assume that a significant number of readers of this book are actively looking or will soon be looking for a job. Therefore, this chapter focuses on development of the resumé.

Update your resumé often, perhaps even quarterly. In addition to reducing preparation time when you need to send it out, periodic updates allow you to more accurately track the projects you've worked on and your accomplishments. Remembering the time frames and specifics of projects can be difficult if you've let too much time elapse between updates. Periodically updating your resumé also allows you to better assess your impact or performance on the job.

Your Ambassador to the Professional World

I have an extremely simplistic viewpoint of resumés and what makes them effective. However, my rules and ideas are just that—my ideas. If you have seen or been advised to build your resumé in a particular way, and you are comfortable with it, do not let me dissuade you. I'll simply throw my ideas out there for your review.

The Purpose of Your Resumé

Resumés primarily serve as your ambassador to the professional world. An ambassador, in the political sense of the word, travels to a foreign country on behalf of his country of origin. Through his understanding of the cultural and political environment in which he is visiting, it is hoped that he will be able to create a positive image for his home country. The hope is that through this representation, his home country will be taken seriously and be worthy of consideration for trade, friendship, and alliances.

Your resumé serves a similar role. By accurately and positively representing your skills to the professional world, you hope that your resumé creates a positive image on your behalf. Countries use ambassadors because of the sheer number of countries to visit. One leader cannot do it all. Your resumé serves the same purpose. It should represent you in as many places as possible.

Determining Who Is Looking at Your Resumé

Just as an ambassador's message might fall on deaf ears politically, your resumé might be rejected. That's okay. The country might not be ready to hear the ambassador's message. The goal is to ensure that it is positively received by as many people as possible.

Also, an ambassador must understand his audience and the social and political mores of the country he is to visit, Likewise, your resumé must take into account its prospective audience. Who is the ideal audience for your resumé?

In short, it is the person who is responsible for hiring you. This might be an information technology (I.T.) manager, an I.T. director, the human resource (HR) representative, the owner of a small company, the chief financial officer (CFO), or any number of other managerial roles who have been so charged.

The fact that there is seldom a single classification of individuals who are responsible for the hiring of I.T. staff—or any staff for that matter—forces you to carefully consider how best to reach the broadest number of people. You must find common denominators and attempt to build your resumé for those commonalities.

The following sections represent a sampling of common attributes for those who might view and review your resumé.

Busy Employers

The person who is responsible for reviewing incoming resumés is busy. In many cases, reviewing resumés is an ancillary function that has been dropped in this person's lap. Perhaps this person has some understanding of technology or technology terms. Alternatively, this person might simply be the only available HR representative.

Whatever the reason, the fact remains that in today's highly competitive environment, few people can afford the luxury of reading through someone's skills and experience and carefully picking up on the nuances brought to bear. The need for your ambassador to quickly and clearly tell your message is critical.

Disinterested Employers

The person who will receive your resumé is probably not that excited about the prospect of going through the entire hiring process (screening candidate resumés, phone interviews, live interviews, administrative paperwork, and so on). This person has other things to do, and resumé sifting detracts from his larger role in the company. When I say this person is disinterested, I'm not indicating that he won't assess your resumé correctly or that he doesn't take seriously the task at hand. It's just that he would rather have the process completed sooner rather than later.

Resumé Basics

I've created a pattern for resumés that I've found to be effective. It conveys, in a succinct way, the key elements that are important to the prospective employer. Keep in mind the points described in the next sections as you prepare your resumé.

Length: Brevity Is Key

Taking into account that your resumé will be reviewed by someone who is too busy and generally disinterested in the task, keep your resumé brief. In fact, it should be one to two pages in length, even at the executive level. That does not mean that you cannot have a more detailed and longer resumé. But the fact remains, your ability to summarize your most important skills and professional experience on a couple of pages will serve you well.

Remember your audience. At best, this person is too busy to review the stack of resumés on his desk. He might do so begrudgingly. Reviewing resumés takes away from the current productivity of the employer's day-to-day job. Your brevity will be greatly appreciated. If your core skills and important accomplishments are properly summarized, the employer who is reviewing your resumé can determine whether more information or further dialogue is warranted.

The objective of your resumé is to interest someone enough to call you for an interview, not to give a biographical accounting of your entire career. The employer is looking for someone to fill some role, solve some problem, or bring some key skills into the organization. A one-page resumé should succinctly convey your ability and fulfill those objectives.

You can use your cover letter to elaborate on why your resumé is short by framing it in the context of consideration for the employer's busy schedule. And you will, of course, explain how a more detailed professional summary or resumé is available if needed.

For now, though, suffice it to say that the resumé constructed in the sections that follow will be short and follow a predictable layout and pattern.

No Paragraphs

Remember your potential audience. This person is busy. He is charged with finding someone who can fill a role, solve a problem, or bring key skills to the organization. Forcing him to sift through a dissertation of past experience to find that word or phrase that identifies how you fit the company's need is the proverbial kiss of death.

Bulleted Lists

You can break down skills into logical groupings, comma separated and organized in bulleted lists. Prioritize these groups as follows:

1. Skills

2. Experience

3. Education and accolades

The single most important item you can provide the person who is reviewing your resumé is an overview of the skills you bring to the table.

> **Note** For those who are just entering the market, the list of skills might be short to nonexistent. Don't worry. Chapter 11, "Breaking In to I.T.," provides input on how to quickly build that list and the types of opportunities that will assist you in that goal.

For example, you might provide the following:

- Professional Skills

    — **Programming**—Visual Basic, C#, Asp.net, Java, SQL Server, Active
    Server Pages (VBScript), JavaScript

    — **Network administration**—Windows 2003/2008 Server, Linux, Exchange
    Server, basic UNIX

    — **Managerial**—Project management, strong written and verbal
    communications, effective presentation skills

Note	The objective of your skills list is to allow the reviewer to quickly find the skills that are most pertinent to the company's situation. The company might need to find someone who has SQL Server experience and some administrative skills on Windows Server. Everything else is interesting but not vital. This simple bulleted list provides a concise and easy-to-locate set of skills.
	You can, depending on the job posting or your understanding of the skills required, modify the order of your list. This accentuates those skills that you believe are the most desired. However, whenever possible, include your broadest skill set—including appropriate soft skills. It's best to review the specific job posting or requirements and ads for similar jobs. Look for key words that indicate both the hard, technical skills and the soft skills that are desired. Make sure your skills list reflects these.

Documenting Your Professional Experience

When you're building your list of professional experience, continue using the bulleted list format. Action words are certainly helpful if they correctly convey the message. More important is that your professional experience relates back to your skills list at the top of your resumé.

In effect, you are going to show the employer how you put those skills in your list to work. He should see the skills at the top of the list and then see a short description of how you used those skills at your last company or job.

Even if you are new to the field and the work was primarily lab work, include it. The employer wants to see that you have not simply *learned about* key skills, but that you have used them in some functional way.

Here's the formula: Show what you know (your skills list), and show how it's relevant (your professional experience).

A Note About Certifications/Degrees on Your Resumé

I don't believe you should place your certifications after your name. It is presumptuous to pretend that your latest certification is the equivalent to someone who has spent four to seven years pursuing a Ph.D. or some other advanced degree. Instead, place your certifications or degrees in a section titled *Education and Certifications*. A Master's degree might be the exception to this rule.

Guidelines for Writing Your Resumé

Following are some guidelines to follow when constructing your resumé:

- **No special groups or unrelated awards**—I know that the tendency of newer job seekers is to list awards received on their resumé. Remember: I am seeking brevity and relevance. Unless you have reason to believe that the person who is reading your resumé has some personal connection to this fact about you, leave it off.

- **Honesty**—Don't pad your experience. However, do emphasize relevant experience. For example, if you worked for a small business answering phones and handled the company's three-computer network when you weren't busy, I suggest placing the computer experience first.

- **Objective**—You don't necessarily need to include an objective. I know this contradicts many popular notions. However, you don't want to limit your exposure for a particular job.

  An objective can pin you into a specific type of function and cause the employer to overlook you for other positions. Remember that opportunity is best found while working. You are exposed to many more people and projects. Therefore, your first priority during the job search is to get exposed to companies and opportunities through interviews and ultimately the work environment.

> **Note** As discussed in Chapter 11, you should not necessarily start your I.T. career in I.T. All departments in a company have technology needs. You might do well to have your technical skills developed within a department other than I.T.

- **Neat**—Layout is important. Remember: The person who is reviewing your resumé is both pressed for time and looking for specific key words. A neatly laid-out resumé makes browsing for information easier and more accessible.

- **Error free**—Review your resumé for errors in spelling, grammar, and usage (for example, *know* versus *no*). You can have all the skills necessary for a given job, but if your resumé contains numerous errors, the employer will question your competency.

- **Experience**—Your summary of experience does not necessarily have to include every employer for the past 20 years. In fact, you should include only those jobs that have pertinent experience.

If you are new to the industry, include one or two prior jobs and highlight administrative and organization tasks over nontechnical industry-specific skills. For example, if you were previously in the construction field, do not highlight your building skills. Instead, highlight your ability to work with other professionals in the industry, to organize project plans, or other skills that have broader application.

The website www.ITCareerToolkit.com has some sample resumés for you to review. You can find hundreds of books on writing a good resumé. Many of them propose a different resumé style for different jobs. I am a pragmatic minimalist, though. Although you might emphasize different skills for different jobs, I believe, in most cases, a single, brief resumé can do the job.

If you are working with a career advisor or have received feedback that contradicts this notion, adjust your resumé per that individual's feedback. I am covering guidelines and ideas that have worked well for me and for other professionals, but I also understand that under specific circumstances, variations are necessary. A career advisor or recruiter might have specific knowledge about an opportunity that you are pursuing, and I would heed that person's advice.

Writing Your Resumé for Electronic Submissions and Online Optimization

Many resumés today are submitted electronically. In addition, they get indexed in HR systems that catalog key terms for retrieval later. For this reason, your list of skills at the top and embedded in the bulleted list is that much more important.

HR systems will often do a keyword match. So, if you are reading a job description and you see repeated terms or an emphasis on certain skills, it makes sense for you to list those skills on your resumé. Listing them in the technical skills section with another mention inside the body of specific jobs or projects helps to increase the number of "hits" when those terms are searched for.

The same is true for putting your resumé on a website. However, your resumé on your website is much more likely to be found if it is coupled with geographically relevant information and linked to from a blog. There are just too many resumés online for the typical resumé to be picked up by search engines.

I cover blogging as a career strategy in Chapter 26, "A Professional Blog."

Final note: Do not just add terms in hopes that your resumé will stand out in an HR system. If they are skills you do not know or are simply grouped together in a meaningless mass, your resumé is likely to be passed on by the HR representative who finally reviews it.

Video Resumés

A few years ago, the video resumé became a fad of sorts. Services and software to help you create a video resumé popped up. To date, it has not truly taken off as a standard way to get the attention of employers. There are likely a few reasons for this.

First, there is no standardized format or guidance for what industry expects. With a paper/written resumé, even though many formatting options exists, the information lays out in a fairly standard and linear way.

Second, people struggle with their presence on video. I've been creating videos for some time, and I still sometimes find it challenging. For many, few things are as nerve-wracking as trying to appear confident and intelligent with a video camera in their face. It can be daunting.

Even so, video is one of the most engaging mediums available. In addition, almost every laptop or smartphone can create high-enough-quality video to be published online. This means that almost everyone has access to this tool.

If you are intent on using video in some way to augment your resumé, the following tips and ideas will help you use video effectively:

- **The video resumé augments but does not replace your written resumé**— You still need a printable and online-submittable resumé. The truth is, many organizations are not interested in filtering through video resumés. They are not keyword searchable. However, as an add-on (perhaps mentioned in your cover letter), you may be able to use a video to give a more personal face to your message.

- **Keep it short and high energy**—Video, like audio recordings, are an interesting medium. You never appear as energized on video as you do in person. This can cause you to appear disinterested and boring. If you are going to use video to augment your resumé and as a job-search tool, use it as an introduction, no more than two to three minutes long. Also, up the energy. In fact, you might use a professional videographer or acting coach to help you energize your presence.

- **Make it personal**—A video resumé is not about listing a bunch of skills and projects. In fact, we might consider it a video cover letter. It is more about introducing you and letting a prospective employer get to know you.

  One tip to make it personal is to use an individual video for a specific job. To do this, you can upload a video to a service like YouTube but make it "unlisted." This means that only those who have the specific link can find the video. This, of course, requires more work, as well, because you will need to go through your script or outline for each prospective employer.

- **Be professional and neat**—I hope this is obvious, but I've seen video introductions with bad lighting, sloppy dress, and poor attention to hygiene and other details.

- **Practice, practice, practice**—And then practice some more. The nice thing about digital video is that you can practice your pitch, creating and deleting videos as necessary. Don't hyper-focus on any one take. Instead, just plan on doing 20 takes, 50 takes, whatever is necessary to capture the message and tone you want.

If you are not going to take the time to make the video standout and present your most impressive self, do not use video.

Conclusion

Remember: Your resumé serves as your ambassador to the professional world. It speaks on your behalf—letting a prospective employer know what you are capable of.

Using the ideas presented in this chapter can help you create a resumé that speaks well for you. It, along with your cover letter, is a vital piece to your career builder's toolkit. It is likely that your ability to get frequent and quality interviews will be based on your resumé and cover letter.

Note, however, that your resumé, although important, will have a much greater chance of landing you an interview through direct contacts. The holy grail of job seeking consists of your cover letter and resumé along with the development of a thriving network of contacts. Review Chapter 12, "Building an Active Contact List," and Chapter 17, "Your Career and Social Media."

Take some time to assess your resumé and modify it to ensure that it clearly communicates your skills, aptitudes, and relevant experience. Take care of this piece of your toolkit today!

Actions & Ideas

1. Review your current resumé: How long is it? Do you have paragraphs, or is it difficult to find your skills buried in job descriptions and experience?

2. Create a sparse one-page resumé. Include only contact information, a skills list, professional experience, and education. Let a mentor—preferably someone who is in an influential position—review it.

3. Make sure your resumé shows what you know (your skills list) and why it is relevant (your professional experience).

4. Create two skills lists: a list of hard technical skills and a list of soft skills. Use your resumé as a tool to assist you in assessing which areas you need to develop.

EXPAND YOUR TOOLKIT

Remember to visit the book's website at http://www.ITCareerToolkit.com for supplemental and ongoing advice, tips, and data relevant to this chapter.

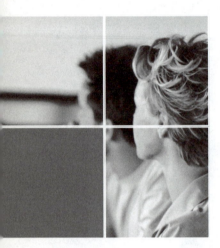

The Entry-Level Dilemma

One of the most frustrating elements of breaking into a career in technology is that initial job. This chapter identifies the quandary facing the entry-level professional.

This chapter analyzes the "need experience to get experience" dilemma that those who are new to the field often encounter. More important, however, this chapter discusses methods you can use to break past this barrier.

CHAPTER 11

Breaking In to I.T.

For many technology graduates, the past few years have been frustrating ones, because they have tried desperately to enter a seemingly shrinking job market. They had bought into the "get a certification—get a job" promise fostered by the marketing of many training programs. These graduates had been excited that their school had placement services to assist them in entering the growing and lucrative field of information technology (I.T.).

Unfortunately, although some technology graduates might have found their dream job as promised, many discovered a different reality.

Having followed the promised path, these eager students have discovered that many colleges have also struggled with placement. Although the schools have programs to help with resumé, and they work diligently to link graduates with employers, the fact remains that a tighter job market and a more skeptical employer pool have made job placement a nearly impossible task.

Adding to a tighter market is the fact that more experienced technology professionals have been forced to take a cut in pay and position. This has increased the competition for entry-level positions. Sometimes new graduates are competing with senior-level technologists for the same job.

Part of the fault of unsuccessful job placement lies squarely on the shoulders of the job seeker. Unrealistic expectations have many believing that a certification or degree qualifies them for positions that require hands-on knowledge.

I know of individuals who received their MCSE certification after attending several months of class. They passed the test, did some lab work, and got into the job market. Many of them expected to be hired as network engineers with salaries of $60,000 to $80,000. Their logic was that they were, as the certification implied, "certified engineers." As they perused want ads, lesser jobs, such as those of help desk or I.T. clerical support, were undesirable to them.

This attitude has contributed to ongoing "certification cynicism" with many employers. Employers hired the "certified engineers" only to discover that many could not complete the most basic and mundane tasks effectively.

A correction has taken place in the corporate world. Companies are no longer willing to provide pay and opportunity to an unproven commodity: the entry-level technology professional. Many new technologists are unwilling to give up the idealistic dream of instantaneous job satisfaction and a high salary. Unfortunately, this is also leading some to listen to the doomsayers moaning about the lack of opportunity in I.T. Talent that would do well in the I.T. industry is leaving to find opportunity elsewhere.

If you are in that group—ready to leave your hopes of I.T. success and find greener pastures—wait!

I understand that you are frustrated and disenchanted, but I ask that you seriously consider the corrective behavior described in the section that follows. In it, I believe you will find a rekindled hope that comes with understanding the reality of the situation.

Correcting Perception

The first battle in overcoming frustration in not finding the "job you deserve" is to correct the perception of the new technologist. As discussed earlier, I.T. will remain a great career choice. However, it is no different from many other good careers. You must make a degree of sacrifice to reach the heights of professional success.

A perspective that places emphasis on long-term career goals and month-to-month personal growth is critical. You must understand where you want to be in the coming months and years. You must also set about creating the short-term plans to achieve that longer-term success.

I'm not necessarily advocating a start-at-the-bottom mentality. I don't perceive that each person's path, even with similar goals, will be the same. I advocate more of a start-where-you-can mentality.

If a company is willing to hire you as a full-fledged network engineer based entirely on your schooling, more power to you. However, beware of overselling yourself without first developing the aptitude that is required. Taking a job where the expectations greatly exceed your production capacity can be just as professionally damaging as it is to take a job that never makes use of, or stretches, the talents you have. In fact, I would say the former is more damaging.

It is more difficult—both mentally and from a perception standpoint—to move down the corporate ladder. It does not look good on a resumé, and more important, it can damage your confidence.

I.T. is an industry that provides ample opportunity to learn new and challenging skills. However, substantial failure early in a career can create a professional timidity that stops you from taking the necessary chances to take on the challenges that come your way.

The perception that you need when breaking into I.T. is one that seeks opportunity over position. If you have been trained as a network engineer but you find an opportunity to take a position in a clerical capacity, consider what opportunities that job might offer.

Some of the factors to consider in whether to take this slight shift in employment are as follows:

- Does the company have an effective training program?

- Is it possible to find mentors in the field you want to enter?

- Is the company growing?

- Does the opportunity exist to greatly expand your professional network of contacts?

Remember: You can safely make this consideration because the job itself is not your career. You have the freedom and ability to move within the company or to a new company when needed.

The most important factor is that you are moving toward a career goal. You might not get the title or job you want right out of school. If you can master those skills at your current position, while simultaneously building your network of contacts that lead to your dream position, you should be satisfied. You must build your career piece by piece. It won't happen all at once.

I.T. Happens Outside of I.T.

One of the most important ideas that I coach is the concept of breaking into I.T. by staying away from I.T. Scratch your head for a moment and get past the nagging thought that what I just said makes no sense. Now move on. I'll explain.

Many who are struggling to enter the I.T. field view their first major career step as getting a job in an I.T. department. This myopic view has been advanced to a degree by the growth of the industry over the past few years. The advent of the chief information officer (CIO) as a corporate executive is a new concept.

In the past, IT largely fell under the watchful eye of the chief financial officer (CFO). Technology managers existed, but not technology senior executives. A somewhat rogue and decentralized culture formerly existed in the I.T. world.

The pressing need to ensure that technology closely aligns itself with corporate objectives drives the requirement for a strategic executive. This tighter level of executive management promotes the idea that all technology jobs necessarily fall under the purview of the CIO.

In a traditional I.T. organization, you might see a senior-level executive (CIO, director of technology, VP of technology), managers over working groups (application development, networking, user support), and their staff. Furthermore, you might be under the impression that you must find a way into this structure to start your I.T. career.

That idea is far from the truth.

For many who are currently at the top of their I.T. careers, their path was much different. In fact, a majority of senior technologists who I know started out working in a user department, not in the I.T. or data processing units. Several reasons can explain this:

- Working in an I.T. department typically provides a higher degree of specialization.

- I.T. often creates a myopic view of the business world.

- You can develop numerous valuable relationships outside of technology.

Working in an I.T. department typically provides a higher degree of specialization. In most cases, you fall under a specific classification, as in *help desk*, *network support*, *application development*, *systems analyst*, and so on. Rarely do the job classifications cross. When a task hits a particular level, it is passed on to the appropriate group.

However, when you are a technologist in a user department, you are expected to handle almost everything. The idea of different roles disappears. You are the in-house technology professional. Whether that places you in the capacity of installing hardware and software, supporting and training users, or writing code, you are expected to take on the tasks.

User departments make no distinction between a help desk/PC technician and an application developer. Both are known as the "computer guy." User departments' lack of distinction in this area makes working for them both exciting and dangerous. You are given charge over all of the technology, whether hardware or software related.

I.T. often creates a myopic view of the business world. It is a well-documented complaint of senior management that their I.T. departments do a poor job of understanding or speaking in business terms.

Many years ago, a study conducted by KPMG and ComputerWorld asked CEOs and senior management about how they felt their I.T. dollars were spent. To a large degree, the CEOs believed that I.T. did not deliver solutions that were well aligned with actual business objectives.

Many went even further, stating that they distrusted their I.T. departments, feeling that in many cases, their convoluted language was being used to hide ineffective projects, create confusion, and pad budgets.

This condition and perspective is still prevalent. As an aspiring or growing I.T. professionally, you must deal with this reality. If you do so, and adopt a more proactive and business mindset, you can separate yourself from the crowd.

Note	This perspective by CEOs is something that I have shared for years. In 1996, I started giving a presentation titled "Why Technologists Must Learn to Speak Business." (You can find an article of the same name at www.ITCareerToolkit.com.) In the article, I admonished technologists to begin speaking to management and businesses in business terms and removing techno jargon from their language entirely.

One advantage to breaking into I.T. by becoming a departmental technologist is that you are forced to speak in terms that the general department speaks. You learn the business from the business unit—the people managing and performing the work. Your work is directly applied to production of the product or service of the company.

This was the path I took, and it has served me well. Many of my clients in my technology consulting practice rely on me for assistance in operations, marketing, and other nontechnology-related ventures. One commented once that he did not view me as a technology professional but as a business consultant and mentor who had extremely strong technical knowledge. I associate that skill with the experience I obtained as a business analyst in a nontechnology department.

You can develop numerous valuable relationships outside of technology. These relationships can easily become the core of your professional contacts network. Many will provide you with opportunities at other companies when they leave or through their extended contacts.

I developed many relationships during my years as a business analyst. Some of those relationships became or referred me to contracts when I became a consultant. These people knew the types of solutions I offered and knew of my professionalism. They were happy to refer me to associates or to recommend me to their employers.

Politically, and from the perspective of production, you often gain much more visibility in a nontechnology department. Your solutions are more apparent to the users, and your name becomes synonymous with what you produce. This, of course, can be a double-edged sword. If you do not produce, this will be apparent, too.

Working in a department other than I.T. offers more interaction with users. This increases the opportunity to develop your interpersonal skills. Over the life of your career, this interaction and the development of the associated skills can pay tremendous dividends.

Given the choice between obscurity and the risk associated with being in the forefront of solutions, I'll choose the latter.

A technologist/programmer who builds an application within the I.T. department typically is viewed as one of many producers in that venue. However, the same developer who is working to create an application in a user department, while working with and within that department, gains a sort of "hero mystique."

The hero stands out because he is providing a valuable service that no one else in the department can. In addition, a departmental technologist is often exposed to technology and projects that would never enter his area in the traditional I.T. department structure.

Exposure to new technology and nontraditional I.T. projects is a key reason not to overlook opportunities that place you outside of I.T. Remember that each job is a progression toward your long-term goal. However, the perks and opportunities offered outside of the technology department can have long-lasting effects on your career. They can provide you with a greatly accelerated path of professional development.

Other Avenues into I.T.

As with most career moves, every turn has options. Part of the challenge facing many professionals is the idea that a wrong decision will have lasting repercussions on their career. I want to alleviate this fear.

Seldom will any single career move make or break you. As indicated in Part I of this book, "Your Career," the idea of a career is based on long-term objectives and planning. Plans can change, and even long-term objectives can be altered without negatively impacting your career.

The fear of changing those objectives and plans is exactly what causes many individuals to effectively freeze in their tracks. They fail to make effective moves, afraid that taking that new position might be the "wrong" move. But a job is always just that: a job.

Typically, if you weigh your decision using the factors of compensation, opportunity, insurance, training, commute, travel, and so on, it is unlikely that you will move to a position that is dramatically worse than your current situation. Even if it turns out that you do not enjoy the work, you can simply begin looking for the next opportunity. In most cases, there is a redeeming lesson or skill to take from every situation. That is the way careers and life work out.

I am not advocating leaving your current job just to try something new. If your current position affords you adequate compensation, a learning environment, access to mentors and peers who are actively advancing in their own careers, and any number of other intangible benefits, I advocate trying to advance within the organization.

If you are a person who is trying to break into I.T., advancing within your own organization requires you to make contacts in your company's I.T. department.

Interning

One of the most powerful ways to create connections and kick-start your I.T. career is through interning. Many I.T. and management information systems (MIS) training programs require this; however, you do not need to wait for a school to place you to begin internning.

Interning may allow you to work in a given discipline long before you have your degree and even prior to receiving any training. In addition, if you go out and find your own internship, you might be able to find one that is geographically advantageous to you.

I had an employee who has gone on to become a senior-level consultant. He approached me while in school and asked if he could intern. This unpaid internship turned into a part-time job with me a month or so later. Soon after, I hired him full time. After my company was purchased by a client and he worked there for a couple years, he went to another employer, quickly becoming a senior developer.

Ask for What You Want

I must give you another piece of advice: Ask for what you want. This is one of the most underutilized ways to help advance your career. For some reason, we feel hesitant to make our desires known.

However, if you are hoping to get into I.T. at your company, your chances improve considerably if the manager of that department knows this. I know that sounds obvious. But I meet person after person who fails to introduce himself to his company's I.T. managers and explain his desired career goals.

Part of this reason might be a feeling of inferiority when considering the seasoned professionals who work there. However, personal promotion is a key factor in how rapidly you rise in your career. In marketing vernacular, personal promotion is referred to as *reach and frequency*. Simply put, get your name, accomplishments, and good attitude in front of as many people as possible.

Ask for Advice

The owner of a small marketing company once told me the most noticed/desirable words for people to hear are *you* and *free*. One strokes our pride, and the other strikes a pragmatic financial chord.

Don't be afraid to ask for what *you* want, but just as important is the ability to ask for advice. When you approach an I.T. manager, ask him what you might do to break into the field. More specifically, ask him how you can break into his department.

Let the I.T. manager know up front that you are asking for his advice. More important, take it. If this person provides you with a profile of what he would like to see in an employee, do what you can to model that profile. Asking advice pays dividends in a few ways:

- **It serves notice that you are serious about your career**—You want to know from the top how to succeed in this endeavor. From this perspective, it paints good public relations. As a business owner, I was always impressed when someone would approach me for advice on my line of work. I considered it a compliment and considered the individual wise for seeking it.

- **You'll probably receive some good advice**—Don't overlook this. If you are asking advice just to paint a good picture, but your attitude is one of disdain for the actual advice received, it will show up somewhere else. Most people in management have actually produced to get where they are. Their advice is valuable and should be heeded.

Don't make the mistake of assuming that the managerial tasks are simpler than the hands-on technology work. I'm here to tell you that the opposite is true. You should aspire to learn from *effective* managers, even if you believe your technical skills far surpass theirs.

Beware Your Online Persona

I cover this topic more fully in Chapter 17, "Your Career and Social Media," and Chapter 26, "A Professional Blog." But it is worth mentioning here.

Even your e-mail address should be professional. Vanity e-mail addresses or those that imply immaturity in an attempt to be clever should be avoided. In addition, fully expect any prospective employer to do some research on you. If you are in the habit of posting information that an employer could find objectionable, just be aware that it could hinder your ability to get hired.

Conclusion

Breaking into the I.T. field can, at times, seem to be a daunting task. However, if you look past the obvious door through the I.T. department and see, instead, opportunities elsewhere, your chances are greatly enhanced. Don't be afraid both to ask for advice and let your desires be known. These two ideas alone will serve you well.

Actions & Ideas

1. Analyze your ideas about breaking into I.T. Do you have the perception that all I.T. careers take place in the I.T. department? Can you see areas where technology expertise would be helpful in nontechnical roles—perhaps even a job you have held?

2. Introduce yourself to an I.T. professional of some influence—whether at your current company, your local church or religious organization, or other sphere of influence. Let this person know your career motives and ask for advice.

3. Create a short-term plan of technology projects that you can perform outside of an I.T. department to advance your skills.

4. Look for ads for I.T.-related jobs (or jobs that require I.T. related skills) in non-I.T. departments. Compare job descriptions, prerequisites, and expectations.

EXPAND YOUR TOOLKIT

Remember to visit the book's website at http://www.ITCareerToolkit.com for supplemental and ongoing advice, tips, and data relevant to this chapter.

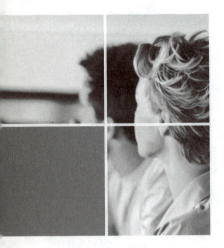

It's Not What You Know—It's Who You Know

It is a cynical stretch to say that what you know is of no value and that getting ahead is more a function of political clout (that is, who you know).

However, a career is built on more than your ability to perform a function well. Your ability to develop relationships is a huge factor in long-term career growth and stability. The people you meet form a natural broadcast medium for your talents and project successes.

In short, the sharing of information and opportunity across a network of professionals will help keep you aware of developments both within your current company and the companies of those who make up your professional network. Modify the old adage to the more accurate, "It's not who you know, but who knows you and knows what you know."

CHAPTER 12

Building an Active Contact List

Few skills are as critical to long-term career growth as professional networking. Your ability to meet and cultivate relationships has a profound impact on your career. Whether it is with your peers, past employers, vendors, or almost anyone else, this factor more than any other will dictate your career growth.

Your professional network is an expansion of this list and should include almost everyone you meet. The primary objective of this list, professionally, is to ensure that you can keep them abreast of opportunities, your career development, and your career goals. In turn, they will have you in mind when an opportunity comes their way.

The mistake common to most people, and this is particularly true of technologists, is that they build their list using industry peers only. They seldom include people from other professions.

This mistake results, in part, because we tend to spend time with those who share our interests. Work is a large part of our life; therefore, our direct peers form a sizable part of our professional network.

However, to succeed in this critical endeavor, you need to expand the reach of your contacts. Most likely, you come into contact with new people on a daily basis. You interact in some way and yet never get beyond the simple hello and goodbye.

Your next big opportunity might be found through the person in front of you when you pick up your morning coffee or as you wait to pick up lunch. Although I don't want you to view everyone you meet as just one more contact for the benefit of your career, the fact remains that each person you meet presents unique opportunities—both personally and professionally.

In many cases, fear is the culprit. If you are shy and introverted, building a professional network is akin to having teeth pulled—if critical, you might do it. If you fall into this category, my advice to you is this: Get over it (quickly). Your ability to create a thriving professional network is critical.

I cannot overstate the impact of a professional network. A professional network goes well beyond the people who make up your personal list. Each person on your contact list has his own contact list. As you search for resources within your contacts, your contacts in turn will look through their own list, effectively extending your reach.

This ripple effect can lead to incredible opportunities. I became chief information officer (CIO) for a small financial services company in just such a way. A friend of mine since childhood had a friend and associate, and he introduced us. This friend, in turn, had a business relationship with another man.

When the business owner was dramatically expanding his business, he asked my friend's friend who he knew who might have the skills to build and run his technology department. A day after that conversation, I was on the phone with the business owner. Two months later, after a short consulting period, I was brought in as the CIO.

Interestingly, I was the only technology professional in this scenario. Almost no competition existed for the role. Expand your reach by networking with a wide variety of people, particularly those who are outside of your industry.

The sections that follow address a list of key elements and ideas I've compiled to help you learn this valuable skill.

Enjoy People

For some people, this is a tough one. You must enjoy people if you are to develop an effective network of contacts. If you do not, and you simply view them as a means to your professional ends, you will always be limited in your effectiveness. People generally know when they are being used.

Develop a Personality

I'm treading on dangerous ground with this one. Everyone sees the world from his own perspective. You might be saying, "I have a personality." However, technologists are particularly guilty of a personality that includes two contact-killing traits: introversion and arrogance.

The analytical nature of technology both draws and cultivates on a somewhat intro-spective mindset. This is particularly true for those in the programmer/analyst crowd.

Many technologists are perfectly happy at their terminal, designing and building their latest creation. Long periods of concentrated effort are required to be effective. For this reason, they come across as aloof.

If you are introverted, you will have to make an effort to ensure that you network adequately. It will be a stretch, but the payoff will be well worth it.

More dangerous, however, is an attitude of arrogance. This is less prevalent during economic downturns, but it is often so bad that it has become the source of cartoons, jokes, and incredibly, an entire character on *Saturday Night Live*.

Several years ago, the popular comedy program *Saturday Night Live* built an entire parody around a computer professional named Nick Burns. The "computer guy" skits might be an exaggeration, but rarely does parody exist without reason. The perception among many nontechnical people is that "computer guys" or "gals" have a superiority complex and treat nontechnical users with the same disdain that Nick Burns, the *Saturday Night Live* computer guy, does.

If you are to effectively build a useful professional network, do not become or appear as a Nick Burns.

Have Other Areas of Interest

Develop interests and points of conversation that are outside the realm of technology.

It is not that I don't enjoy technology. I would not have spent the time and effort developing those skills if I didn't. I'm the first to admit that I am a geek and proud of it. However, I recommend that your conversations take a much less binary tone when in mixed company.

In addition, if you are on the technical fringe, you must develop interests outside of science fiction and obscure collections.

It is not that I mind the obscure or the eccentric. In fact, these can be great personality enhancers if you have some other common interests, too. People will find you interesting and will be likely to remember you if you can mix general interests with those that are more obscure.

Engage in Conversation

I have tried to make it a habit of introducing myself to those I do not know, even prior to a formal introduction. I don't want awkward moments of silence or wondering whom an individual is while I wait for a host or common friend to make the introduction.

This practice has made it easier for me to strike up conversations in various public places. If I catch someone's eye, rather than perform the standard practice of quickly looking away and then struggling not to meet that person's eyes again, I'll simply say, "Hello, I'm Matt."

Such introductions generally lead to conversations. Conversations ultimately lead to the topic of profession and interest. And the conversations can progress from there.

To some, this exchange is natural. These people are natural people persons. I am sure this is how I come across. However, I want to emphasize that this is also a learned and developed skill. If you practice it enough times, it will feel less contrived and more natural.

Just the other day, I was waiting for coffee and started a conversation with another patron. This man, as it turns out, runs a small insurance company. As we discussed our two areas of expertise, we were able to find a natural connection. We traded cards, and although we have conducted no formal business together, we are trading promising correspondence.

I am confident that he or one of his clients will need technology help in the future. But even if that's not the case, the two of us have developed a professional friendship, passing relevant information back and forth over e-mail.

Track and Remember Your Contacts

Keeping business cards in a shoebox is generally ineffective when it comes to tracking your professional contacts and correspondence. Fortunately, you have other alternatives.

The first is to create a tracking database. I developed exactly such a database when I had my consulting company. It tracks vital company information and nearly every correspondence that I, or one of my consultants, have had with a company. In addition, it tracks billable hours spent on project work.

Google's Gmail Contacts is my primary means of contact management these days. Because much of my correspondence is e-mail, it is the primary source of information.

It also synchronizes with my smartphone so that I have my contacts with me at all times.

Act, GoldMine, and other customer relationship management (CRM) companies create products that are specific to tracking and corresponding with clients. Each can be modified to capture the information I cover in the discussion that follows. If you are already using a contact manager and are comfortable with it, simply incorporate the pieces of information that follow. The program or method that you use is less important than your ability to get to the information that you need.

I customized Gmail Contacts quite a bit. I utilize categories and also put contacts into Google Plus's Circles to organize my contacts.

Regardless of the method used, I perform key contact enhancers. I make sure, when I speak with people and get cards, that I write a few short notes about the conversation:

- Are they married?

- Do they have children?

- Did they mention any special areas of interest?

- Did they mention a specific concern?

I then enter this information into the notes for each contact. The notes serve a dual purpose. They serve to remind me of the conversation. In today's world, we have a lot of things to remember. I would love to say that I remember each person I meet. However, sometimes I meet someone and we do not speak again for six months or even a year. The notes jog my memory so that I can recall our conversation.

The notes serve another important purpose. People are flattered when you remember them. Rather than call someone and say, "I have your name here, but I can't remember anything we talked about," you can recall particular elements of the conversation.

You might call and say, "Hello, Jim, it's Matt Moran. We met at Starbucks last year and talked about your insurance company. You had just installed a new conference room. How is that working out?"

Jim is much more likely to remember you, too, with that approach. In addition, your interest in his company and a specific project will have a tremendous impact on him.

I typically enter a next contact date. I can use this to bring up a list of records to contact for the next week. Sometimes these are in the form of a short e-mail. Other times, they are in the form of a phone call. After I make the connection—and based on the feedback, if any—I enter the next contact date.

Other key pieces of information to note with regard to your contacts are as follows:

- **Birthdays**—It is hard to go wrong sending someone a birthday card or a birthday e-mail or making a phone call.

- **Children**—Few things are as near and dear to parents as their children. If someone mentions kids during your conversation, enter the information into your notes.

- **Spouse**—Enter the spouse by name if you can.

- **Special interest**—If the person mentions that he is a fanatical hockey fan (yes, I am, if you have extra tickets), make a note of it.

- **Demeanor and attitude**—This requires some introspection, but I try to list what my impression of the person was. Most important, I want to try to determine the person's style of conducting business. Is the individual a bottom-line type of person? Is he a communicator?

I am sure, as you develop your contacts, that you will determine the information you find important. It is all about making an effective connection. You will find those areas that are effective for you. Mold your contact management and tracking to address those areas.

All the information in the preceding list is to convey the message that you remember that person. Few things are as critical to an individual as personal recognition. If you can recall a conversation or an individual's interest or family information, you will make an impact.

Some might ask whether this is contrived or artificial. I don't believe so. You have the opportunity to meet hundreds of people over the course of a year. It would be irresponsible of you to simply log them into memory and then hope you remember them. That you would take the time to write down notes to help you remember someone shows interest in cultivating some type of relationship.

In fact, when I take someone's card, I tell him that I'm going to write some notes about our conversation. I say, "I'm going to write on the back of your card so that I can be sure to remember our conversation."

No one has ever complained about that.

Typically, I contact people within a few days to a week, just to thank them for the meeting and short conversation. Believe me, doing this will separate you from others they have met.

This is particularly important if the conversation did not produce an immediate opportunity. It is easy to get back in touch with someone who has something you desire. It takes a bit more effort to get back in touch with someone just to say hello.

Ultimately, most people are opportunists. However, you must carry the perspective that you care about the people you meet beyond what they can "get you" in the short term. The long-term benefit of building such relationships is both professionally and personally satisfying.

You *should* care! If not, you will soon be discovered and categorized as a "user" or a "player"—someone who networks and cultivates relationships just for what he can get out of it.

Share Opportunity

The idea behind effective networking is to build contacts with which you can share opportunities. Sharing is the key concept here. If you create a network of contacts hoping that they will think of you for every opportunity, although you never share opportunity with them, you are mistaken.

There is a synergy and general feeling of community that will lend a genuine empathy to your dealings. Make no mistake; a me-only perspective will impact the effectiveness of your professional networking. This is clearly most effective as a two-way street.

Also, when people begin to view you as a person who knows people and can make those connections vital to professional development, they will contact you. This has the added benefit of keeping you in the communication cycle. You will be more aware of what types of opportunities are being developed, furthering your value as a professional contact.

I used to tell my employees that I wanted our company contacted if a client needed a window washer or his carpets cleaned. It wasn't because we provided that service, but because I wanted to be viewed as the company that provided solutions and knew others in different lines of work, with the same attitude. We would facilitate relationships, increasing our value.

I cannot count the number of times I've been contacted by someone in my contact list to find assistance for projects outside of my purview. They simply believe that I will know someone. And when I do not, I scan my list of contacts to find someone I believe will know the right contact.

In the end, I am typically able to assist the person who contacted me.

Professional Networking and Social Media

I cover this in more detail in Chapter 17, "Your Career and Social Media." However, the topic is so important that it bears repeating enough times to ensure you keep these concepts front and center.

I have an article on my website about "Who you cannot be online!"—a warning about abrasive or contentious personalities and activities. It is too easy, in the heat of the moment, to lose credibility, respect, and opportunity online. However, it may be best summarized using my oft-repeated mantra:

Be proactive! Be positive! Add value! Share opportunity!

In fact, whether online or in person, these ideals will go a long way to ensuring your professional network is a valuable one.

Conclusion

Professional networking is the lifeblood of career development. Again, develop your professional network. This skill will become one of the most valuable tools you employ over the course of your career. Work at it constantly until it becomes natural.

Actions & Ideas

1. Look over your list. Have you been adding to it during your employment? Do you regularly stay in touch with members of your list? If not, create a plan of corrective action.

2. Start your list with people from your current company. Include both technical and nontechnical contacts. As mentioned earlier in this chapter, expanding your network to nontechnical professionals helps you learn more how the company works as a whole. It also greatly expands your exposure in the organization.

3. Create a simple location or method to enter and track your professional contacts. A good place to start is to use the Networking & Opportunity Tracker available at www.ITCareerToolkit.com. Plan a time each week to contact several with a courteous and brief note about your current projects and career steps.

4. Prioritize those contacts who have particular influence at their companies or who are also likely to have an extensive contact list.

5. Be familiar enough with your list so that when you recognize opportunities, you can pass them along. This is a great way to be known as a positive networker.

6. Keep track of when and where people move professionally. Part of the power of networking is that as people move to new companies, you gain a valuable information source for that new organization.

EXPAND YOUR TOOLKIT

Remember to visit the book's website at http://www.ITCareerToolkit.com for supplemental and ongoing advice, tips, and data relevant to this chapter.

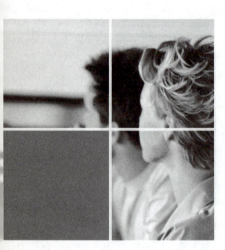

Getting Work: An Effective Method

For many, this chapter will be your focus. Although the varied ideas conveyed in earlier chapters are critical in overall career development, career success finally comes down to finding and landing the job you desire.

Some proven methods lend themselves to an effective job search, and those are covered in this chapter.

CHAPTER 13

The Job Search

Where do you start to create a truly successful job search?

First, understand that the toolkit approach is much less interested in a particular job search. It is covered here because many people have requested assistance in this area.

Many job search books are available. I agree with some of them, but others overcomplicate the issues. A successful job search entails two things: numbers and personal marketing. That's it!

Getting the job you want comes down to creating opportunity by getting your name and talent in front of as many people as possible. As I mentioned in Chapter 11, "Breaking In to I.T.," it is the marketing mantra of "reach and frequency."

Of course, it's possible that you'll hook up with your future employer and your ideal job with the first resumé you send out. To be honest, though, I doubt you would be reading this book if that were the case.

Try not to limit your search to one specific type of position or even a single type of technology. In many cases, the ads show what is needed at the specific moment. The ad might not indicate the total scope of project work you will need to perform. By looking at many possible positions, you are more likely to find the one that is the best fit to your total skill set and desired professional development.

Broaden your idea of what type of job you are willing to, and in fact, would like to have. By doing so, you gain the potential for more exposure and many more opportunities. What at first might appear to be a less desirable position might turn out to be exactly the type of company or role you would thrive in.

Certainly, skill has something to do with the job search, too. When I say *skill*, in the sense of the job search, I don't mean your technical talent—that which is probably most emphasized on your resumé. The skill that will lend itself to your job search is your ability to read people and situations and effectively communicate your message.

Luck also plays a part. Although you shouldn't count on good fortune as a primary job search or career development tool, don't discount it when it arrives. The key is to understand that luck is most readily available to those who are prepared to capitalize on it.

Getting What You Want Requires Wanting Something

The first order of business in your pending job search is to create a mental picture of the ideal situation. What would you, if you could construct it, want your job search to produce?

Ideally, you would want to create a relationship with the person who is responsible for hiring you for your desired position. You would like to have this relationship without the *distraction* of other candidates. You would want to be the "only game in town."

Wow! Wouldn't it be great if this scenario were possible?

It is!

The pages that follow outline opportunities that are similar to this ideal scenario. By following the advice I've outlined in the next several pages, you will have a much greater chance of corresponding directly with the person who is in charge of hiring the position you want. You will have fewer competitive applicants vying for the same position.

It is possible, in many cases, that you will be the only candidate being considered for the job. In the best of all possible worlds, you might be able to provide the impetus for the company in question to actually create a position.

Business owners and management are extremely impressed by proactive personalities. They are hesitant to allow such people to "escape" when they are faced with them. This is how previously nonexistent positions suddenly spring into existence. You want to be there when that happens.

The techniques are simple. They do not involve hard, sweat-of-the-brow-type labor. Diligence and commitment, however, are critical. Follow-through and a willingness to take a truthful look at your skills, objectives, and desires spell success or failure. You must view your job search as a full-time position.

Your payment for this work will be a lifelong and rewarding career in information technology (I.T.).

Defining the Job Search

If the idea of a job search gives you chills or causes you to perspire, you are not alone. The current market hasn't helped quell this fear. The idea of suddenly being out of work and needing to make ends meet is certainly a cause for alarm. Part of this is brought on by the fact that we view job seeking as something we do when we are out of work or when we are greatly dissatisfied with our current employment.

These are certainly times when a job search is warranted. However, there is another great time to begin a job search. In fact, it is during this time that you will be your most marketable. The most desirable time to look for work is when you are happily employed.

I know I'll hear cries that this is disingenuous for your employer, that some sacred bond has been broken. But let me explain.

First, let me define what I mean by *job search*. In the context of those times when you are gainfully employed, a job search really constitutes networking. It is not as much about you sending out your resumé as it is about keeping in touch with your network of contacts. I cover this more fully in Chapter 12, "Building an Active Contact List."

Suffice it to say that your career is a life-long affair. Whether you continue as an employee with your current employer or you strike out on your own to build a business, the contacts you cultivate are your keys to success.

Begin building that network now—this very day!

Remember: *Looking* for Work *Is* Work

Sadly, many job seekers—particularly those who are out of work—have a limited idea of how to perform a job search. They are relegated to spending a day or two updating their resumé, taking an hour or two to post the resumé on a variety of job websites, and then resigning themselves to the depressing drudgery of scanning the morning paper every day for an appealing job post.

They have now applied less than three days' time to their job search. Sure, every morning they scan the paper for new openings, but their job search has shifted into passive mode. The silence of the phone is a reminder of their current unemployed state. But it doesn't have to be this way.

Looking for a job is a full-time job. A friend and mentor passed this wisdom on to me. His own job search, as a highly paid executive, was one of furious activity on a daily basis.

The type of job search I cover will provide you with hope and a feeling of control. More important, however, it has a much better chance of providing you with a better, more rewarding job in a shorter period of time.

Activity that is directed to a clear objective has an amazing side effect. It provides self-feeding energy. It's the type of energy that keeps you eagerly pursuing your job search. This same energy flows into your interviews, contacts, and correspondence.

Take my word for it. If you have pursued your job search in the typical approach, the passive technique described at the beginning of this section, this more active method should be a breath of fresh air.

Again, looking for work is a full-time job. Look back on how you've been performing during your job search. If looking for work was your job description, how would you rank your effort and performance? Are you showing up at work at 8:30 a.m. and ending the day by 9:00 a.m., after reviewing the current job offerings? Would you be able to hold any job working half an hour per day? I doubt it.

You need to plan your job search activities in the same fashion you would your job. If you are normally an early riser, showered and ready by 7:00 a.m., keep that routine. Be prepared to conduct your job, as a job seeker, with a regular starting time.

The dilemma is similar to that of the home-based worker. I have worked primarily from my home for several years. My day starts early. I shower and shave every working day, even when my day will be spent in my home office at my home computer. It helps me mentally "arrive" at work.

As a job seeker, you need to have the same type of discipline. In fact, the amount of success you have in your job search relates directly to your discipline in this area.

In addition, a disciplined routine gets you past the humdrum and tedious days in which your activity is not directly rewarded. Although the method I outline here provides more opportunity than a passive search, it still requires time and effort to get started.

If you land the "right" job at the first place you approach, good for you. You've lucked out, and I am not one to shun good fortune. But for most, time and effort are expended without a direct reward or response. Your discipline and routine are the simplest way to stay on track with your job search.

The Toolkit Approach to Finding a Job

As you read through the toolkit approach, I hope that you are struck by its simplicity. There is no secret skill to master, no complicated formulas, no long and drawn-out analysis of your five most appealing companies.

It is not that I am against such approaches. Certainly, if you are particularly interested in an employer in your area, you should do what you can to discover and create opportunities there.

I am more interested in helping you find opportunities in a broader market. This is particularly true if you are newer to the job market. It is always much easier to approach your ideal employer with some additional clout. That type of clout is bought only with experience.

You will find, as you read the outline and theoretical job searches provided, that there isn't a lot to it. You'll know in the next 10 to 20 minutes how to begin the process. You'll know how to create and discover the opportunities that will lead to a job.

Job Search Outline

The following is an abbreviated job search outline.

   I.   Create/fill your toolkit

       A. Resumé

       B. Cover letter

       C. Tracking log or database

       D. Perspective

           i.   Full-time job seeker

          ii.   I have value

        iii.   I am proactive

        iv.   Remember that the job search is your current job

E. Understand the market

   i. Personal contacts and referrals lead to the best opportunities

   ii. Want ads, job sites, and placement agencies are just a small part of your search

II. Print several copies of your resumé and cover letter

   A. The number of resumé copies you need depends on how active you decide to be

III. Distribute your resumé to local businesses between 9:00 a.m. and 4:30 p.m.—during normal working hours

   A. Attempt to say hello to someone at the company

   B. Track each company

      i. Keep a card, name, time to call

      ii. Find information on the company

         a. Ask about the company

         b. Notice company computers

      iii. Notice signs of prosperity and culture (office space, furniture, autos in lot, demeanor of staff)

      iv. Mark date, time, and information of first visit

IV. Call back in two days

   A. The goal is a short personal conversation

   B. Ask about opportunities

      i. Ask permission to do the following:

         a. Follow up from time to time

         b. Inquire about anyone else who might need your skills

            i. Artificial referrals

            ii. If yes, can you use their name when you call

            iii. Call this other person and refer to Step V

V. First contact (whether while canvassing or calling back)

    A. Introduce yourself

    B. Let the person know you are looking for employment opportunities

    C. Let the person know what you would like to do and what you can do

    D. Find out whether the company is looking for someone and what needs to be done

        i. If the company does not need anything, refer to Step IV B

        ii. If the company does need your skills, find out when you can formally interview

        iii. Be interested, and ask the person's time frame for making a decision

        iv. Be upfront, and ask the person's criteria for making a decision

        v. Ask what you can do to increase your chances of being selected for this position (this separates you from other potential employees)

In short, that's about it. It's simple, really. However, for this to work, your toolkit must be fairly well developed. Action must substitute the romance that is connected with landing a new job.

I make this simple because I don't want you to worry or complain about its difficulty or substitute thinking about your job search, the perfect resumé, the five ideal employers, and so on with the actual work of getting your name into as many potential employers as possible.

This is critical for two reasons:

- Directed activity provides its own energy and motivation.
- Opportunities for career development and growth occur while you're working, not while you're training—and not while you're out of work. Your influence and reach into other professional lives—the extension of your professional contacts—occurs while you're on the job.

A Job-Search Comparison

The following comparison is hypothetical. It is not a promise of results but is indicative of the types of things that can happen with a proactive job search.

Method 1: The Standard "Passive" Job Search

Day 1. John Smith realizes he needs to get a job. He starts to fiddle with his resumé. He hasn't looked at his resumé in almost three years, the entire time he has been at ABC, Co. Looking at it, he realizes how unprofessional it looks. He wants a more presentable resumé, but he's not sure how to start.

John adds his most recent job to the top of the experience section, including the start and end date and the title he held until last week when the company closed down.

He writes two paragraphs on the various tasks he performed.

Then John looks at the objective. It no longer reflects where he would like to go professionally. He tinkers with it but is worried that making it too specific will lock him out of some positions. Although he has specific things he would like to do, his first concern is getting a job so that he can pay his bills.

Day 2, 7:30 a.m. John gets an early start. He has heard the market is tight. A friend of his, in the same field, has been unemployed for almost six months, and John worries about this. He can't afford to be unemployed for that much time.

He gets the paper, bypassing the front page, and immediately opens the classifieds. He begins looking for positions in technology that match his skills. There is one in the field he would like to go in, but he does not meet the minimum experience requirements.

Another ad catches John's eye. It is for a network administrator and covers many of the same tasks that he performed at ABC, Co. At the bottom, the ad says "Send your resumé to A1 Staffing."

He finds a third ad, for a help desk technician. He meets the minimum qualifications, but the pay is much lower than he made at ABC, Co. He circles the ad anyway. He realizes that his friend's predicament might just be his own. There are no jobs to be had.

He sends his resumé to the address listed and puts the want ads in the recycling bin. It is now 8:10 a.m.

John remembers several job sites he has always wanted to try. He goes to his computer and brings up the first. Several testimonials of happy clients meet him. This is the job seeker's heaven—thousands of jobs, and employees finding their prospective employers directly. John creates a profile and begins searching for jobs in his area that match his particular skill set.

Nothing comes up. He broadens his search first in skills and then in geography. Finally, two hits! He clicks the first ad to find out that it has been placed by a temporary staffing agency. The second is for a clerk in an I.T. department.

John then goes to several other job sites, creating online resumé and profiles.

It is now 11:30 a.m., day 2, and John has completed his job seeking activities for the day.

Day 3, 7:30 a.m. John wakes to find a couple of e-mails in his inbox. They are from a few of the job sites he visited. However, it becomes apparent that they are newsletters and advertisements. He notices that one of the e-mails promises to stop e-mail advertisements if he upgrades his profile to the Premium profile. For $6.95 monthly, he can have access to more employers and will receive no advertising e-mails.

John goes through the paper and discovers no new jobs posted. He goes out to the local market and picks up two additional papers. At home, he discovers two additional job postings. He calls the number on one. The voice on the other end answers, "A1 Staffing, how can we help you?"

John is surprised, but says, "I'm responding to your ad in the paper. The one for the technical specialists."

"That's great. Let me get some information."

John spends the next few minutes giving his job experience and contact information. At the end of the conversation, the woman says, "How flexible are you with travel, relocation, and pay?"

John is not sure how to answer, but he doesn't want to cut off any opportunities. He answers, "I guess that depends on the amount of travel and where I would need to relocate."

"Okay, I have your information. We have several positions that might be a fit. I'm going to see what I can set up. It might be a few weeks, but we'll get something going."

John hangs up. The conversation didn't sound too encouraging. It is now 11:00 a.m., day 3, and John has finished his job seeking activities for the day.

Days 4, 5, 6, and 7 are similar. John checks the paper each morning, checks his e-mail for information from the job boards, and waits for the phone to ring.

This is the method most often employed by the average job seeker. It is largely passive, in that you put information into sources and then wait. You have no direct contact with those who can or would hire you. In many cases, you have no idea of the company where the supposed opportunity exists.

Now take a look at a more proactive method. The next section examines the toolkit approach to the job search.

Method 2: The Proactive Job Search

ABC, Co. is closing its doors, and John has been let go. His resumé has not been updated since before he began at ABC, almost three years ago. John knows that this is his first area to correct. After looking over his resumé, he decides a complete rewrite is in order.

He realizes that employers in I.T. are largely looking for producers. Although he holds a couple of certifications, he chooses to deemphasize this in lieu of placing his skills and experience in the forefront.

He restructures his resumé using the formula found in *Building Your I.T. Career*. The emphasis is on brevity and known skills. He makes sure that there are no paragraphs, that all skills and experience are written using easy-to-read bullets. He does not include any job experience before ABC, Co. because he started his I.T. career there, and past skills were adequately covered in that job.

At the bottom of his resumé, John lists his certifications. He then sits down and writes a three-paragraph cover letter. He addresses it "To Whom It May Concern."

In the letter, he expresses his interest to further his career in I.T.. He refers to key points on his resumé, highlighting one key project from ABC, Co. He ends the letter by thanking the reader for taking the time to review his information and invites him to call him with any questions. He also emphasizes that he will follow up in a few days.

John has his letter reviewed for grammar and spelling by a friend who has expertise in this area. He makes the necessary corrections.

With these important documents completed, John makes a list of friends and family who are in professional positions. He then writes a simple correspondence explaining that he is actively looking for employment and asking if they know who he should contact at their company or who they might know who can lead him in the right direction.

He does not ask whether their company is hiring, just the names of who would perform the hiring when jobs arise.

He mails a copy of his cover letter and resumé to those who do not have e-mail. He e-mails the correspondence to those who do.

This has taken him most of day 1 and day 2.

Day 3, 7:30 a.m. John takes a copy of his resumé and cover letter and goes to a local printing/copying company. He has 100 copies of each printed on plain white paper. He realizes that he could splurge for a nicer bond but also knows that most people in a hiring position, particularly I.T., will be more interested in his skills.

At 9:00 a.m., he visits a local professional park. Nearly 70 companies are in a three-block area. Some of these companies are one- or two-person shops, but a few are corporations with several hundred people.

John walks into the first company. The receptionist asks, "Can I help you?"

"Sure, who would I speak to who is responsible for hiring technology professionals for your company? Computers, programmers, technical support?" John adds the qualifiers at the end, knowing that many industries view technology professionals as machinists or engineers.

"That would be Mrs. Thompson."

"Great! Could I speak with her and leave her some information? It will only take a moment."

The receptionist replies, "I'm sorry, but Mrs. Thompson only sees people by appointment. Can I pass along your information?"

"That would be fine. Can I pick up a card so that I can follow up with her?"

"Sure."

John hands the receptionist a copy of the cover letter and his resumé. He takes a card from her and writes Mrs. Thompson's name, today's date, and the words "by appt. only." He then asks, "Is there a good time to reach Mrs. Thompson?"

"Afternoons are normally better. Mornings can be really hectic around here."

John makes a note that afternoons are better for making contact.

"Great. And is Mrs. Thompson the technology director or in human resources?"

"She's actually the VP of operations, but she runs our MIS department, too."

John thanks the receptionist and leaves. He immediately enters the next company.

By noon, he has visited most of the companies and collected 30 cards. He has had conversations with several I.T. managers or senior technologists. Four of the individuals he spoke to gave him names of managers at other companies nearby.

In addition, one of the companies, a small operation, asked if he would work part time to help them set up some computers. John establishes a time to come back tomorrow in the afternoon. He's not really interested in consulting, but work is work, and he knows that referrals are more readily given after performance.

John then takes time to eat some lunch before heading off to another business complex about a mile away. There he spends the remainder of the afternoon handing out resumé and taking names. In each case, he writes any information that he can on the company business cards or in a journal that he carries with him.

Day 4. John prints off another 60 cover letters and resumes. He has 75 names and numbers of local I.T. managers, HR managers, or small business owners. About ten of the companies interest him based on their professional demeanor and a general excitement in the people he spoke to. These he puts in a separate pile with appropriate notes.

He is building awareness of the local business community. One thing is certain: In his perusal of job ads in the past, he could not remember any of these companies posting a position. Certainly, it could be that he didn't notice, but he realizes that this is probably because most job openings never reach the want ads.

John heads out to another large business complex about four miles from his house. There he begins the process again. At the tenth company he visits, he has the following conversation with the technology manager.

"We are just about to begin looking for a new network administrator. Good timing. Tell me about yourself and what you did at ABC, Co."

John covers his experience and adds some of the items he was starting to work on that interested him.

The I.T. manager asks John about a particular technology. He answers truthfully that he has read up on it and understands the concepts, but he has not worked with it directly. The I.T. manager seems disappointed. John asks, "Is there going to be a lot of that type of work in this position?"

"No, but some knowledge will be required."

"I don't want to sound out of line, but I've never had trouble taking conceptual knowledge and putting it into practice quickly. I'd love the opportunity to work with you, and it can be a test of sorts. I can definitely take care of the rest of your environment, and if I can develop the skills for this other technology, we both win."

The I.T. manager is impressed and asks John to come back in a couple of days for an interview with his boss. John thanks him for his time and says he is looking forward to it.

John separates the I.T. manager's card and makes some notes about the conversation. He then continues on to the other businesses in the area. He heads home for lunch and types a quick note to the I.T. manager, thanking him for his time and confirming their appointment in a few days. He includes another copy of his resumé and a more personalized cover letter.

While at home, John checks his answering machine to discover that one of the companies he visited the day before would like to speak with him. He remembers the company. It was one where he spoke to the technology manager.

He calls him back, and they have the following conversation:

"Hi, John. I wanted to let you know that I was speaking to a friend about you this morning at breakfast. He runs the technology department for XYZ, Co., and they are hiring two engineers. I was really impressed with your ambition, and I believe your skills would be a fit. His name is Mike Elliott. I told him you would call, and I took the liberty of passing your information on to him."

"Wow! Thanks."

"His number is 555-5555. He's expecting your call."

John thanks him again and then calls Mr. Elliott. After a short conversation, he sets up an interview for the following day at 3:00 p.m.

John then visits another professional high-rise for the day. He hands out the remainder of his information and takes another 30 cards.

The preceding scenario is aggressive in that I've compacted the contacts into two days of job seeking. However, it is important to note that your job search is largely about the number of contacts you make and what you do with those contacts.

Method 1 Versus Method 2

The contrast of the approaches in method 1 and method 2 is obvious. Method 1 places you in a passive wait-and-see mode, whereas method 2 places you in a proactive make-it-happen mode. Remember: The objective is to build a list of contacts in the shortest time possible.

In addition, you have to remember the employer's point of view. By the time the employer has placed an ad, it has typically gone through the standard channels of tapping internal staff and other contacts. It is never an employer's first choice to go into the random market of people generated via a newspaper ad.

If you visit enough companies, you will inevitably run into a company that has recently lost an employee due to retirement, relocation, and even death. Your resumé appearing on an employer's desk without a sea of other resumés for someone to sort through will be a welcome sight and is more likely to be carefully reviewed and considered.

The fact that you showed the foresight and ambition to personally visit and follow up with a company further separates you from the mass of people in the market. You will appear more professional and indicate to them a go-getter attitude. This goes a long way toward increasing your marketability.

Another benefit of this approach is its effect on your attitude. Waiting for your phone to ring in response to one or two opportunities weighs heavily on the mind. Having several opportunities developing simultaneously is stimulating. You will feel that you have greater control over your job search and career because you, in fact, do.

Method 1 leads to a general feeling of being victimized and being at the whim of a hurting industry. Many individuals I've counseled who were using method 1 tell me they feel as though they've entered the wrong industry.

Method 2 definitely stretches you out of your comfort zone. I know that to many, it sounds like direct sales. And just so we are clear, it is!

You are definitely selling yourself. It is my hope that you feel that you are a worthwhile and valuable asset for these companies. This will make your sales job more convincing—for both the prospective employer and you.

A Word About the Out-of-Town Search

Most of the preceding ideas apply directly to job searches within your city. But what about the worker looking outside his geographic area? Do similar techniques exist for rapidly creating interest when you are geographically distant from your desired location?

I believe there are.

The out-of-area job search poses some unique challenges. With a localized search, your ability to meet someone of influence at a company is much greater. You are also able to stay current with local company news.

When you're out of town, you must make modifications to the proactive method mentioned earlier in this chapter.

First, consider getting the chamber of commerce involved. Most local chamber of commerce offices have publications listing the area employers. Local libraries might have similar lists.

After you have that list, make calls directly to the companies. If your objective is to work in an I.T. department, try to speak to the person who is running that department. If it is a smaller organization, you might want to talk to a controller or the person in charge of finance. Often, these are the people who do the hiring. I.T. often falls under the purview of a financial executive.

I know that what I suggest bypasses the HR department. You will probably be directed back to someone in charge of that role. That's okay, but you might find that you get a chance to have a more direct conversation. Once again, this has tremendous value because you get a chance to create a personal connection.

Don't rule out taking a few days visiting your prospective location. If you do, take the proactive approach diagrammed previously and put it to use.

One thing that does not change is the need to develop reach and frequency. Your ability to make contact with as many employers, peers, and other significant contacts is the single-greatest asset to your out-of-area job search.

Social Media and the Job Search

Social Media is certainly an important part of an active job search. I cover this some in Chapter 12, "Building an Active Contact List," and Chapter 17, "Your Career and Social Media."

Specific to the job search, however, I recommend a few things to make use of social media.

First, have your resumé online on your own website. You could use a resumé written in Google Documents, as well. In short, I want a place you can update and link to, making it easy to reference in social media updates and in direct messages.

Second, if you are out of work and searching, feel free to share your search online. Do so positively, even if the job need feels desperate. Let people know what you are looking for and elicit their assistance and input. Provide a link to your online resumé so that they can easily share your information with their network.

If you are currently employed, publicly announcing your job search might not be wise. In those cases, determine with whom you can safely share your search and send them a message, again with your link to your resumé. Ask them to be discreet and not publicly share your information. Ask them to review your information, provide you feedback, and if they have good contacts or know of a company needing your skills to either pass your information along or provide you with a name.

Gentle Reminders

Due to the noisy and time-driven nature of social media sites like Facebook, Twitter, and even LinkedIn, provide updates privately or publicly—as appropriate—about your search. I do not recommend several times a week, but an update every other week would be appropriate.

Don't Overfocus on Social Media

As with online job boards, the tendency with social media is to stay online constantly in hopes an opportunity comes your way. However, this effectively stops your other job search activities—particularly, the most important tasks of meeting people directly.

Limit your social media time to mornings and afternoons. If there are opportunities, they will wait that long.

Conclusion

It is not my intention to dissuade you from looking for job postings on websites or newspapers. I am not advising you to never use a placement/staffing company. These are additional avenues for your job search.

In fact, use all of them. Remember: Reach and frequency. Your objective is to get your name and experience in front of as many people in as short a time as possible.

What I am advocating is that you take control over all these avenues. Do not be passive in your search and in the marketing of your skills.

Carefully read Chapter 12. A job search is an extension and compressed professional networking opportunity.

It is likely that the best job opportunities you come across will be when you are gainfully employed. To ensure that you are ready and can properly evaluate such opportunities, make sure your toolkit is up to date and that you are networking as you go, not only when you need to. This is the proactive approach to career development in general and to the job search in particular.

Actions & Ideas

1. Evaluate how you have looked for work in the past. How much actual time, per day, did you spend after preparing your resumé and cover letter? If your job title is professional job seeker, would you consider yourself a high achiever?

2. If you have never walked into a company unannounced, visit at least 30 companies tomorrow. It's not painful. Start the process of tracking and corresponding with the contacts you make at those companies using the Networking and Opportunity Tracker available online at www.ITCareerToolkit.com.

3. As you drive around in the next day or so, make note of office building locations and professional complexes. These are areas ripe with undiscovered opportunity.

4. Create a simple map and plan to visit these office buildings, and then immediately act on the plan.

EXPAND YOUR TOOLKIT

Remember to visit the book's website at http://www.ITCareerToolkit.com for supplemental and ongoing advice, tips, and data relevant to this chapter.

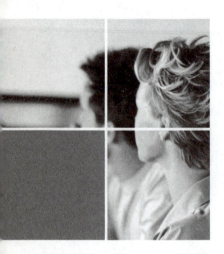

The Big Show

The job interview is the natural culmination of the various tools put into place. The product of effective networking, resumé, cover letter, communication, and so on should result in the opportunity for a face-to-face meeting with your prospective employer.

Whereas the previous tools and methods are part of what can be referred to as the job seeker/career builder's marketing, the interview is the point of the sale.

This chapter offers tips on what to expect and how to deal with difficult questions and have the most successful interview possible.

CHAPTER 14

The Interview

Officially, the interview is not part of your toolkit. It is a product of the effective use of your toolkit. However, the skills that you use during an interview are definitely tools. In fact, your ability to interview effectively is critical.

You might have the perfect resumé, an excellent cover letter, and skills that are well honed by experience and ongoing education, but if you cannot interview effectively, you will be limited in your career potential.

The interview is your moment to shine. It is also the moment when the employer determines whether you are someone to take a chance on. You must understand that this is the employer's perspective. Unless you are interviewing within your current company, where you are well known, the employer is always taking a chance in hiring you.

Your responsibility is to convey a message that says, "Relax, I'm a sure thing. Be comfortable."

Comfort. It's your job to make your prospective employer feel comfortable that you can perform the work needed and that you will mesh well with the environment or culture of the company.

Some key points to remember about the interview are as follows:

- **If you are nervous, let the employer know**—This technique can work wonders to alleviate the pressure within an interview. If you are feeling nervous, tell the interviewer. First, it helps the interviewer understand that you are putting some weight behind this interview (that you feel it's important). Second, it helps you relax.

    When you admit to nervousness, it often greatly reduces your apprehension. In effect, announcing your nervousness removes pressure and makes you less nervous. Also, the interviewer often gives you permission not to be nervous.

- **Ask questions about the job and the company**—Although officially you are the one being questioned and interviewed, feel free to interject some questions of your own. This has two effects.

  First, it gives you valuable information about the climate and culture of the company. This is critical. You want to know as much as possible, without digging, about the work environment. You want to know whether the environment is dynamic, exciting, and fun or whether it is a sweatshop. You certainly want to know, if possible, what other opportunities exist—either for training or advancement.

  Asking about the environment also conveys the message that you are interested in the company. It lets the employer know that you have a vested interest in your career and are interested in knowing more than where your desk will be, how much you'll be paid, and what the vacation policy is. Companies are interested in employees that are interested in them.

- **Be loose, but not too loose**—The best interviews are somewhat conversational. Being conversational conveys the message that you are confident and effective at communicating. You need to be relaxed enough to have some control of the conversation. A conversational style requires you to open up and let a little of your nonprofessional life into the room.

  You can convey personal interest if you can tie these interests into the interview somehow. However, take care not to take the interview too far off task. You do not want your interviewers to leave thinking, "Nice person—I could see going to lunch with him but not hiring him. He's too distracted." Conversational, yet professional, is the rule.

- **Be yourself**—I cannot emphasize this point enough. An interview is where a mutual understanding of both parties must be ascertained in a short period of time. Don't act in a way that is inconsistent with how you would act on the job. Misrepresenting yourself and your personality can be extremely damaging later.

  The interviewer will remember how you presented yourself and wonder what happened. He might even feel he was "sold" a bill of goods. If your personality and style do not mesh well with your potential employer, it is better to find that out in the interview, not two months down the road. Both you and the employer will be disappointed.

However, if your personality is abrasive and difficult, you would do well to work on it. This is not a positive personality trait. Don't protect bad behavior with a "This is just the way I am" attitude. That is, of course, unless you don't mind being limited in your professional growth.

- **Read the interview style**—This is critical. The ability to read an individual's style is critical not only to the interview but throughout your professional career. You need to effectively mold your style to fit the style of the interviewer. However, do this only to a point. (Go back and reread the previous "Be yourself" bullet.)

Some interview styles you might encounter include the following:

- **The bottom-liner**—This person is a "just the facts" type of personality. He wants neither fluff nor personality. He is highly production oriented. When interviewing with someone like this, brief explanations that get right to the point will serve you well.

- **The conversationalist**—This person wants to know about you, your job, and the people you worked with. It is likely that this person runs a highly communicative type of department. This interviewer is concerned with effective human interaction.

- **The silent type**—This person might provide little feedback or input into the interview. You might answer a question and be met with an uncomfortable silence. You might even have to ask the question, "Did I answer your question adequately, or do you need additional information?" Sometimes this might indicate a lack of preparation on the interviewer's part.

- **The friend**—This person might be highly communicative but will steer the interview away from the job and tasks at hand, favoring instead personal anecdotes and insight into your life away from work. At times, such diversion might indicate an interview that is going well and personal rapport. Make sure that you direct conversation back toward the job and the requirements, though.

- **The committee**—This isn't really an interview style. Sometimes you will be interviewed by a committee of some type. Having to answer questions, read the style, and reply accordingly to three or more individuals can be nerve-wracking. You might feel like you are facing a tribunal or that you're under a lot of scrutiny—and you might be right.

The key to surviving the committee interview is to relax. Take time to address the person who has asked the question, but work on making eye contact with all of them.

When I went through my first interview with Blue Cross, I faced this type of interview. I actually expressed that I felt like I was facing a court-martial hearing. All three interviewers laughed, and the interview progressed well from that point.

Of course, that is my personal style. You have to use what works for you to diffuse anxiety and nervousness.

Regardless of the type of interviewer you face, the key skills taught in this chapter can help you make the best of it. Adapt your style slightly depending on the interviewer, but make sure, regardless of interview style, that you are yourself. Also, direct conversation back to the job at hand, the needs of the company, and your questions about the organization.

Practice Your Interview Skills

An interview is, in effect, a performance of sorts. Your composure and poise when answering difficult questions go a long way in setting you apart from others who are being interviewed. Some people interview better than others. Unfortunately, if you have difficulty interviewing—for whatever reason—you are going to be handicapped in your job search.

Note, however, that you can go places to get experience without having to botch interviews. These might stretch you well beyond your comfort zone, but they are worth the time and effort:

- **Toastmasters**—I also mention Toastmasters in Chapter 7, "Communication Skills." Toastmasters is an organization that is dedicated to improving an individual's ability to give presentations. It is not directly geared toward interview skills. However, the organization has drills on how to give an impromptu presentation in front of a group. The practice of quickly thinking on your feet is one that is critical to effective interview skills.

  Typically, Toastmasters groups meet at predetermined times (once a week or once or twice a month). You can find out more about Toastmasters and find local chapters by visiting the Toastmasters website at www.toastmasters.org.

- **Local colleges**—Most local colleges offer courses in speech communications or presentation skills. Once again, these are not synonymous with interviews. However, just as with Toastmasters, you might be able to refine aspects of on-the-fly verbal communications.

Be Prepared to Answer Difficult Questions

I am often amazed at the surprise of many interviewees when faced with a pointed question. Typically, employers throw one or two into the mix. They want to see the interviewee's reaction, to test the ability of the applicant to think on his feet.

In my consulting business, I often interviewed technologists. My first question often threw them on their heels. I would simply ask, "Are you smart or are you stupid?"

My small consulting company placed technologists in a variety of environments on a daily basis. I needed people who were technically savvy but also highly adaptable. I could not have someone who was easily flustered when presented with a difficult situation. That question gave me an idea as to how someone might react in such a situation.

I do not expect that you will ever be faced with such a blunt question. However, I do expect that you might be faced with one or more of the questions described in the sections that follow, in addition to a few that aren't mentioned.

Prepare yourself to answer the following questions. More important, prepare yourself for questions that force you to think on your feet. Poise and confidence go a long way toward helping you answer effectively.

What Professional Accomplishment Are You Most Proud Of?

If possible, use the same piece of information that you supplied in your cover letter. It gives you a starting-off point, and if the interviewer has reviewed your cover letter, it lends itself to a cohesive message.

What Do You Feel Is Your Greatest Strength? Greatest Weakness?

I pose the two together because if you are asked one, it is likely the other will follow. My advice: Be honest. The employer will find out both if you're hired anyway.

If you have trouble with these questions, refer back to Chapter 5, "Self-Assessment."

When it comes to your weakness, however, frame it in a way that demonstrates an understanding of how you deal with it. For example, if you have trouble keeping track of various tasks, explain how you utilize and keep an accurate and up-to-date day planner.

Note	Several great planners are on the market, and I strongly recommend that you get one and learn how to use it. Time management is of particular importance to me. I use Google Apps (Calendar, Tasks, and Documents) to track everything. If I don't do that, I forget things. I keep a notepad and my smartphone with me when I'm away from my computer. As soon as I'm back in the office, I transfer the notes from the pad directly into Google Apps.

Don't use a pseudo-weakness to make yourself look good. For example, I have heard interviewees, when asked about their greatest weakness, say, "I work too hard. Often, I take too much work home or stay too late."

The statement sounds trite and arrogant. It won't go over well. The interviewer wants to see whether you have a strong sense of your abilities. It is the person who understands his limitations and has plans on how to remedy or work within them that brings value.

Why Are You Leaving Your Last Job?

Honesty is your best policy here. For some, the idea of conveying that you did not like the company or a boss is a difficult one. However, I believe this is more a question of how you frame it. Saying "My boss was a jerk" is probably not going to get you points during the interview.

However, claiming that you felt it was time to move on to a company whose direction better matched your career objectives should be acceptable.

When asked why you are leaving one company for another, it is important that you frame your answer so that you don't disparage your prior employer. Try to present uncomfortable situations in the most flattering light. Table 14-1 provides some ideas on how you can portray key situations that might be causing you to leave a prior employer.

In all cases, instead of using the question as an opportunity to speak poorly about your past employer or indicate bitterness or complaint, frame the answers positively. The easiest way to do this is to reiterate what you are looking for in the new opportunity instead of focusing on the problems that existed at your prior company.

Table 14-1   Diplomacy for Explaining Departure from Your Previous Job

Reason for Leaving	How You Might Explain It
Fired	Ouch! This is a tough one. Of course, a company and individual part ways for various reasons. You might say this: "The company was moving in a professional direction that was incompatible with my professional goals."
Bad management	It is almost never a good idea to speak poorly of bad management, even if your current interviewer seems empathetic or disparages the other company himself. Maintain strict professionalism in this case. You might say this: "I am looking for a management team that is better focused on company objectives and who helps its staff achieve them. I have heard good things about your company, and I believe I would make a good addition to the team."
Lack of training opportunities at the old company	This is a great reason to leave a company. If training is not part of a company's plan or budget, consider moving on. A company's commitment to its employees can be assessed not only by pay and insurance. Particularly in I.T., training is a huge factor, one that impacts overall career growth and satisfaction. You might say this: "I am looking for a company that works with its employees to ensure that skills match the required tasks and one that places importance on training and future skills."

continued

Table 14-1 continued

Reason for Leaving	How You Might Explain It
Moral/ethical issues	If your previous company was involved in unethical practices—consider the case of Arthur Andersen and Enron in 2002, for example—you have to assess your interviewer's awareness of this fact. If your prior company's problems were highly publicized, you might need to address them head on—acknowledging them openly in the interview. You might say this: "I need to find a company that is more ethical in its business practices. I need a management team that places a high priority on integrity and honesty."

Although myriad reasons exist for leaving a company, the sampling in Table 14-1 is meant as a guideline. As you can see, I am attempting to frame each situation in light of positives with the new company. Although you are implying subtlety that the prior opportunity did not meet your expectations in this area, framing it positively for the new opportunity allows your interviewer to justify and explain how its company meets your requirements. In effect, the interviewer can begin to see how you are looking for a company just like that one.

There is nothing wrong with looking for personal advancement and financial/professional gain. If the reason for your leaving a company is to find a better opportunity and make more money, let the employer know.

Where Do You See Yourself in Five Years?

"On a white sandy beach in the Caribbean."

That's a good answer, but it's probably not what the interviewer is looking for. Once again, honesty is the best policy. Let the interviewer know your professional aspirations. Motivated employees generally produce better and are more valuable. Contrary to popular misconception, most managers are not threatened by good employees. A manager advances to the degree that he develops others. Good managers will seek out employees who want to get ahead and be rewarded.

If you are unfortunate enough to run across a manager who is threatened by your ambition and talent, it is better to know this during the interview rather than two years into a miserable job experience.

<table>
<tr><td>Note</td><td>If you do not have career aspirations, get some! I talk about this earlier in the book, but to reiterate, careers do not generally happen by accident. They require planning. That doesn't mean you can't change direction and change your plan, but have some idea of where you want to go.

When you are starting out, your goal might be exposure to various aspects of technology-related careers. Your current career goal might be to form a long-term career goal. That is perfectly sensible.</td></tr>
</table>

After the Interview

Here are a few ideas and techniques to put in place after an interview. These are not hard-fast rules, but you should consider them.

- **Ask how you did**—Don't be afraid to ask your interviewer how you did. It is a good way to convey the message that your "performance" was important to you. Normally, the flow of the interview will give you an idea as to how you did, but still ask the question.

- **Ask about the rest of the process and time frames**—It is appropriate to ask how the process works. Are there several layers of interviews? What happens next? How long until a decision is made?

    All of these are appropriate questions. In addition, express an interest in following up with the company. Let the employer know that you will follow up.

- **Write or call to thank them**—Within a day or so of your interview, drop a note or e-mail to your interviewer thanking him for the opportunity. This is true even if you have already been notified that another candidate was selected. The employer did, in fact, give you his time and provide you with an opportunity.

Also, doing so can open many doors down the road. A professional and courteous attitude is a rare commodity. You will separate yourself from others who were interviewed. And who knows—down the road, you might find a new opportunity at the same company.

■ **If you are not selected**—In addition to the thank-you note, I recommend the following courses of action when another candidate was selected over you:

- **Call to ask for a critical assessment**—Try to set up a time to speak to your interviewer and ask for a critical assessment of all aspects of the process. Ask the interviewer what areas you can work on for future interviews. How can you better frame and structure your resumé? What skills or attitudes did you lack (if any)?

  You might find that the interviewer thought you did great. It might simply be that the employer made an assessment between two equally good candidates, and intangibles or personality made the difference.

  Whatever the interviewer's response, thank him again for his time. Process what he has said, and determine what areas you can work on to improve your chances the next time.

- **Create a professional contact**—You have met one or more individuals at a particular company. If you are not selected for a position, you have, at minimum, grown your network of professional contacts. As with the job search, ask the interviewers the two magic questions: Can I follow up with you from time to time? Do you know of anyone else who might be looking for someone with my skill set?

  It is likely that this same company will be hiring another technologist in the future. If you network correctly, your name will be at the top of the company's list.

Conclusion

The interview is the culmination of the job search process. However, just as with individual jobs, no interview makes or breaks a career. If an interview goes poorly, chalk it up to experience and move on. Interviews are mini-performances that require practice.

Actions & Ideas

1. If you can find an interview workshop, take it. Often, your local chamber of commerce or state workforce development center conducts mock interviews.

2. Get a sheet of paper (or open a new document) and make a list of some of your past interviews. Which ones went well and why? Which ones went poorly and why?

3. At your next interview, employ some of the techniques described in this chapter. Take particular note of post-interview questions so that you understand the process and planned time frames. This understanding reduces your overall anxiety as you wait for feedback.

EXPAND YOUR TOOLKIT

Remember to visit the book's website at http://www.ITCareerToolkit.com for supplemental and ongoing advice, tips, and data relevant to this chapter.

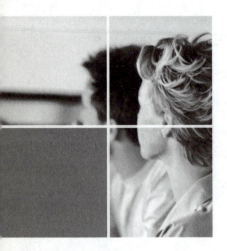

Getting What You Want

As stated elsewhere, employment is an agreement between two parties. Ideally, this agreement should involve trading two commodities of equal value: the employer's money and resources for the employee's time and effort.

Many employees feel they are not in the position to negotiate, but as the saying goes, "Everything is negotiable." As your career progresses and your ability to make an impact increases, you will be in a position to negotiate better employment deals.

This chapter covers some of the basic elements of such negotiation.

CHAPTER 15

Salary Negotiations and Employment Agreements

Well, it has happened. A company is preparing to offer a position. You developed and utilized various elements of your toolkit to get to this point. Your resumé and cover letter were brilliant, your interviews were scintillating, and your follow-up and professional networking were perfect.

Now the employer is starting to press the envelope. The company has expressed interest, and it is time to start negotiating your compensation program. Wait!

Salary negotiations, employment agreements, and performance contracts are critical elements to your overall career success. They can help lay the groundwork for future growth within a company.

Start Early

If you want to maximize your earning potential, you must start the negotiation process early. Don't wait until the offer is laid on the table to develop a clear idea of what you want and how you will get there.

When you are entry level, this is a little more difficult. However, the seasoned professional should have a good idea as to his worth and what the market will bear.

Starting early means placing the compensation package on the table during the interview process. You don't have to get into particulars immediately. However, expect that the subject will come up at any time, and be ready to address it.

The employer might have provided a salary range up front, giving you an idea of what the company wants to pay. Although this is an indicator of where the employer wants to go, it is not set in stone.

Even large corporations, which are traditionally less flexible when it comes to altering job requirements or salary ranges, can make adjustments if the talent warrants it.

Don't let a salary range that seems low keep you from either applying or speaking to the company. You might find, during discussions, that the company simply does not know what the market will bear for good talent. The company's low salary range might even keep others with your level of experience from applying.

If you have extensive experience, you will have little competition in the pool of talent. This will work to your favor.

I'm not saying that the company will alter its salary range. It might not. However, I have seen companies create new positions when the right talent is on the scene. In addition, remember the idea of building your network of contacts.

If you have impressed the management at a company, even if the company chooses not to hire you, you now have an additional source of referrals to other companies.

Know What You Want

As discussed in Chapter 4, "Defining Yourself: Aptitudes and Desires," you need to have a clear idea of what you bring to the table and what you need from material compensation, insurance, training, and so on.

This is critical. Without these ideas in place, you are shooting from the hip. It is likely that you will overlook some important requirement during the negotiation process.

Understand the Employer's Perspective

Two ideas are often misconstrued by employees when it comes to employers. If you carry either or both of these perspectives, you need to alter your thinking.

The first misconception is that businesses are out to squeeze employees. It certainly is true that a business is hoping to get as much production in the time allotted as possible. To do otherwise would be foolish and ultimately lead to failure. However, rarely is this done without regard to the employee.

The second misconception is that there is little or no room for negotiation with an employer. Often, the job seeker feels that the employer holds all the cards, that as a job seeker, he has no bargaining power. You must understand that every employment arrangement is a barter for things of value. Read Chapter 6, "Attitude." Good employees are a rare commodity, and business owners and management are more than happy to make concessions when they see value.

Remember: A business that fails due to lack of production is the same as being unemployed. Ultimately, you must understand that your employment is a cooperative agreement between you and the employer. You are there to provide value; the employer is there to provide a product or service. Both must take part in the success.

This idea should help you in negotiation. If you have a realistic sense of the value you bring to the table, you will be more likely to negotiate from a more powerful position.

This assumes that you are bringing value to the table and that your perspective and actual practice shows that you can produce.

Be Creative

Negotiation is meant to provide a solution when two parties (the employer and employee) have different ideas as to what is appropriate compensation for the services to be provided. Remember first that straight salary or hourly pay is not the sum total of a company's compensation program. You need to look at the entire picture.

Think outside of the box. For example, if an employer states that employment reviews take place one year after hire, but you believe that you will make a dramatic impact early, negotiate for that early review.

I recently assisted an I.T. director during the negotiation process. The company in question had clearly stated salary guidelines below his desired monetary compensation. However, the company also was ready to implement a popular and comprehensive solution.

The company needed his skills. As it got closer to the point of the deal, the employer offered the top end of its salary range. The company conceded that it was below what he desired but expressed that it would provide an opportunity for bonuses and a raise after the first year.

My client liked what he saw at the company but did not want to concede the salary. He felt it would set a precedent that would be difficult to overcome.

My suggestion: I told him to offer to take the company's stated salary but negotiate for a shorter review cycle. In fact, instead of a year, I counseled him to push for a 3-month and then 6-month review.

When presented with his offer, the company returned with another compensation plan. The company offered him a salary that actually met his minimum requirement but pushed the initial review out to 6 months.

Reviews are an administrative hassle, and I was confident the employer would counter with something else. As it worked out, my client got both his desired salary and the opportunity to be reviewed and get a raise in a shorter period than the standard year.

Be Firm

After you have your minimum requirements in place and you have come to the negotiating table, be firm. Although you must be creative and flexible, you must also have a point at which you do not give in.

This can be difficult in the face of a difficult job market or a long and drawn-out job search. But a minimum requirement is not a desired salary. Your minimums should be based squarely in the reality of your current job situation and primary financial needs.

I am assuming that you have not oversold your qualifications and that you have a realistic idea of your worth to the company. Also, if you have been building your network of contacts and getting your name to numerous companies, you will likely have more opportunities in the wings. More opportunity also produces more confidence in the negotiation process.

Your Worth to the Company

Be clear on this. Your worth to one company might not be the same as your worth to another. I bring this up because you might have a salary in mind based on your skill set and experience. But if you are interviewing with a company that will not utilize all of your skills or simply does not place the same worth on those skills, your negotiations will fail.

Negotiations Never Fail

Or do they? If you are disqualified for a position because a company cannot meet your minimum requirements in one of many areas, your negotiations have succeeded.

Negotiations are meant to bring you and the company in question to an agreement. It might be that the company and you are not a good fit. That is okay. It is better to know this sooner than later. And in some cases, the company will come back to you later in its hiring process.

Be Flexible

Being firm is critical in achieving what you need out of negotiations. However, if you enter negotiations without room to concede or be flexible, your negotiations will fail.

You must separate those items that you desire into absolute needs, strong desires, and nice-to-haves. The company might meet every requirement but one, and your ability to be flexible and creative will be the key to negotiation success.

You cannot expect a company to bend at your every request if you are unwilling to budge at any of theirs. Also, don't overstate your qualifications and salary requirements assuming that a company will take a bit off whatever you state. Most employers readily recognize this as amateurish. State what you want as what you want.

Employment Agreements

After you have hammered out key pieces of the compensation and job requirements, it is time to put things in writing. Employment contracts or agreements are meant to provide clearly defined guidelines and expectations for both the employee and employer. A good employment agreement protects both parties.

Typically, employment agreements are reserved for senior-level employees, managers, and executives. It is pretty rare that entry-level employees or even staff engineers are offered guarantees and buyout packages. I am not saying it cannot happen, but few companies are willing to risk guarantees on unproven commodities. With the past failure of so many technology projects and companies, this is even truer now than before.

If you are in a position to request or if you have been offered an employment contract, the sections that follow address items to keep in mind.

Seek Legal Counsel

Prior to negotiations or even a career move/job search, find a competent attorney who specializes in business and employment contracts. When you are offered a contract, always have it reviewed by your attorney before signing it. At the minimum, find a good book or visit your library to look over some employment contracts.

Your prospective employer will view this as normal and will probably view it as a sign of your preparedness. The company certainly will be running the contract by its legal department, too.

Assumptions

Your contract should list key assumptions. These are things you are expected to perform and items the company must produce. These can include working environment, equipment needed, budgetary concerns, and so on.

You don't want to be in a situation in which you are being held to a standard that you can't achieve because of elements that are outside of your control.

Assumptions are your legal recourse when the basic requirements of a job cannot be fulfilled because of external factors. As you might have noticed in Chapter 5, "Self-Assessment," I am not a big believer in blaming factors outside of your control for job failure. However, every given job has basic needs that must be met for there to be a chance of success.

If you are being held accountable for server uptime or system performance but the company is unwilling to act on your recommendations or purchase the right equipment, you are going to have difficulty meeting the objectives.

Assumptions place factors that are outside of your control on the table. Remember: A job is an agreement between you and your employer. Both sides have needs and requirements. It is much better to know up front what each side intends to do for the other.

Deliverables

Your agreement must include some type of deliverables. These include products, services, or performance requirements that you must deliver so that the company can assess whether you are meeting the job requirements. The clearer these are defined, the better.

Bonuses and Performance Perks

A company should put bonuses or performance perks in writing. The company should balance its performance perks with the minimum assumptions so that it doesn't gauge your performance against performance or items that the company or another individual could not deliver.

Of course, your performance might be tied to the performance of a team—something that is unavoidable in many cases. This is particularly true in cases of management or project performance.

Conclusion

When it comes to your salary and contract arrangements, don't agree to anything that leaves you with a bitter taste in your mouth. It's okay to make concessions, but don't take a position believing a company will suddenly alter its agreement when it realizes your value. Doing so is setting yourself up for failure.

Actions & Ideas

1. Create a mental and written picture of the perfect job. This includes pay, working environment, insurance, training, peers, and so on. This is not to dissuade you to turn down a job that does not meet your ideal. Instead, use it as a way to gauge those opportunities you come across. You might find that you sacrifice one aspect for particular strengths in another. The picture you create is simply a guideline for assessing opportunities.

2. At your next interview, begin the negotiation process early by letting the company know factors that are important to you. Don't do this in a pushy, I-need-this-or-else type of way. Instead, your goal is to let the employer know your future negotiation points.

3. Keep in mind that negotiations never fail. In fact, you are better off knowing a company will not meet your requirements on some critical point early. Doing so frees you to move on to the next opportunity. For this reason, create a baseline of requirements that you can use to gauge every opportunity. If, for instance, you cannot or will not travel more than two days per month for your job, and the requirements for a position involve two weeks of travel per month, your decision becomes much simpler. Almost all other factors become moot.

EXPAND YOUR TOOLKIT

Remember to visit the book's website at http://www.ITCareerToolkit.com for supplemental and ongoing advice, tips, and data relevant to this chapter.

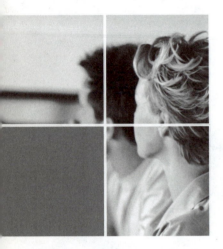

Where Career Building Really Begins

After you are hired, the true work of career building begins. Unfortunately, many people cease putting their toolkit to use after they have landed the job. The danger, of course, is that at some point they will either be out of work again, or they will have stagnated in their position and want to move on.

Promotions might occur based solely on your job performance and without your actively requesting or directing them, but why leave them to chance? When you are working at a job, the ideas of networking and communication become much more critical. These ideas govern much of your advancement and satisfaction.

CHAPTER 16

On-the-Job Promotion

You're hired! Now what?

For many, the job search is the sum total of their career planning experience. In many cases, an employee simply becomes bogged down in the day-to-day work and loses sight of long-term objectives. For others, the job *was* the objective, and career planning from a long-term perspective has never crossed their mind.

The first group of career builders becomes focused on training and skills that help them maintain their current position. They become process-driven, ensuring that their skills meet the current and short-term demands. Although it is important to ensure that you have the skills to meet your current job requirements, if that becomes the total focus of your training and development program, you will find yourself stagnant in your career growth.

Opportunity, the kind that can greatly enhance careers, is developed when you not only meet your job responsibilities, but when you acquire the skills you need to enhance and grow your responsibilities. This increases your sphere of influence and separates you from the rank and file.

In this chapter, you learn some of the skills you need to keep your career moving forward while on the job. This is a critical juncture in career development. Fight the tendency to rest on your laurels after you have landed a job or experienced small successes.

On the Job

Although landing a new job can bring a sense of a high and often provides a financial boost that is greater than incremental on-the-job advancements, your time spent at a given company provides the greatest opportunity for advancing your career.

It is while you are on the job that you get the opportunity to provide incredible value and make a name for yourself. Although in these days of rapid career changes, it is in vogue to move up the ladder by changing jobs, when you do this too quickly, it can just as easily put the brakes on your career.

I will not try to give any hard-fast rule as to how long you should stay in a particular company, but consider changing employers carefully regardless of the time frame. Your current employer is where you are known and where you know the projects and people who make up the opportunities.

Maintaining and Building Your Network

For many, the idea of maintaining and, in fact, building their network of professional career-building contacts becomes lost in the day-to-day shuffle of work. Once again, this is largely because of a lack of long-term career objectives or, at a minimum, objectives being placed on the back burner while handling the tasks of the present.

However, for a career to thrive, you must maintain your professional contacts while on the job. In addition, this is the area where contacts should grow most quickly. This is true for several reasons. One of the most obvious is the sudden loss of employment because of downsizing, a company move, a purchase, or a merger.

Whatever the reason, you will be crippled in your subsequent job search if you have failed to maintain your network. Maintaining your network is critical if for no other reason than to provide you with a readily available list of professional contacts should your employment situation suddenly change.

However, following are some other equally compelling reasons:

- **Ease of networking**—Building your list while you're on the job is much simpler than during the job search. Rather than having to go out of your way to seek out contacts to add to your list, your normal course of working can put you in front of dozens if not hundreds of people who extend your sphere of influence.

- **You're a known commodity**—Those with whom you come in contact will have first-hand experience as to how you work or perform. They will become your most compelling referrals. This, of course, assumes that you have performed well.

While you're on the job, you will work with many different people on various projects. Make it a point to introduce yourself to everyone. Grab a business card and write additional notes about that person on the card. Make sure you leave that person with a card, too.

Identifying Areas for Success

I'll say it again—careers seldom happen by accident. In fact, accidents are usually mistakes with painful consequences. Don't build a career by accident. Take control of your career direction and its future success.

One way to help achieve more success is to identify projects that have a high probability of success. During the course of your work, you will be asked to perform your standard duties. However, additional projects always come up. The day-to-day tasks you perform are the expected elements of your career. Such tasks are why you are there. Although you might be recognized as effective at your given tasks, to dramatically accelerate your career, you need more.

It is critical that you take on some of the additional projects that are not being done. In doing this, you need to identify those projects that will garner respect, have a high profile, and require you to learn new skills.

I won't lie. There are risks involved. When you take on such a project, you expose yourself to the possibility of failure. For me, that has always been an easy task. I've always believed I could take on projects and make them successful. I'm willing to chance the possibility of failure. Without it, the chance of great success is also limited.

As you work to identify which projects you should volunteer for, keep in mind the following:

- **Select areas of interest**—To maximize both the experience gained on the project and the chance of success, attempt to find projects that will stretch you in an area that you are willing to go. For example, if you would like to know more about scripting for automated desktop configuration, get involved with a project that utilizes some of those tools.

  Your chances for success increase greatly when you are emotionally vested in the process. Not only do you stand to put a nice professional feather in your cap, but you also will be learning another skill for your toolkit. This has the effect of keeping you interested in more than just the completed project, but the learning process, too.

- **The makeup of the team**—Undertake projects in which the team members can be trusted to do their part. If you are involved in a project that involves several members, make sure you know the skills and interest of those members. Although you might be vested in the project and the process, it is possible that others were placed on the project against their will.

  If team members are not truly career-minded, they will have little interest in the project's success. This can be the kiss of death for a project.

- **The tools you need**—A project team must have the tools to put its project in place. If you see a project developing, but management has not truly bought into the idea, beware. You need to make sure that management has the same vision and desire for the project to succeed. If specialized tools are needed for the project, make sure management has agreed to acquire them.

  It is not out of line to put in writing your expectation of how the project will work. As part of this document, include the assumptions and predicated factors that impact the project. Although it is good to work at maximum capacity with and beyond your skill set and take on varied projects, you also must be up front with what you expect from management.

Attitude

Attitude cannot be overrated. At times, though, it is. What I mean by this is that you often hear trite phrases about maintaining a positive mental attitude: "Attitude determines altitude," and so on.

These phrases are only a hint at the truth. A great attitude should ideally be driven by an achievable objective or goal and the resources needed to achieve that plan. As mentioned in Chapter 6, "Attitude," if attitude is manufactured without an achievable plan, it quickly fizzles.

Working for a Tyrant and Other Joys

During the course of your career, it is likely that you will have a number of bosses. Some of these bosses will be difficult—almost intolerable.

However, your ability to work for a difficult individual might prove to be one of the most valuable traits that you can bring to an organization. Doing so requires tact, a strong sense of self, and the ability to produce under personal pressure.

Most of us, if we are honest, will admit to shying away from painful experiences. This is normal behavior. Our human nature forces us to react to difficult people with an almost fight-or-flight mechanism. This reaction normally means that we will argue, have personality conflicts with this person, or avoid the person altogether. None of these reactions is helpful from the standpoint of your career.

First, understand that all people, including you and me, are difficult at times. We all have bad days, overreactions, biases, and prejudices that impact our objectivity. In some cases, *you* might be the difficult person.

Assuming, however, that you are typically easy to get along with, what can you do to help you work with a difficult boss? The sections that follow provide some suggestions for overcoming this unfortunate obstacle while maintaining your professionalism.

Determine Whether Your Boss's Actions Are Personality or Personal

Before reacting to a difficult boss, client, coworker, and so on, determine whether the behavior or actions are personal or personality. There is a difference.

Some people are abrasive by nature. In fact, this trait might have helped them reach a level of authority. They might be naturally decisive and have high expectations. Both of these can be extremely desirable for a business.

You must determine whether your difficult boss is difficult for everyone. If that's the case, you can take solace in this fact. Your boss is not personally attacking you. It is simply the way this person relates.

Although it might be difficult to clearly classify each boss's personality style, the following list is indicative of some you might meet. Also, any given boss could have multiple traits.

- **The micromanager**—I'll start with this trait first. It is the Dilbertized caricature of a boss who attempts to get involved in every decision or task you undertake. Usually highly egotistical, this type of boss wants to ensure his ideas are acted upon. For me, this is the most challenging type of boss. I am highly independent and entrepreneurial in nature. I want broad objectives and then to be left alone to achieve them. For employees who do not want to make any mistakes and are risk averse, micromanagers might work, but most employees have a hard time with them.

- **The dictator**—Similar to the micromanager, this person wants everything to be done his way. There is no room for independent thought or action. This person is extremely controlling in his approach and deals harshly with any deviation. In many cases, this person might have been highly skilled in what he did to achieve his position, so an overactive ego resulted. Success with this type of boss involves bringing him into your ideas early so that he views the ideas as something he helped create.

- **The company mouthpiece**—This boss might find it difficult to stick up for his employees. If resources are needed for a project's success, and the company does not want to spend the money, this boss can spell doom for a project. Often, this boss has risen to his position through political maneuvering and is hesitant to take chances or take on even marginally risky projects. If you are like me and want to see dramatic career growth, you must avoid this type of manager.

- **The screamer**—I've worked for a manager who literally banged on tables in anger and screamed. This type A personality can intimidate a staff. Usually, this type of boss is highly driven and is internally stressed about project success. He can become frustrated and agitated when others show similar stress.

  It is important that you separate your activity from this manager's behavior. I used to tell this manager that he stressed out for both of us—and then I would concentrate on the tasks at hand. Some people become highly productive when they are stressed, but in most cases, this behavior is detrimental to the work at hand.

- **Everyone's friend**—This manager can often be highly motivating. He places a lot of emphasis on team building and job satisfaction. That can be great, but if employees are not producing, this person is often the last one to make corrective action. If you recognize this characteristic in someone you report to, you must learn to frame your projects and ideas in terms of how they will clearly help the company and the team. Also, ask for permission to be the lead on those projects—particularly if difficult decisions are needed. You, in effect, remove this manager from having to make those decisions himself, which might be too difficult for him to do on his own.

These manager descriptions are a small sampling. Also, just as you might be classifying your managers and to some extent your peers, remember that you are being similarly classified. I've given some ideas on dealing with various types of managers, but in this book, I place a much greater emphasis on how you deal with yourself. Your reaction to situations and people is much more important than the situation.

Note

When my wife and I visited Manhattan for the first time, we were amazed. I love Manhattan and the energy it exudes. However, as we went out to eat, we discovered something. New Yorkers tend to be direct in asking for what they want. We would be sitting at dinner, waiting patiently in that laid-back Southern California style, for the waiter to bring our check. Many of the other patrons would raise their hands and yell out "Check!"

The waiter would calmly come by and drop off the check and go about his business. Initially, we perceived these customers as rude. In California, unless service is really poor, we wait patiently for our check to arrive. And even when we need the check, we usually try to get the attention of restaurant workers discreetly—as not to offend. But what we viewed as abrasive in Manhattan was, in fact, the way they conduct business. Their behavior was not meant to be rude and was not construed as such.

Following that realization, we could watch other diners and make educated guesses as to whether they were native New Yorkers or visitors.

If you work for someone who is difficult, it is important to know whether that person's behavior is directed at you specifically, or whether it is just his personality. This helps you remain objective.

Understand That People Are "Where They Are"

This has become a pet statement of mine. Having run a service-based consulting company, I sometimes had to deal with difficult people. Occasionally, my consultants would get upset by the statements and attitudes of these clients.

I would remind them, "People are where they are."

What I meant by this was simple. Often, we don't know the situations surrounding that person's workday or life. I'm not making excuses. If you have a rotten day, I still believe you should treat people with respect and kindness. However, my admonition to act professionally in all circumstances does not mean that all people will. In the overall scheme of building your career, curbing negative emotions just makes good sense— even when the other person is out of line.

When dealing with people, you need to understand that there is a difference between what is the case and what you want the case to be. You need to deal with people based on what is actually occurring.

When I say that people are "where they are," I am advocating a view that puts responsibility entirely on you to act appropriately in all situations, not the other guy. If I were speaking to "the other guy," I would be telling him the same thing. However, you are the one reading this, so you are receiving the 10-minute lecture.

When it comes to furthering your career, this is vital. When (not *if*) you find yourself working for or with difficult people, your ability to advance your career is dictated by how effectively you deal with them. Your desire that difficult people should act differently has little bearing.

A counselor told me once that we typically "die in our affliction." What he meant is that people seldom change. That includes you. The only thing you can control is what you do and how you react. Understanding that some people are inherently difficult can help you maintain more objectivity during your day-to-day dealings with them.

Take an Objective Path to Evaluating What They Say

Difficult people or abrasive personalities can often dilute the message they bring. I have found that regardless of their style of delivery, people generally have the ability to provide insight into our careers that we otherwise would not see. The problem is, of course, that when people present something as an attack, we react personally.

But what if the person "attacking" you is actually bringing up some valid points? You might not even "hear" the person because of his harsh approach.

Handling Criticism

A mentor of mine gave me some invaluable advice about handling criticism. I went through a period in which I felt I was being attacked by some of my peers. It was during this difficult time that I was offered the approach to handling criticism that is described in the sections that follow. I have found the approach useful ever since.

Determine Whether What Someone Is Saying Is True

Regardless of the delivery, is what's being said true? If it isn't, disregard it. In most cases, you don't have to defend yourself from wild and untrue statements.

However, if the statement is true, you need to take the next step.

Determine Whether It Is Something You Need to Change

Someone might "attack" you or make a derogatory comment about something that is not critical or does not actually require a change.

A few years ago, my wife dyed her hair a dark red. It looked great. However, a well-meaning friend commented that she felt my wife's hair looked too "wild." My wife's first reaction was to second-guess her decision. She struggled for a while trying to decide if she should re-dye her hair back to its original color.

I assured her that she looked great, but that she needed to feel comfortable. She determined that "wild" was a subjective opinion and that most people loved the color. There was no need for her to argue with her critic or to make a justification.

The same is true when evaluating the input of a person with whom you work. Remember, people are where they are.

If you determine that you should change something, however, do so. Put a plan in action to correct the problem.

Using this methodology provides a relatively unemotional method of dealing with criticism. Even if the criticism was in essence an attack, you can learn from it, make adjustments, and move on.

Talk to Someone About a Behavior

At some point, however, someone's behavior might put work performance at jeopardy. If that is the case, the best you can do is talk to that person. If handled tactfully, you can do this with management, too.

We have been conditioned to believe that correction and input is a boss-down phenomenon. However, most good managers and employers want input from their employees. Most people who are abrasive are aware of their behavior. Some simply choose to remain the same regardless. Others have struggled to change. In fact, you might be surprised at how much better these people are now than they used to be!

However, asking for an appointment with this person and letting him know how his behavior affects you or the department can go a long way toward helping to diffuse the situation.

An attorney I was doing work for once asked for this type of input. He was a well-compensated and high-powered partner. I was doing a high-profile project involving a business transaction worth nearly $1 billion. He was rightfully concerned about the project and interrupted me constantly.

"How is this coming along?" "Is this going to work right?" "Why are you doing it this way?"

The barrage of questions was constant. I eventually had to tell him that he needed to leave me alone for longer periods of time if he wanted me to make headway. Later, over lunch, he said, "Tell me to get out of your face if I become a pest; otherwise, I'll bother you constantly."

As mentioned previously, many difficult people understand this about themselves. They often respect those who stand up to them. But make sure you do it tactfully.

Don't Swallow Your Pride—Control It

One of the benefits of I.T. is the pride you can take in your work. The pride of production is a great fringe benefit. You can go home at the end of the day and know you have made an impact on the functional workings of a business. An overemphasis on pride, however, can make working with difficult people impossible.

I have heard many people, after leaving a company or walking out on a difficult boss, say, "I have too much pride; no one can treat me like that."

I understand their view. I have a lot of pride and also believe people should treat you with respect. However, remember that I also believe that people are "where they are." In a fantasy world, you can breeze through your career without ever having to deal with difficult people.

But I provide a different perspective on this. I believe that if you have confidence and a true sense of pride, you will not be emotionally impacted by those who say abrasive or inappropriate comments. Instead of thinking "I have too much pride to put up with this," you could say, "I have so much pride that I *can* put up with this."

You will take what these people say, filter out the vitriol, leaving only the constructive suggestions. If none exist, no problem—you've filtered everything else out. This allows you to take advantage of the opportunity at hand. That's what I mean by controlling your pride.

Conclusion

Ultimately, your on-the-job promotion is dictated by identifying areas to make a true contribution—above and beyond simply doing your job—and your ability to recognize and deal with the egos and personalities at work. Adopting a solution mindset and getting along go hand in hand.

If you work at a company that is not innovative, growth oriented, or rewarding in some fashion, however, you would do well to find other employment.

This goes back to what I've said about dealing with things as they are, not as you want them to be. Many people continue to work for a company that is in decline or simply does not have the opportunities they desire to take their career forward. Don't follow this pattern. Gainful employment means finding a company where your skills bring a value that is recognized and rewarded.

Discovering that you and the company where you work are not well matched is not something to cause concern. In fact, knowing this can go a long way in helping you identify those companies that are a better fit. It is better to identify this incompatibility early at a job rather than later. Knowledge allows you to take action, proactively building your ideal job, rather than waiting for some magical moment where your ideal job appears.

Actions & Ideas

1. Identify additional projects that your department would benefit from. See if a quick-hit project can be done in a short period of time. Offer to take that project on.

2. Create professional relationships with those who are advancing at your company and those who show ambition and drive. Inevitably, these people become external contacts when either you or they move to a new company.

EXPAND YOUR TOOLKIT

Remember to visit the book's website at http://www.ITCareerToolkit.com for supplemental and ongoing advice, tips, and data relevant to this chapter.

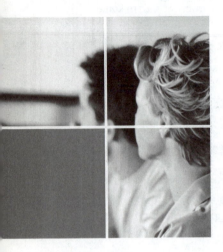

Your Career and Social Media

No technological or cultural phenomenon since the inception of the Internet has so firmly captured the collective attention of so many as has social media. Initially with MySpace and very quickly with the nearly universal adoption of Facebook by individuals, companies, and brands, social media continues to expand its reach and impact into our lives. This reach goes beyond friends and the online communities we are part of. It can very directly impact our professional lives.

This chapter explores that impact—both the positive and negative—and provides some guidance on how to leverage social media to enhance your career. In addition, this chapter addresses some of the mistakes that some aspiring I.T. professionals occasionally make.

Chapter 17

Your Career and Social Media

Over the past few years, one of the hottest topics in career development circles is the role of social media. Management, HR, employers, and employees alike all have ideas about how this technology and the various social media platforms and online communication can be used.

My goal is to help both demystify social media's role for the savvy I.T. professional and help you devise a strategy you can effectively follow to get the best results out of your social media efforts.

I suppose the first question to ask is whether you should be using social media at all as a career development tool.

My answer is an emphatic *yes!*

Currently, and for the foreseeable future, social media and social platforms will play an integral part in our lives. Personally, I do not separate personal life from career; after all, so much natural crossover exists. Facebook, LinkedIn, and Twitter are excellent places to network and enhance your career by extending your professional brand (as well as keep up with family and friends).

Social Media/Social Network Definition

For the sake of clarity, I am providing the definition I use for social media. I think such a definition is important for this conversation (in particular, in the framework of social media as a tool for enhancing your career and professional development).

My definition of social media is this:

Software (typically web based) to help facilitate the creation of networks or communities of shared interest or objectives.

This definition might not be perfect, but the important context is the idea of "communities of shared interest or objectives." One reason for the growth of social media is the need for people to connect in a world that's linked digitally but who may often feel socially isolated.

Busy and competing schedules mean that we do not get together as often with our neighbors and communities. Social media is a way to help bridge that gap. Career-wise, as you see later in this chapter, social media does not replace professional networking, but it is an amazing tool to augment and expand our professional networking capabilities.

Privacy Concerns

Let's address issues of privacy and concerns with online information first. It is a topic some I.T. professionals I know obsess over. Perhaps their understanding of the value of information and the pervasive use of data mining by both professional and government organization makes them more aware of the potential misuse of that data.

To read some people's take on it, you shouldn't post anything online. I know one professional who set up his Facebook account with a phony name and a photograph of a monkey. At the same time, he expressed frustration to me that social media did not seem to be helping him with his career or professional endeavors. Although that is an extreme example, similar fears have been expressed to me to various degrees.

I have a simple set of rules when it comes to what (and what not) to post on social media:

- I rarely post political issues on my Facebook page. I tend to find such conversations rarely lead to useful or intelligent discussion and only serve to polarize people who otherwise might be able to work together.

- I never post any negative information about conflicts with family or friends. I will, however, post about products and brands—both positive and negative experiences.

- I do not call names or use profanity.

- I do not share personal information that is not readily available publicly as part of my professional life. For instance, my birthday is not part of my profile. For me, I do not need professional acquaintances who rarely interact with me wishing me a happy birthday. (I do not post any public birthday wishes, either; I reserve those for private messages to people I know more closely.)

What Is Your Use of Social Media?

What should dictate the type of information you make available and how much personal transparency you express online is your use of social media in general and of any given social network specifically.

Just Personal

If you are only connecting with friends, those you personally know, and you hide your information from all others, you can more freely express yourself within that circle.

Just Business

If you use social media or a given social network for business only, ensure that the information you provide and the interactions you post are primarily professional. You may express opinions on your areas of expertise or on related topics, but avoid those conversations that you would not make part of your professional interactions at your work or with clients.

The Crossover: Business and Personal

This is where the huge majority of people live in social media. Personally, I believe it is the most effective. However, it does require that you remain aware that friends are watching your professional interaction. More critically from a career perspective, your professional contacts are watching (or at least have access to) your personal interactions.

Some people throw caution to the wind and hold an idealistic (and unrealistic) expectation that people should "accept me for who I am" mentality. They post comments and information that is rife with conflict and divisive in nature. Worse yet, they may post personal escapades that reflect poorly on them.

I'm not here to judge your personal life. I think most reasonable people can all agree that our lives behind our personal curtains should remain there. For some reason, however, parts of our lives we would not represent to our boss, co-workers, casual acquaintances, or children become fodder on Facebook and other networks.

My advice is this: Don't let this happen to you.

Not a Professional Networking Replacement

A common and dangerous misconception about social media is that it replaces the need for active and effective professional networking. Let me be clear about this: Social networking does not reduce the need for professional networking via face-to-face meetings, phone conversation, and periodic e-mails. It can, when used properly, augment those things.

However, social media can also negatively impact professional networking. This typically occurs when people cross certain lines and represent themselves poorly in their social networks.

With many employers turning first to Google and social networks to research candidates, think twice about how you represent yourself online.

My hope is that you can accurately reflect yourself online and that your "accurate self" is the type of person a prospective employer would feel privileged to have work for them.

The Seven People You Cannot Be Online

I initially covered this topic during some presentations on effective use of social media for business and career. Later I wrote a blog on the topic, titled, "Social Media Suicide or Who You Cannot Be Online." Originally, I had four types of people represented, but after conversations with other professionals, I have expanded that list to seven.

The following personality types are presented tongue in cheek, as caricatures. Even so, I am deadly serious when I observe that adopting any of these personae online will diminish, and even destroy, the effectiveness of social media as a professional networking tool.

The Angry Individual

This person is usually posting some angry rant about anything from an employer, politics, religion, or just the nature of life. Their response to anything others post online is typically cynical and with an edge. At times, they try to be funny, but in most cases they come across as vitriolic.

The Conspiracy Theorist

Whether the Illuminati, JFK's assassination, the Rothschild's control of global banking, or any of the myriad individuals who "really" attacked the World Trade Center on 9/11, the conspiracy theorist is there to let you know about it.

They have the YouTube videos and grainy photos to prove everything from the secret alien landing spots to the various connections that organized crime has with the presidency.

When I speak on online presence, I express this caveat: In the United States, you are allowed to be crazy; I wholeheartedly support that right. In fact, there is probably a once-a-month crazy conspiracy club you can join. However, when it comes to the impact on your professional credibility and career, my advice is to keep your craziness in that club and off of Facebook.

The Party Animal

I am continually surprised by the number of adults who express something like pride in how hung over they are from drinking the night before. Or those who post pictures of how "wasted" they are.

Again, I'm not trying to impose on your fun—whatever that looks or feels like. I do suggest, however, that if your fun involves large amounts of alcohol or drugs that you make sure that a computer or smartphone is not readily available.

I promise that employers find even the appearance of intemperate living to be a concern. Never mind that it is your once-a-month night to cut loose. Again, I'm not making a value judgment. I'm not saying you don't have the right to cut loose once in awhile and drink with friends. I'm simply advising you that those activities are best if never documented on social networks.

Vulgar Vicky or Lewd Larry

I used to say that MySpace was the network where young men and women forgot that a picture is worth a thousand words. This was in the early days of Facebook. These days, the same could be said about Facebook and middle-aged and older men or women.

This person is characterized by frequent vulgarity or direct or implied sexual content. Again, in many cases, the attempt is at humor. When it comes to your professional life, though, you want to keep such humor between close friends.

The Unwanted Kisser

This is best explained through an anecdotal story but one I see repeated often. Later in this chapter, I explain how and why I try to put relationships in context by sending a direct message to anyone I connect with or who connects with me.

In one particular case, I had connected with a woman who presented herself as an online marketing expert. I wrote her a note introducing myself and asking for more information about what she did.

I didn't receive an immediate response. However, a week or so later, while I was training someone on how to use Facebook, this person accepted my friend request. Instead of writing back, she proceeded to "recommend" about 15 different Facebook pages of clients she represented.

As the pop-up messages came across my screen, I turned to the person I was training and said, "I feel as though she just stuck her tongue in my mouth and we haven't even had a date yet."

While sort of gross, the analogy stuck with me and I use it to this day.

The Used Car Salesman

This person seems to turn every conversation into a pitch for his business, product, service, or expertise. You get the impression that the Used Car Salesman does not listen to any of the "conversation" online but is simply waiting for the next opportunity to pitch you something.

The Family Strife Poster

I am certain that every couple and every parent and child, at some point, gets into arguments. If you are the rare person who has never had family conflict, good for you (but lying is a bad trait).

The challenge is that the immediacy of social networks, always-on Internet access, and mobile devices allows us to take our common dysfunction online before we have had time to consider the consequences.

Husbands and wives air their arguments or complain about each other. Parents and children blast each other publicly to their network. Not only does this undermine the relationship in question, already strained with whatever the situation is, but it also necessarily paints a portrait of your life and your response to conflict.

Employers, potential employers, and (more importantly with social networks) those who might refer you professionally will think twice about doing so if they feel you will take conflicts public.

I spoke with a friend who did this often and explained that I thought it was not a very good way to handle such situations. Her response was that she was getting "support" from her friends. I pointed out that she had 475 friends listed and probably did not need all that support.

It isn't that I don't believe conflict exists or that there is never a time to reach out to a friend when you are frustrated with some relationship. Just do it privately, over coffee or in a phone call.

You run the risk of alienating the person you are having the conflict with. Furthermore, you might alienate those who support that person and cause others to question your judgment. If your judgment about your personal life appears questionable to them, you cannot expect those people to refer you in professional situations either.

How to Use Social Media Effectively

So far in this chapter, you've read about some of the pitfalls when it comes to social media and social networking. Instead of focusing solely on the "do not do's," I want to provide a proactive approach to using social media as a career development tool.

The following are some strategies to help you use social media to enhance your career.

Share Knowledge

This is a common theme throughout this book and when I speak. It may be the one concept with professional networking in general and social media in particular that has the most direct and positive impact on your career.

Educate or entertain, preferably both. I also discuss this idea in Chapter 26, "A Professional Blog." Those two words provide the basic guidelines for social media as a career tool. Adding value to the network means educating your network in your area of expertise.

Don't get this wrong. I'm not saying that you tell them over and over what you do. It isn't about what you do; it is about what they can do because of you. Educate your network on how to better accomplish things, and your name will rise to the top when opportunities come up.

In the area of social media, the truth is that I.T. professionals have an advantage. In many cases, we have knowledge that is highly desirable. If you can effectively share that knowledge in your network, the upside potential is very good.

This can be in the form of a short update indicating how a given technology works or how a problem can be solved. You can also link to articles or tutorials you write and even articles written by others.

Don't think that you need to come up with an original piece to add value to your network. Finding and sharing an article that helped you will also help elevate your social collateral—the esteem in which you are held among your peers.

Share Opportunities

Another way to add value to the network is to share opportunities in your network. If you are working for a company or hear of a company looking for a given skill set, consider posting that need into your network.

If you have a specific individual in mind, you can (in the case of Facebook, for instance) publicly post the opportunity and tag that individual. In that way, you not only publicize the need but also directly contact at least one person you think may be a fit.

The benefit is that others will see that you recognize opportunities and are willing to connect them to individuals. That alone helps others recognize the value you are attempting to bring to the network.

Put Relationships In Context

Some people find the number of friends to be an important metric. They connect to almost anyone who shows up on their suggested friends list or is a friend of a friend.

The number of connections you have may or may not have any value to your professional life. I believe that it is more important to put your relationships in context. Here is what I mean.

Whenever I see someone "interesting" online (perhaps that person left an insightful comment on something I read), I make both a connection request and send a personal message.

My message is fairly standard. It is something like this:

=======================

Hi [name],

I noticed that you are a friend of/I noticed you commented about X topic and saw that you work in [field]. I made a friend/connection request but also want to put the connection in context by letting you know more about me.

I am a business coach and consultant. I am also an author with one book and numerous articles to my credit. I help companies develop content strategies to engage customers and to help with search engine ranking.

Tell me a bit about you and what you do. Do you use social media to network professionally? Are there any questions I can answer or is there anything I can help you with?

I look forward to getting to know you. Thanks and write back.

Sincerely,

Matt Moran

=======================

When they write back and let me know more about what they do, I can add their name to my personal groups and at least have some idea about them and their professional life.

Having context means that I can more easily pass information and opportunities along to them if and when it is appropriate.

Putting relationships in context is a great way to improve your use of social media as a career tool.

Assessing Your Use of Social Media

Take some time and assess how you have been using social media. Does it reflect a positive professional picture? Do you add value to your network? Have you been one or more of the seven people you cannot be online?

I believe in written plans. It might be worth it for you to define what your image will be online and what information you will share. Determine what things you won't share, as well (for instance, personal conflicts with individuals). Set that rule in stone so that it does not come up during the heat of a conflict.

Social Media Conclusion

I hope that, through the information and examples in this chapter, you can see how you can use social media to augment your professional image and grow your professional network. I trust that you also see some of the pitfalls, activities, and information you should avoid.

For now, and for the foreseeable future, social media and its benefits and pitfalls will be part of our lives. Rather than taking a haphazard approach to social media, create both a strategic and a philosophical plan of attack that leverages your knowledge and helps you grow your career.

Actions & Ideas

1. Using my definition or starting from scratch, write a short definition of what you believe social media is. This will help you define how you can or should use it.

2. Do you currently use social media to connect personally, professionally, or both?

3. Of the seven individuals you cannot be online, list one or more you might have been at one point. Define how you will change that.

4. What special skills or knowledge can you share through your network? Think of the people you are connected to via social networking; which ones add value to the network through education?

5. Put three relationships/connections you have that have no context into context by sending them a message. Select three people who interest you.

EXPAND YOUR TOOLKIT

Remember to visit the book's website at http://www.ITCareerToolkit.com for supplemental and ongoing advice, tips, and data relevant to this chapter.

Career Options for Technologists

One of the advantages of a career in I.T. is the ability to do many tasks remotely. This can lend itself to the telecommuting option.

Although telecommuting has become more popular, you, as an "at-home worker," need to be aware of some important factors. In addition, the employer who provides the telecommuting option must understand how best to manage his remote workforce.

CHAPTER 18

Telecommuting

Note This chapter is not meant to provide legal guidelines on the subject of telecommunicating. Your employer should consult with local and federal agencies regarding liabilities, OSHA requirements, insurance needs, and so on.

One of the most exciting aspects of technology is its capability to offer unique career options. Of these, one of the most attractive is working from home, or telecommuting.

If managed properly, working from home offers numerous advantages for both employee and employer. These include issues such as family time, reduced commute time, flexible scheduling, and some tax advantages.

So strong was my draw to this lifestyle that I left a company that had made me a partner, paid me a good six-figure income, and provided me with a significant staff and budget. My second day home, my wife handed me a book she had found at the library titled *The Joy of Working From Home: Making a Life While Making a Living* by Jeff Berner.

Opening to the preface, here is what I read:

> It's Monday afternoon and I'm writing this in my home office, which overlooks the Pacific Ocean. This morning I made some phone calls, wrote five business letters, and finished a proposal for the next book I'm going to write. Soon I'll walk down the hill to my mailbox and pick up today's correspondence. I'll take a mid-afternoon break with a friend to go bicycling in the countryside and probably wrap up the workday answering phone messages and watering the lawn while most of my peers are creeping along the freeway. My own commute is about ten seconds—from the breakfast table, across the living room, to my desk in the office with the big picture window. I look forward to "going to work" almost every day.

I immediately shot off a message to Jeff, claiming that he had stolen my life and asking if I could have it back. That started a correspondence that continues to this day. I have become somewhat of an evangelist for this lifestyle. It's one that is much less rebellious than it seemed 30 years ago when Jeff started his work-at-home journey.

> **Note** A few years ago, Jeff Berner semi-retired as a photographer overseas. His former website about working from home is no longer active, but as of a few years ago, he was still telecommuting. And although technological advances make it a bit dated, his book is a joy to read (if you can find it).

For some, working at home might not be a viable option, or a combination of telecommuting and standard office work might be necessary.

When I made the decision to leave a traditional company/office environment, a huge part of my decision came down to my desire to work at home. I like to tell people that I married my wife and had children so that I could see them. For too many of my peers, their day consists of departing for a one-hour commute in the morning, putting in a full day at the office, and returning in time to tuck their kids in bed.

The advent of new technologies is rapidly making this option a standard part of the economy. With technologies such as high-speed Internet access, virtual private networks (VPNs), terminal application servers for remote desktop access, and a better understanding of the tools and skills needed to manage the at-home worker, the opportunities for telecommuting will continue to grow.

As an author, coach, and performer, telecommuting affords me the opportunity to continue to coach clients, write, and stay in touch with family and friends from my home or from the road.

It is not uncommon for an entire workweek to pass without ever walking into a client site, with my most consistent coworker being my Labrador retriever, Beaux.

Careers That Lend Themselves to Telecommuting

Technology careers are particularly well suited to telecommuting. This is because they generally require less support from the home office for problems that might arise with telecommuting equipment and software.

Within the technology professions, some careers further lend themselves to working from home. These include the following:

- Programmers
- Network administration
- System engineers

Programming, in particular, is something that an I.T. professional can easily do from a remote location.

The Benefits for the Employee

Following are just some of the benefits of telecommuting for the employee:

- **Less stress**—This is certainly true if done properly. One of the benefits of working at home is the ability to plan my workday around my life. Certainly, I must be available when my clients need me, but taking care of personal items becomes much less complicated. Doctor's appointments, family matters, and other appointments can be worked into your schedule without concern about taking time off from your job.

- **More family time**—Once again, this is true if managed properly. You do have some freedom in this area, but I know many consultants who, when in the midst of project work, work longer hours than many other professions.

  Although you have control of your schedule, you must control your schedule. Try to schedule your day as though you were still an employee, and work to keep your work at the office (even if the office is in your home).

- **Reduced expenses**—Working from home means you spend less time commuting. Less time commuting means less spent on gas. In addition, when you work at home, you are much less likely to go out to lunch.

  These can greatly reduce your expenses.

The Benefits for the Employer

Following are a few of the benefits of telecommuting for the employer:

- **Reduced office expense**—I have worked from home for several companies. In all cases, I used my own desk, my own computer, and other resources. Although I billed back to those companies appropriate expenses, the fact is that those companies were relieved from allocating full-time desk space, parking, and other expenses.

  Typically, the technology to allow such arrangements is already in place and is pennies on the dollar compared to setting up a brick and mortar office space.

- **Happier employees**—I have spoken to several telecommuting employees (some full-time, some part-time telecommuters). In every case, they cite telecommuting as one of the most critical elements to their job satisfaction.

  Many are willing to trade higher pay for the option. Why? Just two days per week can save a telecommuter anywhere from an hour to four or five hours in commute time.

  In Los Angeles, I have met employees who commute three hours every day (back and forth). That is 15 hours per week, or more than 60 hours in a month. In a very real sense, telecommuting would give these people more than two full days each month.

- **Less sick leave**—Studies indicate that telecommuters work more consistently without taking sick time. This might be in part due to less exposure to other sick employees. However, these same studies show that some employees, who would normally take a day off for illness, are willing to work out of their home office without taking that time off.

The Concerns for the Employee

Some of the concerns that telecommuting employees have are as follows:

- **Family guidelines**—This one is critical. Working at home has the benefit of providing more family time. For example, I regularly have lunch with my wife and kids.

However, I am also "available" during the day to deal with household emergencies. Incidents ranging from a family dispute to clogged-up plumbing no longer wait until I get home from my traditional office.

My family has had to set up rules for when I can be interrupted "safely." My wife and children need to be reminded of the rules as often as is necessary to create a cohesive work environment.

- **Self-discipline**—Along with increased freedom comes an increased need for self-discipline. Telecommuting often creates a more discretionary schedule, one where you can start earlier, take longer lunches, or get work done late at night. However, the telecommuter must be careful to put an emphasis on work first, and then reward.

  If you want to take off early on Friday, simply work later Thursday and start earlier Friday. Don't put the work off until the following Monday. Doing so can lead to incomplete projects and derail the work-at-home arrangement.

- **Need for recognition**—Some telecommuters have told me they feel their lack of presence might lead to a lack of recognition (an "out of sight, out of mind" dilemma).

  If this is a concern, simply create a correspondence that you issue weekly to the people you work with that covers a summary of completed work and a summary of upcoming work. Don't do this in some overt grab for glory, but as an information piece. It can ensure that your contribution is recognized. Beware: On the flip side, if you are not producing, this summary report exposes that, too.

The Concerns for the Employer

Concerns that employers have about their telecommuting employees include the following:

- **Lack of control**—Many employers believe that they have less-effective control over employees who telecommute. Their concern is that the person might exploit the situation, putting in fewer hours or failing to complete necessary work.

Certainly, it could turn out that way. Note a couple of things here, though. First, not all employees are suited to be part of a telecommuting force. A lack of commitment and discipline can kill the arrangement.

The second, however, is much more critical. The company that employs an at-home workforce must reevaluate its method for gauging employee success. A general shift from an hourly perspective to a project perspective is necessary to make telecommuting a success. You'll find more on this in the section "Keys to Successful Telecommuting."

- **Disassociation with the team**—This is another real issue for some employees. Some employees need close interaction with their peers. Without this interaction, they can become depressed and much less productive. This is something that the employer and employee must have an open discussion about.

  The employer must watch for signs in the employee that indicate a negative response to the isolation of working at home. In addition, tools such as conference calls, effective e-mail, and instant messenger (IM) services can alleviate some of this.

  In fact, communication in a telecommuting environment often improves because its importance is emphasized.

Conclusion: Next Steps

Working at home is not for everyone, even though each of the concerns addressed in this chapter can be effectively addressed. Telecommuting, whether you are an independent contractor or a corporate employer, requires a greater degree of trust and self-discipline—on the part of both the company and the worker.

The nature of the work must be evaluated more by its effectiveness than the time it takes to complete. In effect, even the person who is employed by a company must view his work with a project/contract mentality. Work-at-home employees must be responsible for achieving key project milestones in a given time frame. Whether the employee performs that work between 6:00 a.m. and 2:00 p.m. or between 9:00 a.m. and 5:00 p.m. becomes much less relevant.

I, for one, thrive in a work-at-home situation. My day generally starts sometime around 4:30 a.m. Early mornings are my most productive time. For others, late evenings are best. The benefit for many telecommuters is that they can find their productive time and adopt their schedule accordingly.

One professional I know created an incredible business working as a consultant for companies on the East Coast. He had two small children and was a widower. The need to make a living, while at the same time being available to his children, forced him to get creative.

He would start his day early—very early, perhaps 4:30 a.m.—while his children slept. He would perform work until it was time to get his children ready for school. After taking them to school, his day would continue. He would be finished with work typically well before his kids' school day was done.

Certainly, his schedule required discipline, but the dividend was an increased level of satisfaction with his life as a whole.

If you believe that the work you perform can be done at home, propose the idea to management. It might be management is simply not ready for it. Perhaps your manager does not understand the benefits. Or perhaps there is a pragmatic need for bodies at the workplace. However, using a little bit of creativity can make the possibility of telecommuting work, even if it's only part time.

Before you approach your employer, have a plan in place that addresses the concerns from the company's perspective, while proactively addressing the concerns from your perspective.

Keys to Successful Telecommuting

Working from home can provide greater satisfaction and lead to increased productivity. To make it work, though, you need to consider a few things. The items that are covered in the sections that follow are important keys to make the work-from-home experience a successful one.

Project-Based/Free-Agent Mindset

You must, if working from home, be even more disciplined when it comes to producing a final product for your employer. The fact is, when you are at your place of work, part of your performance is based simply on your appearance. Managers typically do not look over your shoulder to see what you are working on.

When you are working from home, management does not see you. It sees only the work you produce. Employers are much more critical of project time frames. You must develop a free-agent mindset that places production above "busy-ness."

You must document additional tasks more meticulously and more effectively track your time. Communication between you and your employer must also be more effective. Notice that I did not say more *frequent* or *quantitative*, only more effective. You must be able to concisely keep management apprised of the work you have done, what you are doing, what has to be done, and when.

Apply Discipline

Working at home requires intense discipline. The draw of family, little projects around the house or, worse yet, the television, must be set aside. If not, you will fail in this endeavor. Telecommuting requires much more discipline than is needed when working at the office.

At the office, it is unlikely that your spouse will ask you to fix the television. You will not hear the kids playing in the pool and feel compelled to put in some "quality family time." These types of situations certainly do arise in a work-at-home environment, so if you are not disciplined, don't consider working at home an option.

Clear Expectations

You must establish clear expectations for what constitutes an effective working relationship with your employer. These include what hours you must be available via phone, how to communicate on projects, what a minimum schedule entails, and so on.

Establishing clear expectations right from the beginning is a key factor in work-at-home success. Doing so greatly reduces the possibility of frustrating misunderstandings.

If you have a history of great work with your company, it, of course, will be more willing to approve telecommuting as an option. If your company's past experience with you is not a positive one, your telecommuting is unlikely to be approved. Telecommuting requires a great deal of trust on the part of the employer. Give the company a reason to expect continued production regardless of where you work.

Technologies for the Telecommuter

The sections that follow cover some of the key technologies used in the work-at-home environment.

VPNs

A virtual private network (VPN) is a secure network connection to a private network (the company local area network or LAN) through a public network (the Internet). A VPN provides a way for an external computer or resource to connect to resources on the private network. This can be access to company e-mail, files, and applications.

As an example, I connect from my home network, across the Internet, to the networks of several of my clients. This provides me relatively high-speed access to their LANs without having to pay for leased lines or other expensive telecommunication links. I can administer their servers, perform troubleshooting tasks, or even develop applications on their private systems directly from my home system.

With recent advancements in network-based telephones, you can even connect a phone to your home network and, through a VPN connection, have calls to your office routed directly to the phone at your house. This lends to the professionalism associated with telecommuting.

IM Services

Although they're often cited as a source of abusive practices, IM programs can be extremely valuable in telecommunication settings. I use a combination of Instant Messenger to stay in contact with remote developers and key clients. When I have my IM applications running, I might be logged in to Skype and Gmail (Google chat) simultaneously.

Note, however, that IM can be extremely detrimental to performance. I have had employees who had day-long conversations about virtually nothing "between moments of production." The problem is that technology work, when done well, requires concentration.

Programming takes anywhere from 15 to 30 minutes to shift into "high-productivity" mode. Every distraction resets this clock. IM, if used incorrectly, can kill productivity if you're not careful. In fact, any interruption can.

You need to set time aside that you are not available except for emergencies. This means turning off IM and e-mail.

Web Cam

Web cams fall under the IM category. However, they provide an even more intimate and direct way to connect with your employer, employees, peers, and clients—not to mention family and friends.

I use Skype and Google Voice chat extensively, and now Google Hangouts and Tinychat.com have introduced group video chat.

I have two programmers overseas I video with a couple times a month and a fellow songwriter whom I've coached who has lived in London, Qatar, and now Manchester. We Skype regularly.

Webinar Software

Several companies have introduced webinar software (both free and low-cost) that are great tools for technology professionals to showcase project work and train and connect with employees and clients.

I've used AnyMeeting, WebEx, Citrix's GoToMeeting and GoToWebinar products, and several others. Even video streaming services like UStream, LiveStream, and newcomers JustJamIt.com and SpreeChat provide great tools for productive telecommuting.

When writing, I turn off Gmail and put my phone into Airplane mode. I also shut down my web browser so that I am not tempted to browse the Internet to see the latest news or research something. All of these distractions are much more available and dangerous for the telecommuter.

It is not that these technologies cannot play an important role for the telecommuter. In fact, I use them daily for my work. I have a network of peers who specifically use IM to stay in touch and quickly resolve work-related issues. For instance, if I run into a problem programming, I typically have one or two programmers online whom I can ask a question of. If they are busy or unavailable, they simply log off the system, and I know not to interfere with their day.

The point is that you must use the technologies wisely and when appropriate. Distractions greatly hinder productivity, and a lack of focus can kill any telecommuting opportunity.

Resources for the Home Worker

Many resources are available for those contemplating or currently working at home.

Don't forget to check out the library for other books discussing everything from office space, tax implications, and other work-at-home arrangements.

Conclusion

Telecommuting is a great option for the technology professional. Many technology professions lend themselves to remote work. The underlying technologies are available and relatively inexpensive to put into place.

I've addressed the challenges and benefits in this chapter, but should issue one additional warning: Although telecommuting can greatly enhance your lifestyle, it is still subject to overwork and a lack of life/work balance. The home office is readily available 24 hours per day. Often, the telecommuter might find himself wandering back into the office in the evening and on weekends. This can lead to resentment from your family and ultimately can lead to burnout. Understanding the benefits and creating necessary boundaries can go a long way toward making telecommuting a highly productive option for your career.

Actions & Ideas

1. Find out whether your company has a policy on telecommuting. Check to see who is telecommuting effectively and ask those people about their experience.

2. If you are interested in telecommuting, create a list of those things you do that can be done remotely. If the list is small, you need to modify your career to match a remote workforce.

EXPAND YOUR TOOLKIT

Remember to visit the book's website at http://www.ITCareerToolkit.com for supplemental and ongoing advice, tips, and data relevant to this chapter.

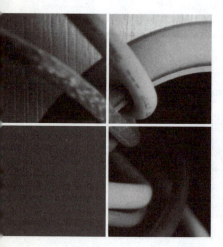

Selling Your Time and Talent

Consulting has become one of the most popular options available to the technology professional. As the economy fluctuates and companies look to mitigate long-term costs (read full-time employees), opportunities will abound for astute professionals to sell their talent on an as-needed basis.

This chapter offers some simple, yet effective advice on how to make the transition to consultant/contractor. In addition, this chapter identifies and explains some resources to assist the consultant.

CHAPTER 19

Consulting

In this chapter, I speak of the consultant in the framework of the independent, self-employed individual. Staff consultants, those who are employed by technology companies, are no less consultants, and some of this information certainly applies to them, too. However, a good portion of this content relates to those issues specific to the independent consultant.

The path to consultant is one that many technologists have taken. However, with a tighter job market, many are finding that the move, once so attractive, is more challenging. It's not because companies aren't hiring consultants; rather, it's because technology professionals who are currently employed are hesitant to leave the perceived security of their current position.

The consulting/contractor industry, despite being slightly less appealing of late, will continue to serve a valuable purpose. In addition, those who can create the "complete consultant" package will still garner high pay and find ample opportunity. In fact, Bruce Tulgan's book *Winning the Talent Wars* indicates that the economy is moving closer to a true free-agent, talent-driven workforce. This is good news for those who are interested in consulting.

In short, companies commonly staff for projects and talent, not for long-term commitments. This means that the need for independent contractors will continue to rise.

During the technology boom between 1995 and 1999, many technologists were drawn into contract agreements. Large hourly rates and a glut of projects made the move simple, requiring little personal marketing and, in many cases, even less hands-on ability.

Corporate America became caught up in the technology craze, abandoning more conservative models of profit and return on investment. Because of their need to ensure that their technology was up to date, these companies began throwing large sums of money at ill-advised and poorly planned technology projects.

This created an artificial salary curve that skewed many technology professionals' view of their long-term worth. A veritable industry gold rush ensued, with college students quickly shifting majors from anything to information technology (I.T.).

The seemingly endless need created a talent hunt that left few out of its sights. Consultants popped up everywhere, many of whom had never worked previously in corporate America or implemented much in the way of technology.

But as quickly as the boom began, it ended. Contractors who had previously had their phones ringing with prospective projects suddenly found themselves reducing their rates. And instead of referring to themselves as consultants, they more accurately stated that they were out of work.

This is often the case during economic downturns: When the market rises and companies struggle to find talent, technology professionals enter the market, believing consulting to be lucrative but not truly prepared to maintain a long-term consultancy. However, consulting can prove rewarding both financially and personally. A truly effective consultant can take satisfaction from knowing that he provides excellent advice and implementation skills to his clients. Few industries warrant a need for consultants the way that technology does.

This is because of the transitory nature of technology. Normally, a company implements technology and then grows the usage of that technology until such a time that business growth or technology direction warrants a change. It is during these times, when the company's technology must change, that a company finds itself in a transition period.

During these transitory periods, the in-house staff, saddled with maintaining the day-to-day operations, has neither the time nor the necessary skills in the latest technology. Consultants serve the valuable role of introducing new technology effectively into an organization. They might be involved in the recommendation, the implementation, and the training of in-house staff.

In addition, smaller companies—those that don't warrant a full-fledged I.T. department—can use a consultant or consulting company to outsource their I.T. functions.

The Consulting Life

I have found the consulting life to be particularly rewarding. My expertise has been sought out and well rewarded. However, I want to give you a fair assessment as to what the consulting life entails—some of the perks and some of the pitfalls—in hopes of providing a complete picture. With this complete picture clearly in view, you can decide whether consulting is for you.

I'm not going to spend too much time on the mechanics of the engagement, marketing techniques, or how to identify the hot new trends in technology. These are important, to a degree. However, once again, I defer to the myriad of books in libraries and bookstores that can assist you in these areas.

You can find a number of book and articles in the "Reading List" appendix and online at www.ITCareerToolkit.com. Also on the website, you'll find some videos on the subject. These resources can serve as a virtual mentor of sorts.

The Benefits

Joining the rank of the independent or staff consultant can be exhilarating and boost your career both financially and in professional development potential. The sections that follow describe just some of the benefits associated with consulting.

Respect

Good consultants are treated with respect. Of this, there is little doubt. However, please understand that excesses in the industry have created a healthy skepticism in businesses' attitude toward consultants.

Consultants in general, and technology consultants in particular, have suffered from costly projects gone awry and a sometimes-dismissive attitude toward the needs of the client. Individuals with little experience or practical knowledge (and so resulting in failed projects) are an ongoing bitter taste that impacts the industry.

I view this as a positive to the technology industry in general and to the consulting field in particular. It weeds out those who did not actually produce, leaving the industry healthier for those remaining.

The respect you gain from consulting comes from providing a business with tangible benefits from your advice or technical skills. In many respects, good technology consultants garner the same type of mystical respect that was formerly reserved for doctors. You perform tasks that others simply do not understand.

In the past, I recommended a book titled *Dangerous Company*, by Charles Madigan and James O'Shea. The book is geared toward the management consulting industry, but the message applies to technology consulting, too. The authors discuss the largely misguided trust that many businesses place in their consultants—leading to failed and costly projects and, in some cases, failed businesses.

Although a bit dated, the book's message is still very much relevant. If you want to succeed long-term as a consultant, you must be providing exceptional value for your client's dollar.

You should take very seriously the stake that a business owner or management places in your work. Good advice can help build a business. Bad advice can be devastating.

Schedule

I mentioned already the perspective that consultants make their own hours. After you're in the field, you will understand how untrue this is in practice. However, you do gain a certain degree of freedom in the consulting profession. Ultimately, though, you have to work many hours to be profitable.

However, you do get to determine the projects you take on and the hours you use to complete them. If you're disciplined and like working in the evening, you can do some of your work then. If early morning is your optimal production time, as is the case with me, you can perform your work then.

This can leave time for you to take care of other matters during the day. Of course, if your clients need you during prime working hours, the relative freedom of your schedule is affected.

It is important that you schedule appropriate gaps during working hours. If you don't, even small emergencies or setbacks with one client can suddenly have you overloaded and unable to complete your day's work.

Exciting Projects

One phenomenon that I find interesting is the stake that management places in a consultant's advice. In many cases, I advocate ideas that the in-house I.T. staff has already suggested, but because I am a consultant—one who advises for a living—my advice is more readily heeded.

This also leads me to more exciting projects. Many I.T. departments, burdened with the daily upkeep of company technology, cannot undertake new projects. Their current workload is spent maintaining existing technology. Consultants are often brought in for the initial thrust in new technologies.

The by-product is that consultants often have the privilege of working with the latest and most innovative technologies. This becomes a self-perpetuating advantage in professional development. As you complete one project and gain that experience, you become more valuable to the next prospective client hoping to do the same.

It is not always that your talent is superior to the in-house staff; it is simply that you have the opportunity to apply your talent to the newest technologies.

Compensation

Although the pay for consultants and contractors has fallen off a bit in recent years, the fact remains that good technical consultants are still landing profitable projects. In fact, my rate after the boom has risen on average. This is in part because of a greater understanding by clients of the need for *proven* experience.

In addition, I market myself to niche technologies wherever possible. I look to capitalize on those things I do extremely well that are often overlooked.

The compensation for consulting can certainly lead to a six-figure income. However, to develop that type of income, you must be extremely effective at both project work and personal marketing.

The Pitfalls

When I discuss the pitfalls, I'm not making a positive or negative comment about any of the items. I merely mention them as areas that are often overlooked and can create anxiety or pressure in the consultant's life.

Where possible, in each pitfall I offer suggestions on how to mitigate this particular area becoming an actual problem.

Business Planning: Taxes, Legal

As a self-employed individual, often working from his home, an independent consultant has some real planning to do in the area of taxes and legal matters. I will give my strongest recommendation right up front: Hire professionals.

Yes, I know, they are expensive, and an assortment of books is available to assist you in these areas. I ask you, however, to apply the same logic you apply to those companies that hire you. These companies could, theoretically, grab a book on the given technology for which you have been hired and implement their own solution.

But you are aware of the problems that can arise. You know about things that someone will overlook or not understand. Your expertise is needed if the company wants the project to be a success.

The same logic applies to planning for taxes and legal matters. Incredible opportunities are available for tax savings, deductions, and creative ways to keep your money. However, if done incorrectly, the impact can be financially devastating.

I am not implying that you not be involved or read up on these matters. In fact, I recommend the opposite. You should be able to bring to your tax professional's attention an article about some tax law change and ask how it applies to you. You are creating a partnership.

However, in the final analysis, your time is best spent winning and finishing billable work. That is where your money comes from.

Billing

Other than providing solutions for your clients, the most important function that you can perform as a consultant is billing. This is not a matter of greed. It is a matter of survival. Many consultants put off this function for a number of reasons—namely current workload and inaccurate records.

Current Workload

When the current workload is high, the consultant becomes consumed with completing that work. Billing and paperwork seem like a tedious and expensive endeavor. If you are billing, of course, you cannot work, and while the work is available, you should do it.

However, if you don't perform billing regularly, you'll find yourself quickly in a cash-flow crunch. Soon you'll begin funding your client's projects by pulling money from savings or credit cards. Both serve to reduce the actual dollars per hour you earn. Don't get in the business of funding your client's project.

I try to bill weekly, on Monday mornings. I know others who bill twice a month. Find a schedule that works for you, and stick to it. In addition, for projects that have a set number of tasks, I use a project initiation fee and then progress billing every week.

My personal model for projects of less than one month duration is a 50 percent work initiation fee to start the project and the remainder due at project completion.

If the project is longer than one month, I do a work initiation fee of 50 percent of the first month's estimated billing and then progress billing for specific milestones or specific time periods.

> **Tip** Negotiating terms upfront is vital. Many companies employ a Net 30 accounts payable. This means you are paid 30 days from the day they get your invoice. If you are billing for work from the prior week, and you consider time for mail and processing, you might not see your money for 45 days or more.

I negotiate extremely aggressive terms as a matter of course. Much of my work is done on a Net 5 or Net 10 basis. At times, I'm paid against a retainer fee. Have a frank discussion with your client. If the client's terms make life difficult for you, and the client cannot or will not change the terms, drop that client.

Even if a client pays well, the most difficult one can become a drain emotionally and lead to burnout.

Inaccurate Records

Some consultants do a poor job of tracking their billable hours. They put off billing hoping to be able to go back and re-create the hours from two weeks ago.

I was taught by a mentor of mine to fill out a daily timesheet. It seemed silly at first; here I was an independent consultant, reporting to nobody, filling out a daily timesheet. However, I found that a timesheet helped me track the time I spent on billable work and, more importantly, the time I spent on nonbillable work.

A timesheet helped me gain a better understanding of what time was valuable and what time was wasted. I recommend this exercise for anyone.

You might be able to produce the most amazing solutions for your clients, but if you do so at a loss every month, it won't be long before both you and your clients lose out. Invoice regularly!

Trading Time for Dollars

One of the nicest parts of consulting is the rate. You can certainly earn hourly rates that, if extended over a full-time schedule, equate to a nice six-figure income.

However, remember that you are in the ultimate trading-time-for-dollars position. This means that when times are good and work is plentiful, you are in fat city. But when the work runs out, times can be lean.

I know that working in a traditional job is also trading time for dollars. However, the difference is that business expenses, marketing, billing, and other ancillary functions are spread across a group. When work is slow, you are not as severely impacted.

Also, you must beware of the mindset that views all nonbillable time as lost wages. This is an easy mindset to adopt. In fact, I used to take every Friday off when I began consulting. I would take the time to have breakfast with my wife and spend time with my kids.

But eventually, as project work increased, I found myself viewing the time as having a greater cost than the two cups of coffee and scones we had purchased. I started to calculate the two hours of quality time in terms of the lost revenue.

This is a serious danger. Ultimately, I corrected it, but I mention it because many consultants I've spoken to share the same perspective.

Schedule

I mentioned schedule before as a perk. However, it's also an area of concern. You must be disciplined with your time. To be profitable as a consultant, you need to schedule your work time carefully. It is easy to get caught up in busy work that produces no income.

At the end of the day, you will have put in a lot of work but have little to show for it. Consulting hours, when you are handling all aspects of the work, can be extremely long. Don't get caught up in this idea of the freewheeling maverick who answers to no one.

Others mistakenly believe the same thing. Many individuals who hold traditional jobs tell me that I don't understand their scheduling problems because I can make my own hours.

Although my initial reaction was a desire to strangle them, I came up with a more diplomatic response. I learned to smile and tell them that they were right. I made my own hours, which were 4:30 a.m. to 10:00 p.m.

If you are one of those who believes that you will have tons of free time by starting your own consulting practice, let me dissuade you from making a big mistake. There is certainly an amount of freedom in the consulting life. However, time is not really one of them. You will put in your time somewhere.

Although I was taking Fridays off, I was working 12 to 15 hours daily, Monday through Thursday.

Enter consulting because you have proven expertise, enjoy and can manage the freedom (*not the free time*) it affords, can perform all aspects of a business, and are not afraid to go it alone. If those things appeal to you, definitely consider consulting.

Ongoing Marketing

Depending on which book you read, between 15 percent and 25 percent of your time as a consultant is spent on nonbillable business functions. A good portion of this time is spent in some form of marketing. In many ways, the consulting life is only as profitable as the next engagement.

To ensure a steady cash flow, which in turn reduces pressure, ongoing marketing must take place.

Marketing takes the form of cold calls, referrals, and publications:

- **Cold calls**—These calls are exposure to new prospective clients without referrals. Certainly the most difficult, cold calls require a commitment to ongoing calls and discussions.

- **Referrals**—These are by far your most effective and simplest marketing. When you are referred into a company by other clients, you stand a high chance of landing that client. This is similar to what I cover in Chapter 13, "The Job Search," where I explain how to get your resumé out.

- **Publications**—The phrase "Publish or die" is common in the academic world. Professors and those who are pursuing advanced degrees understand the impact that publishing an article means to their career. An automatic sense of prestige is given to the professional whose ideas have been considered sound enough to put in print.

    The same is true for the consultant. Having an article published provides an excellent discussion point for you and your potential and existing clients. You can forward a copy of your article to them with a note explaining how this idea or technology might be useful to their business.

    Later, when you call to follow up, you are no longer the no-name computer guy, but the distinguished and published author. You now become a noted expert who the company should listen to. I cannot overemphasize the importance of publishing.

Ideas on Getting Published

If you have the ability to organize your thoughts and can effectively put them on paper, you can get published. Magazines are on a constant hunt for content. Every month, for every magazine, an editor is frantically trying to keep his advertisers happy by publishing articles that draw readers.

As a consultant, you are typically exposed to many different technologies and a variety of business models. Even the staff technologists can benefit greatly by having something published. Use the projects that you are exposed to and the solutions that you have developed as the jumping-off point for publication.

You must understand, however, that being published rarely equates to monetary gain. It is about professional exposure and the sense of prestige that you gain—which in turn will assist your career as both a technologist and a consultant.

The Process of Getting Published

The following lays out in simple terms how to find an editor who needs content.

First, you are probably already reading several magazines that you find valuable. If you like one particular magazine both in content and in style, start there.

It is likely that the magazine lists the editor or editors who are in charge of content. The magazine might also include submission guidelines or provide you with a website where you can find them. If not, simply call the paper or magazine and ask for the editorial or submissions department.

Submission guidelines list the format for the piece, the general length, and perhaps some pet peeves or personal suggestions from the editor. After you have these, create an outline for the article.

You can choose to write the article first or to query the editor first. I have taken both approaches. Personally, I like writing the article first. I'm confident in my ability to sell the article. If the article doesn't sell, though, I can use it personally as a newsletter/ promotional piece.

The query letter should introduce you and the piece to the editor and should suggest both the length and content of the piece. For most magazines, especially those of a technical nature, e-mail is an acceptable way to query the editor. In fact, most now recommend electronic submission.

If you want tips on how to effectively write your query letter or e-mail, pick up a copy of *The Writer's Market* at the bookstore or library or visit their website (www.writersmarket.com). It contains numerous suggestions and examples of query letters.

After the magazine has accepted your piece, the work starts. Let me caution you: If you don't have strong self-confidence, the editorial process might kill you. Editors have a way of taking what you consider some of your best ideas and reducing them to a sentence or two—or, worse yet, cutting them altogether.

However, editors are experts at both their readership and at what the magazine needs. Expect your work to be cut significantly. In hindsight, you will find that editors' alterations are typically correct. Avoid the mindset that every sentence you write is a sacred cow—not to be touched.

My wife edits much of what I write, and a single suggestion from her gave my writing its greatest boost. I tend to draw out my ideas. I believe they are so good that I must explain completely the train of thought leading to my idea. After reading one of my earlier pieces, she gave me this advice: "Write shorter sentences."

Now as I write, and more important, when I do my second draft, I keep her edict in mind. And I pass along the same to you. Short and to the point is understandable. It leads to becoming an "easy read," which will help you publish more writing.

If the idea of writing terrifies you, or if you would like to write but need assistance in the craft, consider taking a course. I have a short section on improving your writing in Chapter 7, "Communication Skills." The ideas I present in that chapter are not earth shattering, but they are effective nonetheless.

Don't be concerned if you don't or can't write. Certainly, writing isn't for everyone. Play to your strengths.

Marketing is, however, without a doubt one of the most critical functions you'll perform as a consultant. If marketing doesn't appeal to you, the consulting field is not really an option.

Good consultants are treated with respect and benefit from excellent word-of-mouth marketing. But becoming a consultant/contractor takes more than an effective grasp of a given technology—that is, if you want your business to last.

A consultant must have good technical knowledge, have an excellent understanding of his client's business, and most important, be able to promote himself without crossing the line into a gimmicky sales rep.

Numerous books have been written on the consulting field. It isn't my intent to add to them. Instead, I'll offer suggestions from my experience and point you to resources that will be valuable if you're thinking about or have already entered the consulting field.

Resources for the Consultant

I've provided a list of resources in the appendix of this book. Also, make sure you check out the Consulting Tools at www.ITCareerToolkit.com.

In addition, Chapter 27, "Twelve Weeks to Profitable Consulting," covers a highly focused approach to marketing and getting your consulting business started quickly.

Online Supplements for the Consultant

At the website www.ITCareerToolkit.com you'll find numerous resources for running an independent or small consultancy. They range from sales and marketing material to time tracking, billing, and a proposal template.

You can find instructions and videos explaining the materials on the same website.

Conclusion

Consulting can be the most rewarding career for a technology professional. It has the potential for pay, prestige, and the most innovative projects available.

Consulting also means taking responsibility for all aspects of your professional life. If you're planning to become a consultant, I recommend starting part time, which is an excellent way to work through time tracking, billing, and managing your clients and yourself.

Actions & Ideas

1. View the video online or read the primer on "Marketing & Billable Hours." How does this information impact your understanding of the relationship between time marketing and billable hours on yearly income?

2. Create a simple case study example of work you have performed. Have a nontechnical manager or business owner read the document for clarity. Use the case study outline and instructions provided on the website to guide you.

EXPAND YOUR TOOLKIT

Remember to visit the book's website at http://www.ITCareerToolkit.com for supplemental and ongoing advice, tips, and data relevant to this chapter.

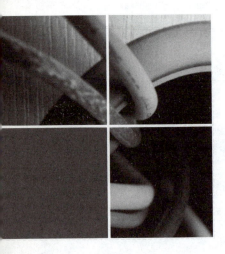

Management of Projects and People Requires Specialized Skill and a Certain Degree of Risk

Moving into management typically means spending less time working directly with technology and honing those purely technical skills. For some technology professionals, this is a scary and difficult proposition.

However, for many, assuming a management position is the natural progression in their career. Developing the skills and attitudes necessary is critical. Even if you don't want to take on an actual management role, the skills are vital to continued career growth.

CHAPTER 20

Management

This chapter discusses the phenomenon of management and emphasizes skills and ideas that are necessary for the successful manager. The first thing to do, however, is to define *management*:

Management (noun)

1. The act, manner, or practice of managing; handling, supervision, or control; management of a crisis; management of factory workers.

2. The person or persons who control or direct a business or other enterprise.

3. Skill in managing; executive ability.

What this definition lacks in creativity, it makes up for in accuracy. Quite simply, management is either the act of, the skill required, or the people who manage, direct, and supervise a process or organization. Whether you have a desire to move into management, the underlying principles should be well understood.

Good management is hard to come by and can be richly rewarded. This fact is critical and should give you pause as to why you should consider developing the organizational and leadership skills to manage both projects and people.

Bruce Tulgan, author of *Winning the Talent Wars*, studied the dynamic of management. He concluded that undermanagement was a "disease of epic proportions."

In his research, Tulgan discovered that although organizations often create programs to engage the employee, they do little to engage the manager to engage the employee. What this means is that the idea is passed down to staff but has not been modeled and directed by management.

Good management requires a high-level combination of time and process management, leadership, and organizational insight. Typically, we are naturally proficient in one area and must work to develop the others.

I know that personally, leadership is my strong suit. The ability to motivate and drive ideas forward is a place I can hang my hat. However, I have, through notable failures, discovered that time and process management are equally important.

This chapter discusses each of these areas in relation to your I.T. career. The goal is for you to start developing those skills now. Whether you aspire to become a mid-level manager, a vice president, a chief information officer (CIO), or just better understand the management process, these skills can provide a huge boost to your overall value in an organization.

Leadership

Leadership is most often associated with a dynamic and motivational style. However, you can achieve the same effect through a more reserved or conservative style.

Great leadership is primarily concerned with providing the resources that are necessary to enable staff members to get their job done.

If you have a desire to manage, you must be able to enable your workforce.

Enabling your workforce means giving them the resources, motivation, and direction to complete their projects and tasks.

Enabling can take many forms. It can be as simple as making sure that the physical resources for a job are in place. If you are a programmer, ensuring that you have the programming tools to get the job done is part of enabling. If you are an engineer or technician, ensuring that you have the equipment necessary to work and succeed is part of enabling.

Enabling can mean giving the appropriate amount of leeway to allow employees to accomplish their task without interruption. This might mean that a manager notifies others when an employee is unavailable for one of his projects.

Enabling also takes the form of project ownership. Turning over projects to staff members—allowing them to create and innovate—is key to effective management.

When I worked for a large law firm, I was privileged to see an excellent management style. The I.T. director did not assign projects to those whose title naturally fit the tasks. When a project or need arose, he would call everyone to a central location and explain the issue.

In the short conversation that followed, he identified those who had good ideas and teamed them up. These people were then assigned the project. He would request a list of resources or tools to complete the job—identifying those that were not already in our toolkits. He would then ensure that those tools were quickly located and purchased. At that point, ownership—success and failure—was the responsibility of the team.

This manager expected results and typically got them. Once, he asked whether I could deliver on a given project in the time frame the attorney needed. I answered, "I think I can."

He replied, "I didn't ask if you thought you could do it. I'm about to stick my neck on the line and say that it will be done. Can you do it?"

I answered that I could, and he made sure that I had a laptop and the necessary software before the day had ended.

If you are to succeed as a manager, you must be comfortable with the idea of turning projects over to your staff. You must be effective at gauging your employees' skills so that you can mitigate risk of failure, but you must also allow for some growth—forcing employees to stretch their abilities with each project. Doing so keeps them interested and makes them more valuable.

Process and Time Management

Process and time management are also critical for the manager.

Some of my peers might tell you that I cover this topic in theory only. There is truth to that. In particular, time management is my Achilles heel. For that reason, I have to spend a little more effort in this area.

If you have problems meeting deadlines or keeping track of significant project or work milestones, you might need some remedial help in this area.

This goes beyond writing things down on sticky notes or on the back of your hand. Time is our most precious commodity—and it is a commodity that we can only spend. You cannot save time or bank it. You must master its use.

Following are some ideas that I have found critical regarding time management:

- Keep a single journal or book for your tasks and appointments.

  Although you don't necessarily need to go out and purchase an expensive time management binder, you should try to keep information about tasks, appointments, and projects in a single location.

  I have worked with many professionals who have multiple notepads with notes and contact numbers in each. Later, finding key pieces of information is difficult.

- Take a few moments at a designated time to plan your day's critical tasks.

  This can occur at the end of the day or early in the morning. Use whatever time is effective for you. Sit down and make a list of critical tasks for the day, and then prioritize those tasks.

  Of critical importance here is to look over your schedule and see whether you have overbooked your tasks and appointments. Although it is great to be ambitious, your day might be encumbered by many unplanned distractions. If you schedule and plan for tasks without room for delays, you'll find that you're constantly failing to finish your list.

  Make sure that your list is ambitious but achievable.

Critical Skills You Need Now

A key to making the move to management is the adoption of skills before you have a formal title or responsibility. Fortunately, if you have read this book sequentially, you likely have started to identify and work on some of the skills.

The sections that follow cover several key skills in relation to their role in a management career.

Presentation and Meeting Skills

The ability to hold an audience and accurately convey your message is critical. This is true whether it is a large corporate gathering or a small departmental meeting. Project ideas are typically presented by management. The ability to be concise and engaging during a presentation is a must, as is the ability to be persuasive.

You don't have to be Tony Robbins or Zig Ziglar. However, you must understand how to best structure a presentation for your audience. You need to understand those things that are important to them. You also need to be able to clearly explain how your team can successfully address your audience's concerns.

If you can add a little flair or humor, that's even better.

When you're creating presentations to management, remember the following:

- **Management has little time**—Get to your point quickly, and let managers know what you want from them. I have taken part in many presentations in which managers have been convinced of the importance of a project, only to have the presenter fail to explain his desire to undertake it.

- **Keep the culture and personalities in mind**—I have a tendency to be theatrical at times. I have a lot of fun giving presentations. However, I am also aware of the particular personalities of my primary audience.

  If I am meeting with a new executive, I often ask his coworkers and peers about his style. If the executive is stoic and conservative, I rein myself in a bit. If he is demonstrative and dynamic, I up the energy and edginess.

- **Maintain a strict agenda**—Meetings often flounder because of lack of direction. The meeting facilitator (most often a manager) lets tangential issues take over the agenda.

  Once, while working with a client whose meetings often went longer than planned and seldom stayed on the agenda topics, I helped draft a meeting primer. It helped reduce the time of meeting and helped keep the client on agenda.

  Here are some of the key ideas my meeting template included:

  - Most meetings should be less than an hour.

  - Place high-priority items at the beginning of the meeting.

  - Place as few items on the agenda as possible. You have to recognize what type of items require a face-to-face meeting and what requires only some e-mail communications. Don't place the latter into a meeting agenda.

    If during the course of the meeting you come across an item that cannot be answered quickly, don't spend too much time on it. Assign it to one or two attendees with the charge of getting the necessary information and briefing those in attendance via memo. If another meeting is needed, you can schedule it then.

    If the two attendees are able to make a decision based on the knowledge they discover, give them that authority during the meeting. This reduces unnecessary communication down the road.

  - Based on meeting information, assign roles of projects to appropriate individuals.

  - When your meeting ends, summarize the findings, the tasks that need to be completed (*action items* in management-speak), and the feedback you expect. When people leave, they should feel that items were either removed from the agenda or have become a task for someone to complete.

Team-Building Skills

The ability to coalesce a team of individuals into a common purpose can be one of the greatest skills a manager can possess. Doing so requires an ability to see and diffuse potential personality conflicts and the ability to create and communicate a vision that multiple people share.

This is no small task. Office politics are often petty and yet stubborn and pronounced. Individuals who otherwise share skills and interests might, for any number of reasons, have a problem with one another.

In addition, people are selfish by nature. Although working with a team is ultimately a superior career strategy, you will find some who work against the team concept in hopes of bolstering their own career.

You must learn how to recognize and deal with all these situations while remaining distant enough not to get caught up in them.

In both analyzing management styles and anecdotally looking at areas where I've done well and areas where I've struggled, I've created a short list of simple methods or techniques to foster team building, as discussed in the sections that follow.

Give Credit Where Credit Is Due

I often hear people complain about their manager taking credit for their work. Although I have rarely seen this in practice, I know it exists. A good manager gives more credit to his staff than he takes himself. He understands that his ability to create high producers is what he is held accountable for.

Promote Your Team and Its Members

Career development necessarily includes some self-promotion. In a management role, however, promoting your team is of far greater value. Doing so accomplishes several objectives:

- **Your team is held in higher esteem**—As a manager, your success is largely gauged on your group as a whole. If you promote your team (their strengths and their accomplishments), your team will be viewed as stronger. A stronger team is looked to for better projects. This can end up being self-perpetuating. As you solve more problems, you get the better problems to solve.

- **Your team members develop loyalty**—My son had a teacher who was emotional and, at times, bitter. Eventually we moved him to the only other available teacher.

The teacher we moved him to was known as the strictest teacher in the school. Later, knowing how strict she was, I asked my son if he was happier in his class.

"Yes," he replied.

"But isn't she strict?"

"Dad," he replied, "she's strict, but she's fair."

A hard/demanding boss, one who pushes his staff but is fair and promotes his team's successes, is typically okay to work for. You know that you are required to work and to achieve, but you also know that your manager will go to the mat for you and recognize your contribution. This creates loyalty.

Foster an Environment That Allows for (and Even Celebrates) Failure

To create the type of environment in which innovation and creativity flourish and where people take initiative, you must allow for and even celebrate failure. The fear of failure is the single greatest hindrance to initiative and innovation.

When staff members are afraid to take calculated risk because of fear of repercussions, they are unlikely to push for new and innovative solutions. Creating innovation is necessarily risky. If you are to have a department and team that are viewed as innovative, you and your staff must be able to fail with some degree of safety.

Of course, this does not mean or require you to allow for foolish and blatantly risky projects. Putting a company's data or operations at risk is irresponsible.

In creating a culture that allows for failure, you must emphasize the need for logical controls and strong backup and recovery options. In addition, creating segregated lab environments is a wise course of action.

Although you are ultimately responsible for the actions and success of the team, your employees must have the authority, tools, and responsibility to correct their own mistakes. The idea is to give them the ownership of the full project—they own the success, and they own the failure. If a project or task goes awry, your staff must have the mentality that immediately creates a corrective action plan and puts it into place.

Create a Project/Contract Mentality with Those You Report to and Those Who Report to You

I've mentioned Bruce Tulgan's book titled *Winning the Talent Wars*. In it, Tulgan creates the case that corporate America is no longer interested in hiring employees. Instead, companies want to bring on talent when needed. They are interested in project skills for project success.

To have a team that is successful and that is viewed as a valuable addition to the corporate team, you must foster a project-based mindset.

You must be able to assign the projects to your staff—along with the responsibility of that project's success. When doing so, the staff member becomes the de facto project manager, and every other member of the team becomes a resource for his use. It is then the staff member's responsibility to manage the scheduling of those other resources.

Of course, with newer employees and those who struggle with this type of project ownership, your allocation of responsibility should be according to their ability.

It is a recipe for failure to assign too much project ownership to someone whose abilities do not match the responsibility. Your success as a manager rests with your ability to assess, develop, and manage that ability in your staff.

Conclusion

Although the list of skills to move to management is not long or complicated, the acquisition of those skills is a lifetime of work. It is no mistake that good managers are well compensated and highly valuable.

To make the move to management, you need to make a commitment to yourself. You need to commit to personal growth, largely remove yourself from emotional office politics, and create a plan in which you develop the key management skills discussed in this chapter.

And you need to start managing and leading now! Good managers appear because their actions make them natural choices for the position. If your plan is to take a management role only when the pay and position are presented, you might never get your opportunity.

Actions & Ideas

1. Do you have aspirations for management? If so, what can you do now to adopt a management approach to projects and your career? Record your thoughts in the space provided.

2. Identify a project that has no clear manager—even a small one. Offer to take ownership of that project. It's not important whether you're called a project manager, just that you own the success and resources needed for the project.

3. Do you think in terms of projects or of daily tasks? Work to create a holistic project mindset.

4. Consider purchasing project management software, such as Microsoft Project. Tutorials are available online to help you master its use.

EXPAND YOUR TOOLKIT

Remember to visit the book's website at http://www.ITCareerToolkit.com for supplemental and ongoing advice, tips, and data relevant to this chapter.

Indispensable Does Not Mean Always Employed

With the advent of outsourcing, increased competition, and a tighter job market, the technology professional struggles to ensure that he remains gainfully employed. Using the techniques and ideas in *Building Your I.T. Career* can go a long way toward ensuring your ongoing profitability and growth in the field. This chapter discusses key ideas to increase and ensure your value within the organizations you serve, the goal of which is to make you indispensable.

CHAPTER 21

Make Yourself Indispensable

I would love to tell you that the information in this chapter will ensure that you are never out of work. I cannot make that claim. Too many intangible factors make such guarantees impossible.

However, the ideas that I share in this chapter go a long way toward ensuring your ongoing marketability to a broad range of organizations. Together with strong professional networking, the job/project search techniques covered previously in the toolkit, your ambition, and a strong commitment to excellence, these ideas provide greater overall career stability and growth.

Many of these ideas involve some level of professional risk. However, failure to enact these strategies is equally risky. If you are to build a career that places you at the top of your profession and positions you as a problem solver who has organizational value, you necessarily must incur some risk.

Not doing so means that you are not at the top of your profession and are not perceived as a problem solver who has organizational value. Making one of the following two choices seems relatively easy on the surface:

- Incurring calculated risks to achieve dynamic career growth
- Assuming the default risks that are associated with more passive career activity

However, you must assess this important decision for yourself.

A Word About Value

The idea of value is one that I have attempted to infuse throughout this book. Your value is a central theme in the toolkit approach to career development. Understanding your value to an organization and how to increase that value is critical.

This understanding can help you model your career, actions, and focus. It can ensure that the work you do brings value to the organization that you serve. This understanding also helps you find the right type of employer. Your understanding of where an organization places value can help you determine whether you and the company are a good fit—if those items, tasks, and projects that the company values match your desired career path.

This understanding of your value can also help alleviate the frustration I hear many technology professionals express in regards to compensation. I've counseled many technology professionals who complain about their low compensation. However, in speaking to them, these professionals indicate that their organization does not pay well in general.

Although salary surveys abound, they do little to help you in your current situation. You will receive the best compensation by finding an organization whose idea of what is valuable matches yours. You might be excellent at user-level automation, and you might be building great solutions for your employer; however, if their perception of the value of such solutions is low, you will remain undercompensated.

I often state that if I take the skills I've learned as an I.T. professional and go to work for a one-person automotive shop, I can still put many of my skills to work, but I cannot expect to be compensated in the manner I desire. Such an organization will not and cannot place a high value on what I provide.

You need to match your skills and desires with an organization that both needs and values those skills.

If you are persuasive, you might be able to help build a case for the value that you and your solutions provide. This is an excellent way to build your career within an organization, but it requires the ability both to quantify the results and tie them to the business case for the organization.

As you read through the ideas in the sections that follow, keep in mind your own career, and evaluate steps you can take to improve your value in your organization.

Being Proactive

Business owners and managers need proactive people. You must be able to make decisions and take responsibility for the impact of those decisions—whether positive or negative. Many employees seem to work on an "I will act only when directed" mentality. They do so with the assumption that management will frown upon independent ideas and action.

To be honest, if you work within an organization that does not foster independent and proactive ideas and actions, you need to consider other employment options. Unless you know of some convincing reasons to remain in place (pay, training, and so on), such organizations are unlikely to provide true growth opportunity.

If you have not been proactive in the past—always waiting for specific directives to move on a project or specific tasks—make a change now. If you have an idea for a technology or process that would improve operations or create a level of automation or efficiency within your job or on a current project, act on this idea.

Demonstrate your idea's benefit to management. Let your manager know of other ideas to improve process or information flow.

Understanding Technology's Role in the Organization

A large part of making yourself indispensable is a clear understanding of technology's role in the organization that you serve. Of even greater importance is helping define and expand that role in a way that provides business value.

In most cases, business value is tied to improving profits, lowering costs, or increasing efficiency, consequently providing more production throughput.

Your ability to define your role as someone who helps technology provide value in the areas of profits, costs, and efficiency is critical. To do so, you must understand how the company works. Excelling only within your direct job scope with the technology is not enough. You must perceive how the technology that you build and support works seamlessly in the organization.

Maintain a Business-First Mentality

Understanding that technology is, first and foremost, a business enabler (something that enhances the ability for the organization to perform its functions) helps your longevity in the field and at your company.

Too often, technology professionals become so focused on their specific technologies that they fail to grasp their impact within the greater organizational structure. This is particularly true with back-office support roles.

Placing vital importance on the optimization of the technology is a mindset that most professionals can plead guilty to. Although such optimization can be extremely valuable and important, it is only so because of how it supports the business, not because of the technology.

Maintaining a business-first mentality can help you see the importance of your technology within that context.

Create Standards, Automation, or a Programmer's Toolkit

One of the single greatest areas of impact is that of standardization and automation. Technology is, if nothing else, a tool to automate the mundane tasks or provide better and simpler access to good information.

To have the time to build the best technology possible and have the greatest impact on the organization, you must first find areas of your own job that can be streamlined. You can best do this through standards, automation, and a library of code, files, and ideas.

Also, stay current with new ideas, tools, and methods in the industry. Subscribe to appropriate journals and professional magazines and see what others are doing. Adopt those items that fit within the work that you do. You can find a list of some popular journals and online resources in Appendix A, "My Reading List."

Standardization removes the guesswork from many areas of technology. New projects and systems become more self-documenting because the environment begins to look and feel "the same." One of my past network engineers and I used to tell our clients that we build "boring" systems. They always look and work the same.

Standards also greatly improve maintainability. Technologists who are new to the organization can learn and support the standards more quickly. Standards reduce errors and make reengineering projects much simpler.

Automation is of critical importance, too. Many tools can help automate back-office functions and functions at the user's desktop. Some of these tools are free, whereas others can cost thousands.

Some automation tools are built in to the operating systems and can provide excellent automation. Many of the tasks that you and other users do every day can be reduced or completely removed. This results in a more effective use of your time.

If you find yourself repeating certain tasks over and over, consider writing a macro to automate them. Macros effectively reduce time and errors from tedious and repetitive tasks. Macros are a simple example of a time-saving technology.

When it comes to how things are done, don't be satisfied with the status quo. We as technology professionals should be the first to apply automation and technical tools to help get our own jobs done. If not, how can we demonstrate the effectiveness to the organizations we serve?

As a general rule, user-level automation provides greater direct/tangible benefit to the organization. However, to be able to provide user-lever automation, you must first automate the tedious tasks in the back office.

User configurations, software configurations, server maintenance, and so on can be automated. This leaves you time to provide support directly to the users. When you create user-level automation, you greatly increase your exposure in the company.

Create a Peer Knowledge Network

This might be the most useful piece of advice in this chapter. As you meet other technology professionals, you will naturally meet some who you believe have great skills. You need to create the most effective method to stay in touch with them.

I am not a big user of online chat programs. Usually they are a distraction and a waste of time. However, in the context of your peer network, these programs can provide instantaneous information.

At a minimum, you could use any one of the online discussion/forums software packages to track conversations with your network. Group communication websites such as LinkedIn Groups, Facebook Groups, and Yahoo! Groups can provide e-mail notification of messages and are free.

You must also take part in thriving technical forums. When I say thriving, I don't mean constant friendly banter. I am talking about technologists who post and respond to legitimate questions.

Such a network increases your available intellectual capacity. You become part of a larger, more experienced community.

Be Known as the Go-To Resource

Never take a not-my-job attitude. You want to be the first person that your company thinks of when it needs answers. Having a strong peer network and having a thriving professional network is critical in meeting this objective.

In addition, you need to have a good list of online resources, knowledgebases, and discussion lists. Your ability to quickly find solutions for the problems thrown your way will cement you as a go-to resource.

Read more about becoming a resource in Chapter 17, "Your Career and Social Media."

Be Ready and Willing to Take On the Necessary Responsibility

Your willingness to take on responsibility can go a long way toward making you indispensable. In general, management and business owners want individuals who make their jobs easier and more productive.

Your willingness to take on responsibility for projects and people is a critical factor in career success. This is a key career ownership attitude. Wherever and whenever possible, you need to find projects that you can be responsible for.

As stated in Chapter 20, "Management," the risk is that you must take responsibility for the failure of a project. However, I view this as less risky than taking no responsibility at all.

If you work within an organization that doesn't provide opportunities for project ownership, I recommend making a move. Your career will always be limited in such companies. To make moves into management or other higher-paying roles, you need to be able to take responsibility for and push the success of many projects.

Have Experts You Call On for Your Organization

You might fear that if your company knows of a resource that is technically better than you, your job is in jeopardy. This might stop you from referring your peers into your organization. The fact is, you can't have all the information and expertise. Being able to have access to other experts and willingly refer them to your company when needed positions you as a solution provider.

It doesn't matter that you did not directly solve every problem. It's more important that you understand the resources that you have available and make the right connections. This understanding is critical for several reasons.

First, your company will come to identify you with a great list of resources. That alone is a career-enhancing perception. Second, however, is how you will be viewed with those professionals you refer. They, too, extend your professional network. They will perceive you as someone who passes opportunity when appropriate.

Maintain an active contact list that identifies available resources. Make sure these individuals share your passion for solving problems, have great attitudes, and communicate well.

Be Passionate About Something!

This is a critical life skill. I'm not necessarily specifying that you be passionate about technology or about business. I'm merely proposing that you have deeply rooted passions in life. Make them a driving force in your professional life.

I find that people who don't have passions or interests often have lackluster performance at work. It is as though their entire life is marked by a general disinterest or lack of focus.

Carrying a passionate attitude about something can help you separate yourself from those who are not so internally motivated.

I'm passionate about many things. In the business world, I love understanding what a client's business is. I enjoy catching the vision of the executive management and then helping to crystallize and realize that vision. This isn't contrived or artificial. I actually take an active interest in what a company produces.

This helps me create better, more proactive solutions. Coupled with a passion toward solution-driven technology, I join the company vision with the possibilities in technology. Following this model will put you on the top of the list of producers at the company.

Never Blame, and Always Have a Corrective Plan

Sometimes things go wrong. This is inevitable. When this happens, don't pass the blame on. Most business executives understand that mistakes happen. What they struggle with is an unwillingness to take responsibility and then move forward with a corrective plan.

I recently spoke to a group in which my message was to work with passion and to work decisively toward a solution. If you do so, when you make a mistake, you might find that you can correct it before anybody notices.

Although I was making a humorous point, the underlying message has some truth to it.

If you are decisive and moving forward, you will automatically separate yourself from your peers. The ability and willingness to make decisions is one of the most sought-after qualities in an employee. And yet, many people don't do that. In many cases, this is because of a fear of failure.

Informally, here is the model I used. I believed that I would make the right choice or decision 80 percent of the time. I created a course of action and then put it into place. Usually it worked out great. However, in those instances in which something went wrong or didn't work, I quickly adopted corrective action and moved forward.

By modeling that attitude, you demonstrate both initiative and responsibility. If the company that you are working for doesn't want that type of employee, I recommend looking for other opportunities.

Adopt Concept Over Process

Concept Over Process (COP) is a rapid analysis tool. (See Chapter 22, "Concept Over Process," which is entirely devoted to this idea.) People are going to view technology as either a necessary expense or a value-add within your organization. Your ability to help others perceive technology as a valuable contributor to the organization's success is critical in making you indispensable.

COP provides a methodology for helping you see where the greatest positive impact exists. Then it's up to you to develop the skills necessary to make that a reality.

All of these ideas form a holistic picture of what makes an employee indispensable. It isn't that any one of them is "the key" to your career growth and stability. However, when you match these ideas with your technical skills, they are powerful.

Analyze those whom you see advancing rapidly in your industry. Identify which of these ideas they seem to put into practice. It is likely that the top producers you know are practicing many or all of these ideas. Your objective should be to do the same in your career.

Conclusion

Remember, it isn't that learning skills to become indispensable means you will never be unemployed. What it does mean, however, is that you are committed to developing skills and attitudes that are value rich—that contribute to your company or client.

This commitment will separate you in the quality and quantity of work you provide. You will be known as a producer and will be viewed as a valuable resource. Even if a company you work for shuts doors, downsizes, or moves to a new geographic area, you will have a readily available list of professional contacts and excellent referrals to bring you your next opportunity.

Start today. Work to become indispensable!

Actions & Ideas

1. Evaluate your peer/mentor network. Do you have a way to rapidly get in touch with other members? Do you see yourself as a contributor to this group? If not, start today to correct that situation.

2. Create a short list of websites that include active technical discussions and a searchable knowledgebase for several technologies. Don't pick sites that are primary meaningless discussions. Refer to Appendix A for some ideas.

3. Look at your professional contact list. Identify key experts that your company might be able to use now or in the future. Maintain this list.

4. Determine whether you have something that drives you, a passion. If you don't, identify why and work to remedy that situation.

EXPAND YOUR TOOLKIT

Remember to visit the book's website at http://www.ITCareerToolkit.com for supplemental and ongoing advice, tips, and data relevant to this chapter.

Becoming a Value-Added Technologist

It should be obvious, after reading the previous chapters, that I place a huge emphasis on soft skills. In fact, nothing in this book pertains directly to identifying technical skills or particular trends.

I hope to help the ambitious and directed career builders develop those transcendent and technology-independent skills, the value of which remains pertinent for a lifetime.

The development of such skills makes the adoption of a given technical skill set simpler to attain while simplifying changing career direction and focus.

Strong conceptual knowledge is a defining talent. This chapter attempts to lay the foundation for strong conceptual knowledge without diminishing the technical know-how to implement any given process.

CHAPTER 22

Concept Over Process

Concept Over Process (COP) is a project development methodology. Much has been written on project management, the monitoring and measurement of the resources and tasks in the project. However, less information is available on the actual analysis and creative process—the process that occurs prior to and during a project's life cycle.

Most project management books include sections on defining the project. They explain the importance of identifying the project scope. The actual thought process involved in the analysis, however, is less readily available.

Throughout my career, I have created a simple, yet powerful method for generating the creative/analytical thought that must occur prior to and during a project. This method has been formalized into COP to provide a starting point for those who perform project work.

What to Expect

COP is largely conceptual in nature. It is the intellectual precursor to a variety of task-oriented processes. Certainly for the technologist, it is a critical step in helping to define tangible solutions.

You can expect (as you adopt a COP mindset and approach) to think differently about your projects. You will find that you become largely agnostic about which technology or process is critical and more focused and interested in the overall business objectives and project impact.

What Not to Expect

COP is *not* project management. Although COP is a component that is often missing from the project management cycle, it does not involve measurement and tracking per se. It is an ancillary skill and tool to ensure that a project is more closely aligned with actual business objectives.

Highly organized and technical individuals often provide project management. However, innovation and solutions are often abstract concepts that require a more creative, almost artistic mindset. Both ideals are critical in creating true solutions:

- Highly analytical, process-driven detail
- Creative/innovative thought

These two ideals are often viewed as two competing forces in the project. The creative individual might be part of the project team and provide tangential input. Or the creative input comes from management in the form of vision and a big-picture perspective.

COP provides the basis for highly technical project managers and technologists to have a greater understanding and ability to provide the creative direction and input. The primary objective of COP is to ensure that projects of all types are more closely aligned to the business and its objectives.

COP Objectives

The objectives and results of COP are as follows:

- More solid project development (pre-project planning)
- A stronger grasp of a particular business model in as short a time as possible
- More accurate and meaningful project analysis during a project life cycle
- Greater focus on a project's final impact versus mid-project tasks and milestones
- Greater innovation in thought and technical implementation
- Proper relegation of technology as a tool used to achieve carefully defined business objectives
- Greater breadth of knowledge and learning capacity as a result of reducing technology and tasks to their most common elements

The section that follows discusses the origin of COP so that you can understand the COP mindset. This discussion provides insight into my development of COP and its value as seen in numerous projects.

COP Origins

During my time with Blue Cross, I had the opportunity to work in a unique and valuable environment. I was a technology professional who did not work within an information technology (I.T.) department.

Initially, I wanted to to make that transition, interviewing for positions within I.T.. None of these positions offered either the pay or opportunity I was seeking. For a period of my career, this frustrated me. I initially coveted an I.T. title. I discovered, however, that I truly wanted the opportunities I was already being faced with every day.

I worked within a user department. By that, I mean I worked in a department with the users of my programs and technical solutions. For this reason, my title had to be one available to the department. Corporate edict mandated that all technology positions were available only to technology staff.

Instead, I held positions of junior data clerk, business analyst, senior business analyst, and so on. My day-to-day tasks, however, involved application development, network administration, and other I.T.-related tasks.

My unique position provided me with incredible opportunities—opportunities that probably would have been lost working for the MIS/I.T. department.

During this time, I developed a comprehensive, yet simple project development methodology. The methodology first creates a strong understanding of the underlying business model. It is a dual creative/analytical process that fosters innovation and results in a unique business/solution-based focus for your technology projects.

I titled this methodology *Concept Over Process*.

COP has become the backbone to my career as a technologist, consultant, and mentor to other technologists. Many have found it instrumental as a career development tool. Its unique approach properly emphasizes strong conceptual knowledge over straight technical know-how.

Technology professionals who adopt a COP mindset are better able to produce comprehensive business solutions and are more adept at proactive analysis and recommendations. Management recognizes these people more quickly because their solutions, language, and focus are unique in the business model orientation.

What Is a Process-Driven Mindset?

Technology professionals put an incredible amount of time and energy into understanding the how-to of technology. They understand methods. They perfect the process-driven tasks that make their technology implementations optimal.

However, technologists are far less interested and often do not understand the why of technology—what the technology is for. By that, I don't mean the tasks that a given technology performs. Once again, that is the process.

What technologists overlook is a comprehensive understanding of the business challenge—the business model, how it makes money, what products or services it produces, the interrelationship among vendors, departments, clients, and so on. These were the items that were of utmost importance to me and to my boss.

Technology, when understood in this context, is simply a tool to achieve some optimization of an already existing or developing business model. The technology is not the business; in fact, technology is the wrong area of focus for developing good technical solutions.

Before you read any further, I need to make a disclaimer: I am not implying that technical skills are unimportant. In fact, the contrary is true. However, I am convinced that understanding the underlying reasons (business reasons) for technology will lead to far greater technical skill.

A simple example of this is the initial exercise that nearly every programmer goes through when exposed to a new language. Programming books universally give a short tutorial that when completed presents a message box to the screen that says "Hello World!"

Although this exercise exposes the programmer to the language and development interface, it does little to actually develop the programmer's skills in the language. Expertise comes through the application of these skills in solving some business challenge.

However, COP goes beyond a cursory understanding of the business challenge in isolation. To fully understand COP's benefit and impact, you need to have a more complete understanding of business in general, the industry in which you are working, the specific entity for which you work, and the various relationships leading to your solutions.

If you are a technology professional, an understanding of how you approach technology, an understanding of the role of technology, and adopting strategies that further technology's role in your organization make you much more valuable. Increased personal value ultimately equates to increased responsibility and pay.

The ideas that are discussed in the sections that follow are meant to foster this understanding. They are meant to provide you with tangible ways to change the manner in which you think about business, your company, your role as a technologist, and your understanding of what technology is and its impact on commerce.

The Role of Technology

Understanding why technology exists is a good starting point. After you understand that, I will move into the actual steps of the COP process.

I reduce useful technology into two simple roles, although additional subroles or subsets might exist for each role. In conversations with a number of business owners, managers, and technology professionals, however, the following roles have proven to be effective in categorizing why we use technology.

Role 1: Storage and Retrieval of Information

It's about information. Often, the focus of technology is incorrectly placed on the technology. But the fact is that information is the commodity of value. This is the first role that technology plays.

Technology provides the storage and retrieval of information, specifically, for analysis and decision support.

The rise of segments within I.T. that are dedicated specifically to information analysis indicates that the industry is aware it must give special attention to this area. *Decision support* and *knowledge management* are two such segments, and more seem to be developing daily. These segments function, in some way or another, to advance this first critical role of technology.

Role 2: The Automation of Delivery of Product or Service

The second role that technology plays is one that you can use to greatly enhance your value and propel your career. Automating the delivery of product or service is one of the most important facets of technology.

This can, of course, take the form of automation in the traditional assembly-line type of automation. Robotics is the type of automation that is readily visible in business situations. However, what I term *micro-automation* is also of extreme value within a company. In addition, micro-automation is available to technologists early in their careers.

Micro-automation is the automation that takes place in the office. It can assume the form of document assembly, reporting, automated information distribution, or any other manual tasks that take place within a company.

In many cases, this type of automation receives a low priority. Company business systems, network upgrades, and big-money integration projects tend to gain the bulk of the attention. However, this type of automation can be put in place quickly, does not require the big project lead times, and has tremendous visibility for personal career growth.

Approaching technology projects with a solid understanding of these roles can help bolster your career. They produce positive exposure for your career and real value within a company.

Keeping your company's business model in clear view as you perform your work is what COP is about. It makes you more aware of the impact that technology has and should have in the organization. Your solutions become much more proactive and more closely aligned with the business as a whole.

COP also helps you adopt and learn new technologies. No longer do you view new technology as something you must learn. Rather, you view new technology in relation to its differences from what you already know well. You effectively reduce what you have to learn.

Adopting a COP approach during your career makes you more valuable because you not only understand the technology but also operations, marketing, distribution, and other critical business functions. You soon separate yourself from those who view technology as the primary focus of their career.

From the standpoint of career growth and possible paths you can take, COP provides a much broader possible spectrum. You can move from straight technologist to system analyst, manager, consultant, or business owner.

This idea has transformed the careers of several technologists whom I have trained and mentored. Their increased confidence in dealing with management—because they can speak intelligently about the business—has provided them with numerous opportunities. Most have been offered significant compensation packages. More important, they recognize that they are better able to make a difference in their organization.

This might be the best byproduct of COP: the satisfaction gained from knowing that you are equipped and able to make a positive contribution in your company.

Moving from Process Driven to Concept Driven

How do you move from a process-driven mindset? This can be difficult for the rank and file technologists because so much of their perceived worth is driven by their hands-on technical skills. Remember, however, that my objective with COP is long-term value and the ability to quickly adopt new technologies based on a clear understanding of their role or usefulness.

The sections that follow take you through the methodology that forms the underpinning of COP.

A Concentric View

You will find a common theme throughout this discussion of COP. In all things, I start with the broadest view possible. I am at heart a minimalist. Broad concepts typically answer many of the basic questions, and the minute details are simply tweaks, or details, that are meant to optimize the big-picture view.

Picture a series of concentric circles. COP starts on the periphery, the outermost circle, attempting to capture and see as much information as possible. It then works inward to the greater detail. Each circle is another level of analysis, until you arrive at a detailed understanding of the process or project with which you are involved.

The problem facing many of us as technologists—and truly any highly skilled professional—is a myopic focus on a particular concentric circle or process with which we work. If our starting point is too narrow, we risk losing sight of the impact that our work or project has on the organization as a whole.

Figure 21-1 illustrates the starting points for clearly putting COP to work. The starting points form the concentric circles of analysis:

- Business objective/goal ($)
- Industry analysis: trade publications/mentor
- Organization's role in its industry
- Workflow (money, information, product/service)
- Interaction/dependencies
- Congruencies, incongruencies, omissions
- Project definition
- Solution/implementation

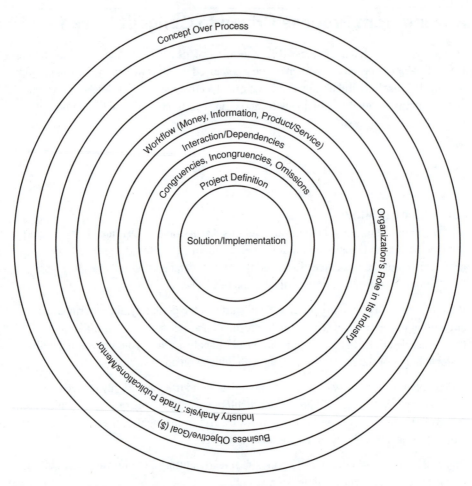

Figure 22-1 COP: Concentric circles of analysis.

A Note About Time

COP typically requires more upfront time in project definition. This was often difficult for my clients to understand. I placed a premium on the analysis at project inception. However, we found that projects ran much more smoothly and more quickly when we performed the COP analysis. In addition, projects had fewer costly mistakes and missing components—changes to be added later.

The size of the overall project dictates how far into each of these areas you should go. Certainly, if you are writing a small script or process to perform a niche function for your client, I wouldn't suggest that you spend four days in analysis. The actual project size determines the amount of detail for each segment of COP.

The COP methodology is something that you can employ as an overall client relationship process, too. Although you might not be performing workflow analysis or large system implementation, you can work at gleaning this understanding as you provide day-to-day support for your client.

Developing Proactive Solutions

A key byproduct of COP is the development of a *proactive solution ideology*. As you work with a client or your company and have a greater understanding of the industry, business, and operations, you begin to see where technology can best make an impact. You can intelligently suggest good technologies that fit the company's business and strategic plan.

This takes you out of the position of being a straight technologist—one who implements what the company directs you to—to becoming a solution provider—one who works with the company toward its strategic objectives.

The impact on your career is immeasurable. CEOs and management are often jaded in their view of technologists. They believe that technology departments in general and technologists specifically do a poor job of "aligning I.T. with business objectives"—a phrase similar to many that is creeping into formal job descriptions.

Because COP starts with business objectives as the standard and basis for all understanding, it lends itself to better business and technology alignment.

A Warning/Suggestion

Critical in adopting COP is a desire to have a true understanding of the business. If you don't really care, you will find COP to be tedious, and you will be poor at it. If your idea is to adopt COP to push your particular technology more effectively, you are missing the point.

COP Is Not About Technology!

Although COP is currently framed as a methodology for technology projects, it is just as adequate as a methodology for marketing projects, accounting projects, or manufacturing projects. COP is about clearly defining business in general and then molding your project to that business.

The particular project implementation is the process. COP is so named with reason. It is not *Process Over Concept*. Keep that in mind at all times!

Start with the Goal of Business

This might sound trite or simplistic, but the first idea to grasp is the goal of business—in particular, the goal of your company, client, or organization.

In his landmark book, *The Goal,* Eliyahu Goldratt identifies a key problem facing many companies. His book is focused on manufacturing, but the idea holds true across industries. In the book, Goldratt's protagonist is brought in to help turn around a manufacturing company. From the outset, he asks the various managers what their departments' goals are.

They answer that their goals are efficiency, higher production, fewer mistakes, and so on. He points out that if each of these goals is met and the product sells for a loss, they will have met their goal and the company will fail.

He eventually gets the managers to understand the simple concept that their organization exists to make a profit. That is the goal.

Understand Your Objective as an Employee

Your objective is also profitability. Once again, you might want to provide your services for a worthy cause and not for high personal compensation. That's okay and worthy. But if you can't eat or take care of your basic needs, you won't continue at that worthy endeavor.

What About Mission Statements?

Mission statements for companies were the craze ten years ago. Lofty statements covering ideals and ethics were created to give the corporate culture meaning as it went about its day-to-day operations.

The same is true today with individuals, and that's a good thing. Certainly, having a guiding ideal—a moral compass—that forms the underpinning of your professional and personal conduct is good.

However, as Goldratt pointed out, for many companies and individuals, the mission statement became the goal. A goal is not the same as a mission statement. The mission statement is composed of the underlying ideals with which a company works to achieve its goal of profitability. It includes the values that drive meaning into the achievement of profits.

A personal mission statement can and should be a positive guiding factor in your career development. But it is the way in which you achieve your goal, not the goal itself, that is of critical importance.

From Goal to Analysis

After you have correctly identified the goal, it is time to create the strong conceptual understanding of your particular project. COP is a holistic methodology. As such, it requires more than a simple cursory view of your project objectives. Remember: COP is meant to help you better define the project objectives. Therefore, you must start broader than the project.

A project impacts more than the systems or workflow it replaces or optimizes. A project impacts the people in ancillary departments and even outside the company. For that reason, to correctly and effectively define a project, you must see beyond the scope of the project work itself.

This is a huge point of failure or disconnect on project work in general and specifically in the technology and integration business.

Understand the Industry

The first level of understanding is the industry in which you are working. This can be healthcare, manufacturing, legal, professional services, and so on.

When a new company or new project is being defined, find out what trade journals exist for that industry. Pick up a few and read them. In addition, ask the department head, client, or prospective client for any books that might help in understanding the industry or department. Finally, simply ask this person for time to discuss the industry in general.

This serves a few different purposes. First, you will begin to adopt the language of that industry. You will be able to better speak and understand the particular terminology. Although you might never become an expert in that industry, during subsequent meetings or phone conversations, you will adopt the vernacular and win the industry's trust.

Second, you will gain a much deeper understanding of that particular department or business's position and role in the industry. The client no longer must "dumb down" its conversation about industry-specific topics. It will be comfortable in knowing that you have a grasp on the big picture.

Understand the Business: The Organization's Role in Its Industry

After you have done some research and gained knowledge of the industry, you must delve deeper into the client's business as a whole:

- What is the service or product?

- Where does the client stand from a market-share perspective and its role in the industry?

- Is the client an industry vendor—selling within its industry, or producing product or service that leaves the industry for general consumption at completion?

Then you can work to understand, as quickly as possible, the broader objectives of the company within the industry. Is the company looking at growth within its specific segment or market share? Is it planning to spread to other sectors or roles in the industry?

Because you understand the industry first, what you learn at this step will make sense. Without the industry knowledge, the business-specific knowledge is much less meaningful.

Understand the Workflow

Now you must delve into the how (process) of the company. In this step, you are looking at how the company delivers its product or service. You want to understand, from start to finish, how the company creates, markets, delivers, and ultimately pays for the product or service.

Understand the Relationships: Interactions/Dependencies

Although your project might involve a particular department, it is critical that you understand the relationships that are impacted. This includes relationships both inside and outside the company:

- **Internal**—Relationships within the department, between individuals, and relationships between two or more company departments.

- **External**—Relationships with vendors, clients, suppliers, contractors, and so on.

The objective is to see the impact that even a small project might have on these groups. If you develop a project that makes life easier for a single individual or department but hinders access to key information or makes processes more difficult for a related department, others will view the project broadly as a failure. You don't want to have 3 people pleased for a short time, while alienating 100 others. That's an irresponsible career move.

Workflow Analysis

To understand these workflow and relationship issues, you need to analyze some key items. Each item lends greater understanding to the previously discussed areas of COP—the concentric circles of analysis:

- **Follow the flow of money**—I mentioned this in passing earlier. However, because our stated objective is profitability, the flow of money provides a good way to analyze how a company works.

  The flow of money is twofold: It includes money that the company makes and money that the company pays out.

- **Follow the flow of data**—How do the company's information systems currently track their product or service? How and where does information from all sources get stored, retrieved, and analyzed?

  If you remember that the storage and retrieval of information is one of the two roles of technology, you will understand the importance of this step of the process.

- **Follow the flow of production**—From raw product to finished product, from information to service delivery, whatever the company does to ultimately produce income is where you start.

  I'm not claiming that you will understand each person's role or step in the process. But you must understand in general how the company produces its revenue.

  This moves from the company perspective to the particular product or service that a department or an individual provides. You will be able to see, for your particular project, the impact on the company as a whole.

- **Find the incongruent or problematic pieces**—The overall value of the previous analysis is the ability to locate those areas that create a disconnect. If, during the storage of information, all data is stored in a centralized database, except for customer service requests, you might have discovered incongruence.

Project Definition

With an understanding of workflow analysis in place, you are ready to more clearly define your project. COP is largely a creative/analytical process. It is not purely analytical. In fact, broad concepts tend to be big picture/creative items. They involve sharing and developing the "vision" of company leadership. As you delve further into the analysis of the particulars, you are moving to the analytical side of things.

Project definition is also not rote analysis—it is largely creative and innovative. Project management as a process is often solely a process-driven/analytical exercise. COP attempts to meld the creative/innovative process with the analytical steps of project management.

Myth of Limitation

As project development begins to take place, it is critical that you, as a technologist, understand and remove the myth of limitation.

The myth of limitation is most often seen when a company or department's nontechnical staff approaches its I.T. provider (either internal or external) and asks for a particular technology:

> "We need an Access database to track customer service requests."

> "We need X product installed on each system."

The requestor might be correct in the stated need. However, you'll often discover that the requester is only partially correct. He will have come to I.T. defining the technology, not the business process to be solved.

A company might need a database to track customer service requests. But what about other department access to the information? What type of request? What is the objective of this data? How will it be used, and are there other desired customer service functions it should track or be able to respond to?

The myth of limitation is the partial understanding by nontechnical staff of what is available. In many cases, departments have heard of a technology being put in place at a similar operation. An identified benefit might exist; however, more comprehensive solutions might be achieved at just a little more cost.

Removing the myth of limitation involves a what-if mindset.

What If?

In meetings with clients, I often frame my question this way:

> "If time, resources, and money were no object, how would you like things to work?"

It might be that clients' requests become too outlandish or expensive to implement. But it is just as likely that when properly defined, technologies are available to meet a good portion of clients' needs with little to no impact on costs.

Whether the broader solution is possible or not cannot even be discussed unless you remove the myth of limitation.

To be able to do this, you need to be able to speak and understand the clients' language. I cover this in more detail in my article "Why Technologists Must Learn to Speak Business." You can download a copy from www.ITCareerToolkit.com.

By speaking in clients' business vernacular, you make them more comfortable to approach you as a peer in business, not the technology pro. Although you want to be the technology pro, you first must understand the clients' business need. Remember: Technology is just a tool used to provide that need.

Congruencies, Incongruencies, and Omissions

As you move further into project definition and your solution, the following steps become the standard for identifying and clarifying the solution. You will use them over and over again for each project step and to analyze project changes.

Congruencies: What Currently Works

Quite simply, what technologies are in place and what workflows currently work well with the individual, department, related departments, and external relationships? Does the technology in place and workflow work in unison?

Incongruencies: What Currently Does Not Work

Is there currently a discrepancy in technology and workflow? Is it technology related (bad product or information), or is it workflow related (how the client goes about its operations)? Is it both? How can the incongruency be addressed or solved? Are tools in place to help with this?

Omissions: What Is Currently Excluded or Not Addressed at All

What does the client not track, automate, or perform as part of its operation? This aspect is a little trickier to identify. It often involves information not being tracked in relation to a current workflow process or automation. The information might be available but not used. Often, these discrepancies are because of a status quo ("We've always done it this way") mentality.

Conclusion

COP is ta valuable tool for project development. As stated earlier, the larger the project, the more detail you will use when employing these techniques. As you apply this ideology more and more, you will find that you begin to do so intuitively. Proactive solutions will become the norm and create a distinct advantage in your career advancement.

In addition, your ability to analyze business and projects for their value will be greatly increased. Those technologists whom I have trained in COP have shown the ability to perform a broader role for the organizations in which they work. Often they are included in marketing, business development, and general planning.

COP is not technology-centric; therefore, it is one of those transcendent skills that you take with you from year to year. This reduces some of the *stress* associated with the constant pace of change and learning required to stay up to date with the latest advances in technology.

For the technology professional, one of the most powerful aspects of COP is its capability to reduce the learning curve for new technologies. As you begin to become focused on the business concepts to be solved and technology's role, you will begin to view new technologies for what they are—new tools to adopt.

The impact is that you can better focus on the uses for the tool, instead of the tool itself. This helps you understand how or why a tool is useful and how it's conceptually different from another tool. You no longer need to learn all aspects of the new tool. Instead, you can study key differences with other well-known tools. What you need to study or learn is reduced as a result.

If you are interested in a further discussion of COP, register at www.ITCareerToolkit.com.

Actions & Ideas

1. Think about your career to date. Have you been largely process driven—focused on optimal technology without regard to the conceptual picture?

2. Look at a current project (solution) and quickly analyze the myth of limitations and congruency, incongruency, and omission. Do these concepts help you to better define the possible solution?

3. Analyze how you learn new technology. Can COP help you to better learn technology starting at a broad vision of its goal or purpose?

EXPAND YOUR TOOLKIT

Remember to visit the book's website at http://www.ITCareerToolkit.com for supplemental and ongoing advice, tips, and data relevant to this chapter.

Mentoring: An Active Learning/Teaching Model

As we further develop the idea of building a career, it makes sense to understand the role that mentoring takes. The idea of a few trusted advisors is not new. In fact, you can find accounts of mentors and advisors in virtually every notable individual throughout history.

The question then becomes how to identify mentors for your life and professional development, and how you should consider serving as a mentor, too.

CHAPTER 23

The Role of Mentoring

The idea of the self-made man is a myth. Although notable figures in history and in business seem to have made something out of nothing, the fact is, we all fall back on influential people throughout our lives. These people might be direct acquaintances or those who have influenced through writing or other less direct sources.

From a career perspective, mentoring is a critical adjunct to your professional network. However, it takes the professional network model a step further. More than a peer or acquaintance in the industry with whom you share information and opportunity, a mentor serves in a more vital and encompassing capacity.

The word *mentor* is notably present in Greek mythology. In particular, when King Ulysses begins his protracted quest, he leaves his son in the care of a friend named Mentor.

The word has expanded to mean one who is a trusted advisor on life and careers.

We all learn, use, and need advice and assistance from others. This need takes on varying degrees during different points in our lives.

In the area of career development, the need for a mentor cannot be overstated. Unfortunately, we often view the need to go to a more experienced peer or to acknowledge that we are stuck on some problem as a weakness. We errantly believe this can potentially damage or slow our career prospects.

I want to dispel this myth and give you some input on the art and science of finding mentors to help you advance your career. In addition, I explain why you should become a mentor to others.

The idea of mentoring is not new, but in the past few years, personal coaching has become a multimillion dollar industry. Celebrities have taken to hiring personal coaches for all facets of their life. You only need to look as far as Oprah to see the rise of Dr. Phil, Oprah's popular life-coach.

A mentor is one who provides advice and serves as a sounding board for ideas. Hopefully, the mentor is able to provide some value to situations, either because of his own personal experience or through his education and insight on the topic in question.

Mentors are often older, although this need not be the case. Having years of experience is not necessarily the criterion for a good mentor, either.

Mentor Characteristics

The list that follows discusses characteristics to help identify mentors in your career. Chances are that certain people, whether you have identified them or not, are providing you with mentoring.

- **A mentor should be accessible.**

  For someone to provide you with guidance in your career or life, he needs to be available to you. This does not necessarily mean in the form of face-to-face meetings. However, phone calls, e-mails, or requests to meet should not go ignored for extensive periods of time. If you are never able to receive input from an individual, that person is a poor choice as a mentor.

- **A mentor does not need to be a senior in your chosen career path.**

  Wisdom and honesty are the primary commodities that a mentor provides. I am not talking about instruction on the latest programming technique or how to configure the latest Cisco firewall product. My mentors have taken the form of managers, a building contractor, a manufacturing executive, and so on. In fact, only one person that I consider a mentor is a technology professional.

- **A mentor should, at times, make you uncomfortable.**

  Someone who approves of every choice you make, without question or analysis, is not going to be a very good mentor. Those who play the role of mentor in your career should, at times, play devil's advocate in conversations about careers and profession. They should provide alternative points of view and make you question your decisions. I don't mean in a way that undermines your confidence and makes you fearful of presenting the mentor your ideas, but ensuring that you have taken reasonable steps to see the broad impact of your decisions.

  A mentor makes you uncomfortable not because of his attitude, but because he demands good, solid judgment.

- **You can have multiple mentors.**

  A mentor is simply someone who you regularly go to for advice. When you are stuck or unsure of your next step, whose input do you seek? You likely consult several people. These people are, whether identified formally or not, serving as mentors.

  In fact, I would advocate having several such people for weighty decisions. There is no rule stating that you must seek and take the advice of only one. You might find that three different individuals, all of whom you respect, provide three different perspectives. You might even receive conflicting advice.

  This is okay and should be expected. A mentor is not there to make decisions for you, but to provide you with insight into a situation.

  Mentors help you see subtleties in situations that you might have overlooked. Remember, however, in the final analysis, the decisions you make are your own.

- **You might never have personal contact with a mentor.**

  I broaden the definition of mentor to include those you have never met. For example, significant authors and publications can fall into a career mentor role. They are part of the network of advice you should seek when you are faced with difficult decisions.

Mentoring Others

I said at the start of this chapter that it was important not only to find mentors, but to become a mentor, too. The reasons for this are both pragmatic and philanthropic.

By providing advice and assistance to others, perhaps newer technologists, newly graduating students, and others, we're better able to evaluate circumstances. When we try to apply such analytics to our own situations, we tend to have predetermined views and outcomes. By serving as a mentor, we become better at advising ourselves.

Perhaps as critical is the simple fact that it is right to give back to the professional community. I appeal here to decency and responsibility. Few experiences are as enjoyable as seeing your input and advice helping someone attain a degree of success.

What Qualifies Me as a Mentor?

The question that often comes up is this one: What qualifies me to mentor someone else? In truth, little qualifies you, except that you have more life experience than you know. Often, life experiences are emotional events that we react to but do not analyze.

When confronted with someone else's career or life questions, you are not as emotionally vested. This detachment can create a much broader perspective that can be extremely valuable to the person who is seeking your input. In addition, in providing this less emotive input for someone else, you invariably gain the benefit of your own insight. In effect, it allows you to analyze your past situation in a less reactive manner.

The Role of Mentor Is Not a Power Position

Consider it humbling when someone seeks your advice, and don't take the responsibility lightly. The sections that follow represent a few concepts to remember when you find yourself in the role of mentor.

Encourage and Stretch

When serving as a mentor, you must provide encouragement, while stretching the individual to achieve more. The role of mentor is truly a coaching one. You want the person to view you as a safe place to bring his ideas. Although you might play devil's advocate to help the individual strengthen his ideas, if you are consistently undermining those ideas through contrary advice, the person will cease seeking your input. When an individual's ideas are good, let the person know.

Point to Other Mentors or Resources

Mentoring is not necessarily about your direct experience or advice. Many times you might simply know someone or some resources (book, magazine, or seminar) that can help the individual. I can provide advice with less apprehension when I point the person to other resources for consideration. I don't hold the corner on good advice, and I want to ensure that the person gets the best input possible.

Conclusion

Finding mentors and becoming a mentor are career-long endeavors. Doing so pays valuable dividends in career growth, personal networking, and professional development. If you have not identified those people in your life who serve as mentors, take some time to build that list.

Also take the time to identify those who have routinely approached you for input. Whether the label of mentor is used or not, that is what you have become. Take the responsibility seriously. The positive career impact cannot be overstated.

Actions & Ideas

1. Identify those who have served as mentors in the past. Formally recognize their role as mentor and find one or two who will actively allow you to meet or correspond with them for this purpose.

2. Create a list of career questions and concerns to bring to your mentors. In particular, identify areas or skills with which you struggle, and get input into those areas.

3. Identify those who have placed you either officially or unofficially in the role of mentor. When they seek your advice, let them know of your own mentoring activities. Foster an understanding in them of the importance of ongoing mentoring relationships.

EXPAND YOUR TOOLKIT

Remember to visit the book's website at http://www.ITCareerToolkit.com for supplemental and ongoing advice, tips, and data relevant to this chapter.

Career Coaching

Career coaching has grown more popular as both a service and a career path. An effective career coach can help you understand your strengths, crystallize goals, and create a personalized plan of action to help you plan, execute, and grow your career.

Like an effective coach in sports, an effective career coach can help you maximize your existing skills, help you develop new skills, and help you recognize challenges and opportunities on the career playing field.

Chapter 24

Career Coaching

This chapter covers both the idea of hiring a career coach and career coaching as a potential path in your own career. Much of the information is germane to career coaching in general, but I also address specific areas where a career coach can assist the I.T. professional.

Although career coaching is popular, many professionals struggle with how to use a coach in their own careers. The struggle is often just understanding their strengths and weaknesses and having a clear idea of where they want to take their career. These are the exact topics that a career coach can help them work through.

Career Coaching Topics

The following list represents some of the topics a career coach might address:

- The development of an all overall career path and strategy
- Adopting more proactive and positive day-to-day actions
- Personal marketing
- Interview skills
- New or improved resume
- Professional networking
- Professional skill development
- Personal aptitudes and desires
- How to deal with a difficult boss, coworkers, and employees

This is just a short list of topics a career coach can help you with. In fact, if you are unsure how a career coach might work with you, a career coach can help answer that question.

A career coach goes may go beyond discussions about just your professional life. They often take on the role of confidant and friend, helping you define broadly applied life goals in addition to specific career-focused action plans. The goal should be to more closely harmonize your professional life with your personal goals and lifestyle choices.

What to Look for in a Career Coach

While the credentials and the background of the career coach are important, his demeanor and approach to your individual concerns and situation are just as important. Some coaches are more encouraging, whereas others are stronger taskmasters. If you are going to look for a coach, it is important that you interview prospective coaches to get a feel for their personality. If you contact a career coach and he or she does not encourage this kind of discovery, consider that a red flag. A coach should be prepared to discuss with you their approach and method before you engage them.

I tend to be a very demanding coach and even a demanding consultant, but first and foremost for me is taking a genuine interest in my clients, their situation, and helping them arrive at a positive outcome.

Fortunately, most of the career coaches I speak with have a similar connection with their clients. Many career coaches enter the field simply because they have a passionate desire to help others. If, during your interviews, you do not sense a genuine desire to help, I recommend continuing your search.

For a career coach to be effective, there needs to be mutual trust and respect (both the I.T. professional for their coach and the coach for his client). Without established mutual trust and respect, both coach and client are generally disconnected from the outcome. This negates the effectiveness of a coach. Both parties need to be interested and engaged in producing a well-defined and measurable outcome.

What to Expect from Your Career Coach

In addition to an initial interview where you can determine a coach's method and demeanor, you should expect several important things from a career coach, as outlined in the sections that follow.

A Methodology or Approach

I coached soccer and hockey for many years. At the start of every season, I held a mandatory meeting for all players and their parents. In that meeting, I introduced myself, my approach to the game and to coaching, my expectations for players and parents, and what they should expect from me. I gave each parent what I called my "nag letter."

This gave both the parents and the players a clear idea of how I would coach the team. It also let them know what I would and would not do and gave them a way to contact me with questions or concerns.

As you interview potential career coaches, one of the things you should ask for is an overview of their methodology or approach. It is not important to me whether it is one page or a small booklet, just that it gives you a clear idea of what their coaching entails.

Coaching Styles

There is no doubt that Bobby Knight's somewhat bombastic style as a basketball coach was much different from Phil Jackson's, the more laid-back "Zen master" who coached the Chicago Bulls and the Los Angeles Lakers. Both had tremendous success but were dramatically different in their methodology and demeanor.

Similarly, as you begin looking into coaching, it is important that you both assess and specifically ask prospective coaches about their style and demeanor. In the same way that bosses have their own individual traits, coaches do as well. Note that when it comes to hiring a coach that you are the consumer. You are in complete control here (whereas you have less control over the type of boss you work for).

Make sure, however, that you do not select a coach solely for a personality type that is "easy" for you to deal with. You need to find a coach who both encourages you and at times pushes you past self-imposed barriers to advancement.

Coaches come in all colors and sizes, so to speak, but there is typically a dominant trait they are identified with. Here are some traits that I've seen in coaches I know or have worked with:

- **The motivator/encourager**—The motivator is a popular coach with a natural ability to encourage and mobilize his clients to action. The motivator is an excellent choice for professionals who are already good at creating their own action plan. The support they need is less the tasks and more the day-to-day/week-to-week encouragement to work their plan.

- **The taskmaster**—The taskmaster emphasizes helping her client create a well-defined a course of action and then cross those items off her list upon achievement. The approach of the taskmaster can, at times, be pragmatic, with an emphasis on achievement as its own source of motivation. The taskmaster's ideal client is similarly pragmatic. She largely knows what she wants to accomplish and is seeking assistance in developing her plan and accountability in completing her tasks.

- **The dreamer/goal setter**—The dreamer helps professionals identify the age-old question "What do you want to be when you grow up?" They emphasize a vision or help uncover their client's personality traits and aptitudes. From that, they help their client first establish broad goals before moving into more specific plans. Their client might be professionals wanting to transition to another field or even those seeking a second, more personally satisfying career.

I'll emphasize again that all coaches should have all three of these characteristics to some degree. I personally am more of a taskmaster and work well with the same. This is because I have a clear idea of what I want to accomplish and I usually find my own motivation in reaching those well-defined goals. In addition, I find that when my clients achieve a set of tasks, they are similarly motivated.

As you look into coaching, keep these traits in mind. It will help you find the coach best suited for your individual personality.

An Initial Assessment

One of the first steps to a successful coaching relationship is some type of initial assessment. For some coaching programs, this initial assessment might take place before a formal engagement (before you even hire them). For others, the assessment might take place during the initial session.

The assessment is important for the coach to understand where you are in both your hard skills and soft skills. More important, he or she will gain insight into what drives you. It is likely, through this process, that you will gain a similar insight. The initial assessment will be built upon as your coaching progresses, but it provides the framework for the coaching going forward.

A Positive Attitude

If you've read my blog or listened to my podcast for any period of time, you know that I am not a fan of positive mental attitude in and of itself. A feel-good "rah rah" experience that lacks any pragmatism or actionable items usually leads to frustration and discouragement. It ends up killing motivation and the exact positive mental attitude it pretends to build. However, it is critical that your career coach have a positive attitude both toward you and your career aspirations.

If he is a professional coach, he will most likely work with you to develop a plan. As you implement the plan, run into roadblocks, and reassess your actions and outcomes, his attitude will play a critical role in how effectively you work together. During tougher times, a coach with a negative attitude can hinder your career advancement.

Caution A warning: Do not confuse a coach who strongly admonishes you into fulfilling your obligations and seeing your actions through as having a negative attitude. Personally, I prefer a coach who does not mince words but who is instead willing to say it like it is. Sometimes I do not need them to say to me, "You can do it," but instead need them to say, "You need to do this."

Clear Communications

To get the most from a career coach, the coach must be an effective communicator; clearly outlining the work that you must do and clearly stating objectives. Without this clarity, it will be difficult for you to determine whether the coaching is successful.

The Limitations of a Career Coach

Although an effective coach can be an amazing tool in your career toolkit, he is not a panacea. This section covers some things your coach cannot do for you.

Fix Irresponsible Career Mistakes

A career coach will work with you starting where you are right now. However, your coach cannot erase bad judgment and irresponsible behavior. If you struggle with personal issues, alcohol or drug use, or personal conduct that has resulted in you being fired and even legal ramifications, you need to work on the underlying issue through some type of counseling. This falls outside of the purview of a career coach.

A career coach can help you put together a strategy to begin rebuilding your professional reputation. This can begin even as you are addressing the underlying issue.

Improve Your Skill Set

You are in charge of improving the skills you bring to your job. Whether those are technical skills (a better understanding of networking, servers, security, programming) or whatever hard skills your job requires or soft skills and business acumen that transcends your job, the career coach is more of a skill magnifier.

The coach's role is less about directly developing your talent and more about helping you recognize which talents you should be focusing on given your career objectives and your current situation.

Land You a Job

A career coach is not a placement specialist. Typically, she helps your job search through a combination of focus, motivation, and helping you learn how to recognize the best opportunities—once again, based on your objectives.

The career coach will, however, help prepare you for things such as interviews, understand how to more effectively network, and help you improve your personal marketing.

Individual Coaching Versus Group Coaching

Coaching can come in the form of individual coaching (one on one, just you and the coach) and group coaching. The type of coaching you receive depends on personal preference, your budget, and the desired outcome.

Group Coaching

Group coaching is exactly what it sounds like. You are usually grouped with professionals with similar objectives. The group may be as small as 5 or as large as 15 or more. I try to keep group coaching down to a manageable 10 or fewer clients.

While it might seem that group coaching gives you less individual attention, you gain the benefit of a group of peers with whom you can share ideas, challenges, and successes. The group typically works to encourage each of the members and to keep them accountable. Friendships that begin in group coaching often continue throughout people's professional life.

Group coaching is also usually less expensive because you are spreading the hourly cost of the coach across several individuals. If it is an option, it can be an affordable way to get introduced to the idea of coaching and to get acquainted with a particular coach.

Individual Coaching

Individual coaching is when you work one on one with your career coach. It is often more intense and individually focused, catering to your specific situation and your desired outcomes. In contrast with group coaching, individual coaching is more expensive; however, you and your situation becomes more known to the coach.

This familiarity will help your coach devise better goals, strategies, and action plans. In addition, it might lead to better, and more quickly achieved, results.

How Coaching Is Structured

The way you work with a career coach will vary, depending on where you are with your career. You might choose to work on specific goals and issues, particularly when up against difficult problems or close deadlines. Or you might decide to participate in some kind of coaching program. Often, this means a set number of coaching sessions over a period of several weeks or months.

Many professionals sign up for coaching programs that usually run from four to ten weeks, with ongoing access to their coaches on an as-needed basis thereafter. This kind of approach offers a nice benefit in the short term while the program is underway, with the opportunity for check-ins and tune-ups thereafter.

How Much Does Coaching Cost

The fees associated with coaching vary dramatically. You may receive coaching for as little as $50 an hour or for as high as $250 an hour or more. The higher fees are usually associated with executive-level coaching or for those professionals looking to break into an executive position.

Is it worth the cost?

I'll offer an emphatic yes!

The coaching I've received continues to pay dividends years after the coaching session is over.

A better understanding of how to deal with conflict or sudden changes in the workplace and a greater understanding of a proactive approach to your career are priceless skills. In addition, we often become overwhelmed when we look at the possibilities or challenges we face, viewing our options and specific issues as overly complex. Or we just get stuck in how we view a situation.

A coach can sometimes strip away the nonessential items, reduce confusion, and expose the one or two truly critical issues. The "missing the forest for the trees" metaphor comes to mind. As you more effectively deal with situations that arise, you learn to put to use the skills and techniques taught by your career coach. Over time, you will need your coach's assistance less often. This is the true value of a career coach.

As you master those skills or mentor other professionals in your industry or career in general, you may develop an interest in coaching as a career path.

Coaching as a Career Path

Becoming a career or business coach can be rewarding both financially and personally. In particular, in the I.T. field, there is a great need for effective coaching.

Whether it is new students entering the field who need guidance and direction, more seasoned I.T. pros who are transitioning into management roles, or those I.T. executives who must bridge the gap between company management and executives and their highly technical staff, there are many opportunities for professional career coaches.

During my time as a career and business coach, I've had the pleasure of discovering professionals with a knack for thinking on their feet and providing excellent and actionable feedback. That is one of the most important traits a career coach can possess.

The Traits of an Effective Career and Business Coach

As mentioned previously, the ability to quickly assess a situation and provide a plan of action is a trait almost all career coaches possess. Here are some others:

- The desire to help
- A belief in career ownership
- The ability to listen
- A passion to see others succeed
- A natural motivator
- A willingness to offer and forward and opinion
- Confidence
- Natural leadership

The Benefits of Being a Career Coach

Similar to consulting (see Chapter 19, "Consulting"), career coaching can be a dynamic, challenging, and rewarding career. The rewards include helping people advance their careers, working in an exciting and changing professional environment, and the receiving good financial compensation.

In addition to those benefits, consider the rewards in the following subsections.

Working with Motivated and Driven Individuals

Typically, those who hire professional coaches are more motivated than the average professional. I find that I learn a lot from my clients. Other coaches I know have expressed similar sentiments. In many cases, they have achieved tremendous success both in life and in business. While working with them and watching them execute the plans we put into place, I gain tremendous motivation and insight. The fact is, it is usually the high achiever and the most intelligent who reaches out to, and understands the value of, coaching. It is said that the company you keep is a great determiner of your own success. Professional coaching allows me to keep great company.

Flexible Options on When and How One Works

Some career coaching occurs onsite, at the client's business or place of work. However, the majority of the coaching I do occurs via the Internet. I use Skype, Google Chat, or one of the other remote communication tools to have "face-to-face" meetings with my clients.

This flexibility also means that I can work with clients virtually anywhere in the world. I can provide coaching from my house, a coffee shop, or a hotel room. Similarly, my clients can receive and benefit from my coaching wherever they are.

For more information, see Chapter 18, "Telecommuting."

Working on New Challenges and Opportunities Every Day

I've never been satisfied going into the office and working on the same thing day after day. Business and career coaching provides me with new challenges and opportunities on a daily basis. Every client is different, as are their situations and their goals. In addition, as clients achieve a success or some objective, they are almost always setting new ones.

Although common themes (or oft-repeated ideas) appear throughout my coaching and the advice I give, the individual's application of that advice and the response that they get in their career is always new. This is both satisfying and interesting.

Getting Started as a Career Coach

This section addresses the independent or entrepreneurial career coach. This may be the I.T. consultant, I.T. manager, project manager, I.T. executive, or quite simply any I.T. professional who has identified an aptitude for training and coaching and a desire to pursue the field.

What Makes You Special?

In your current role, what is it about your personality or knowledge that has placed you in a position to coach your fellow employee? Whatever your answer, this is the natural starting point for building a career as a professional coach.

In fact, if you're looking to do this as a part-time or secondary endeavor, you may be able to use your current job as an effective training environment. Many businesses are discovering the value of having coaches who are knowledgeable about their business. There is no reason you could not pitch some type of coaching program within your current organization. That could be in the form of a short once-a-week meeting where you meet with a group of your peers and cover a specific topic where you have a recognized aptitude or ability to improve that ability in others. It might be training on communication or helping fellow programmers better communicate with managers and end users.

If you are already independent and working as a consultant or contractor, understanding the areas where you are best at helping others help themselves is a natural area to focus your coaching efforts.

The Importance of Published Material

If you want to build your reputation and credibility as a professional coach, I cannot overstate the importance of written material and presentations. The most successful coaches I know have created a body of work on their topics of expertise. This can be in the form of training presentations, published articles, blog entries, and other media such as YouTube videos.

Of course, having a book published (like the one you are reading now) is certainly helpful in this regard. Although beyond the scope of this book, I have several blog entries about writing a book and getting it published.

If you have not published material already, I suggest you start immediately. However, do not make it complicated. This can sometimes prove to be a challenge if you are an I.T. professional. There's a great emphasis placed on technical knowledge, and by nature we tend to want to overexplain. In most cases, a one- or two-page primer on a single topic is a good starting point.

If you have done some training and have a slide deck (PowerPoint), you can likely use that presentation. If the presentation is lengthy, try to reduce it to 8 to 12 slides. This is typically enough to introduce a concept and leave the reader/viewer with two or three important facts.

Your Coaching Offerings

It is important that you be ready to answer the question "What do you do?" or to address the request "Tell me about your coaching."

I have been guilty of overthinking these exact questions. Don't let the creation of a detailed coaching program stop you from getting started. Instead, identify three to five objectives or challenges you can help your clients overcome.

Begin letting your professional network know about your work in solving these problems. If you have any testimonials or quotes, even if from a job where you were not officially a coach, get those as well. If you're can, a great way to get testimonials and clients is to offer your coaching pro bono to one or two individuals or organizations in your network.

This is similar to what I teach consultants who are starting out. In fact, much of what I teach to the consultants I coach applies directly to developing a career as a business or career coach. You would do well to take time and go through Chapter 19 and Chapter 27, "12 Weeks to Profitable Consulting."

Sales and Marketing

Once again, I defer to Chapter 27 as a more complete treatment on launching and marketing your coaching business. However, at minimum, you need the following:

- **A website**—Preferably blog based.

- **Business cards**—Keep them simple (your name, your number, and what you do).

- **A one-page handout**—Again, go for simple and try to give a valuable piece of advice.

- **A video introduction**—I'm writing this in 2012. People want to know who they're working with, and video is the easiest way for you to show yourself short of being in front of them personally.

Setting Rates

This is the magic question. Determining what you can charge is important. We usually undervalue the knowledge we have to share, and this comes through in the rates we set. We believe by setting a lower rate we will pick up more clients. At times, this can be true, but let me explain about the perception of value and the types of clients you will attract.

Almost every professional coach I've spoken to has discovered this to be true: When their rates were lower, the clients they attracted spent more time trying to negotiate a better rate than those clients they attracted as their rates increased. This is true in consulting as well.

I am not suggesting that you price yourself out of the market. And when you are starting out, it makes sense to set a lower rate. But when you set that lower rate, stick to it; don't make it negotiable (at least not easily).

As part of 12 weeks to profitable consulting, I have some supplemental tools online to help you visualize the impact of changing your rate on your income. You can also go online and find sample coaching program outlines and take a look at the coaching offerings I provide.

A Final Word on Coaching

Chapter 23, "The Role of Mentoring," covers the importance of both having and being a mentor. Coaching is the next step beyond mentoring. In fact, most coaches I know have coaches of their own. They recognize the value of that professional relationship and they understand that a second pair of eyes and ears dramatically improves their chances of success and their ability to overcome obstacles.

Topics of Discussion

- Did you play sports or some other activity where you were under the guidance of a coach? Did you find that input helpful?

- Have you ever sought out professional coaching previously? Was the experience positive or negative?

- Have you considered hiring a career or professional coach? What has stopped you?

- What areas in your career would you like to improve? Do you believe a coach might be able to help you with those?

- Are you considering coaching as a career path? Why?

- What type of advice do you frequently give your peers or others in I.T.?

EXPAND YOUR TOOLKIT

Remember to visit the book's website at http://www.ITCareerToolkit.com for supplemental and ongoing advice, tips, and data relevant to this chapter.

What Do Finances Have to Do with My Career?

Financial challenges can become the most daunting in creating a rewarding and profitable career. The pressure of money, debt, and overspending actively works against the career builder—making decisions reactionary.

Understanding the role of your finances in relation to your career development (and adopting some key strategies) goes a long way toward helping finances become a career enhancer.

CHAPTER 25

Financial Control

You might be asking why a chapter on financial control is included in a career book. Numerous books, written by financial planners and consultants, provide excellent resources for gaining financial control.

However, the objective of this book is to provide a single source of information geared toward comprehensive career enhancement. That doesn't mean you don't need to check out some of the excellent resources on financial control—you should!

The goal of this chapter is to emphasize the importance of financial control as it relates to career building. In addition, I provide you with some resources and tools to help you in this area. These resources and tools are not meant to provide comprehensive financial planning, but to provide an excellent starting point.

To be able to correctly lay the groundwork for the information in this chapter, it's necessary that you understand the need for financial tools and controls. This chapter also covers some prevailing attitudes toward debt and spending.

Finally, this chapter introduces you to the tools that are included on the website accompanying this book and how they can help.

The Impact of Finances on Career Building

This book is a career toolkit that is meant to help you achieve dynamic career success and growth by teaching you attitudes and techniques that you can use daily to enhance your value and your marketability.

If you've come this far, it's likely that you've learned a lot. You've learned how to better present yourself, how to better market yourself, and how to identify opportunities both at your current company and at the companies that you are approaching for work.

In addition, you've been introduced to ideas about telecommuting, consulting, and conceptual project development. These topics are directly related to your day-to-day operations as a technology professional.

Financial control is another type of topic tool entirely. It's not directly related to your work life or the effective application of your knowledge; however, it can play a significant role in your career-building efforts.

Finances, if handled properly, can help produce great career opportunities. Similarly, financial challenges can disrupt career growth and greatly reduce your ability to take advantage of the opportunities that come your way.

Financial Control Creates Options

In career development, the need for options is critical for dynamic growth. When you are in financial distress, you effectively reduce your available options. Your ability to make good career decisions (decisions that reflect more than incremental pay increases) is removed. Career decisions become reactionary, based purely on financial need.

Finances are a huge source of mental noise. It's inevitable. If you struggle to meet your monthly expenses or if your debt is too high, your mental capacity is diminished. Financial trouble can have a dramatic negative impact on your current performance and on your ability to make good decisions.

In addition, your available options are greatly reduced. When money is the primary factor driving your career decisions, you cannot entertain a position or opportunity that might have greater long-term benefit than a higher-paying position. You cannot entertain lower-paying positions, regardless of the opportunities they present. Remember: I believe that sometimes you should consider trading pay for opportunity. However, that's difficult to do when you are living paycheck to paycheck.

Gaining control over your finances remedies the reduced performance because of mental anxiety and allows you to take advantage of opportunity-rich career moves.

Financial Control Is Largely Mental

Gaining control of your finances is usually less about what you earn and more about your attitudes toward money, spending, and things—material possessions. Understanding this fact can go a long way in helping you develop better financial control. In addition, the steps toward maintaining a strong financial position fall into place more easily with the philosophical groundwork in place.

Money Is a Tool

Money is a tool, just like technology. And just as many technology professionals focus entirely on the technology rather than its function within a business context, so we also focus on money as having value to buy things, rather than its functional role in our lives.

But money is simply something you trade for something of value. In addition, the money you receive has been similarly traded. You apply your effort and knowledge in return for the ability to trade for various products and services.

If you are honest, you hope that you provide value and that your employer or client recognizes and rewards that value. You are similarly aggravated or upset when your work is undervalued.

Yet, when you spend foolishly, you are, in a real sense, devaluing your time and effort. It does little good to create a strong sense of value for your time and effort only to turn around and sabotage that value through foolish spending or mismanaging your finances.

To illustrate this point, consider the following theoretical example.

If you are paid $40 an hour, you make somewhere around $80,000 per year (assuming full-time work). This is a fairly decent wage, and your time is being valued. Now assume that you spend 5 nights per week eating dinner out at better-than-average restaurants. Assume that your monthly total for dining out comes to $800 per month.

Although you might argue that you have had decent meals, you can prepare a decent meal at home for $7 to $11. If you went out to eat only one time per week and prepared meals the other nights, you would save $480. If you are paid $40 an hour, that equates to 12 hours of your life.

I'm not making a value judgment regarding eating dinner out. What I'm trying to emphasize is how attitudes toward money and spending might be in conflict. If you want to have financial stability and yet place eating out and buying things as priorities—if not in words, in actual practice—you are in financial conflict.

I state this only as an idea of how people devalue their labor and the money it produces through ill-advised spending habits. If your career is where you want it to be, you are flush with cash, and you easily meet all your financial obligations, go out to eat. I am addressing those, the majority, who are in far different circumstances.

Debt and Spending

Your attitude toward debt and spending can also create financial conflict. Certainly in the United States, debt is considered a natural byproduct of spending. This attitude is quickly becoming the norm in other cultures, too.

In addition, we have a habit of turning wants into needs. This was emphasized in my house recently.

Several years ago, we left a home with a pool for a less-expensive and pool-less home in another state. Our decision fell in line with the "trade pay for opportunity" mindset that I advocate. I was leaving a corporate environment to pursue additional writing and speaking opportunities, taking on consulting projects as needed.

Recently, we decided to move closer to our children's school. In the ensuing search, my wife saw a house with a nice patio and pool. Soon after, she had added a pool into the requirements for every home we looked at.

When asked about this, she made the case that we "needed" a pool so that our kids' friends had something fun to do when they came over. She also said that our dogs could use the pool to cool off.

Although my wife had not stated that the pool was an actual live-or-die need, by including it in our home requirements, she had made it a de facto need.

Once again, I am not advocating a lifestyle in which you enjoy no leisure activities or material comforts. That's not the point.

I only want you to evaluate your motivations and attitudes toward money to ensure that they don't become career stumbling blocks.

Some Basics of Financial Planning and Stability

The scope of this book does not include space for a comprehensive treatment of financial planning. Financial planning can be complex and requires the proper analysis of your particular situation.

However, some basic components should be part of every financial plan. A few of these are covered in the sections that follow. In addition, some forms and spreadsheets are available on the accompanying toolkit website to help you in putting these basics together.

Regardless of the method you use to track and control finances, it is important that you, in fact, use it. Tracking your finances should be a simple and disciplined part of a weekly or daily routine.

Remember: Financial pressures can create a huge drain on the energy and options you need to build a dynamic career. Your diligence in this area will pay great dividends.

Defining a Basic Budget

The single most important aspect of financial control is a budget. Dave Ramsey, the noted financial planner, author, and radio talk show host, refers to a budget as "telling your money what to do." However you refer to it, a budget is a vital component to your overall financial health.

To create a budget, you need to assess your core needs, create at least a cursory spending history, and divide your spending into meaningful categories. Doing so provides you with a clear picture of where your money goes and can help you identify areas where you can save money.

Defining Your Core Needs

The starting point for your budget is core needs: housing, food, clothing, and transportation. All these areas are identified in the budget spreadsheet located on the website.

Create a quick snapshot of your core needs and compare that to your current income. If you notice a huge disparity (that is, if your expenses come close to or actually exceed your income), you must take immediate action.

Only two courses of action are feasible:

- You must reduce your expenses.

- You must raise your income.

It is likely that you will need to do a combination of both. This might require taking a second job, selling a more-expensive car for a less-expensive one, brown bagging your lunch, and so on.

The idea is to bring your core needs to a base list that is manageable. Once again, this book is not a comprehensive financial planning book. It is not meant to remedy extreme financial hardships. If you are in an extreme financial hardship (you are considering bankruptcy, receiving numerous creditor calls, and so on), you need to get professional assistance right away.

Note You can find additional resources online at www.ITCareerToolkit.com.

Establishing Your Spending History

Tools for tracking spending history are readily available. Intuit's Quicken helps you to track checking accounts, investments, and cash flow and can provide accurate spending histories. You can even use a simple spreadsheet program or a manual ledger.

The most important aspect of the entire exercise is to use the tools that are available. Simply having the tools is not enough.

The website that accompanies this book includes a simple Weekly Cash-Flow Planning spreadsheet that uses key spending categories and allows you to compare monthly spending against a budget (also included).

Creating Your Budget

Some mistakenly think that a budget restricts the freedom that is associated with your finances and spending. This is the opposite of the actual truth. The fact is that a budget provides the ability to have true control and freedom in your spending.

A budget is not judgmental; it does not assess what you spend your money on. It merely provides a tool that allows you to plan where that spending occurs. If you decide to budget $1,000 per month for dining out, you can do so. Although I might question the wisdom of that allocation, if you are able to meet your other financial obligations and the funds are available, at least you have planned it out.

The budget isn't meant to restrict your spending as much as provide direction on where to spend it. Of course, a budget does provide an honest accounting of where your priorities are. This, in and of itself, might be frightening.

Ultimately, the idea is to use the budget as a way to help refine your attitude toward spending. In doing so, you can control your spending, create a financial plan, and open the door to more creative career options.

Cash-Flow Summary: A Weekly Plan

The weekly cash-flow summary is a tool that is essential for both business and personal use. It's a short-term budget tool that you can use to plan your spending for the coming week.

If you utilize it accurately, this tool is a precise spending plan. It can show you where you are spending your money and lets you see what will be left over at the end of the week. It also allows you to see the impact of the current week's spending on subsequent weeks.

You can download a Cash-Flow Planning spreadsheet with instructions from www.ITCareerToolkit.com. I created categories that suit basic budgeting needs. I also included blank areas for additional categories, if needed.

Conclusion

Remember: The idea behind financial control is for you to have as many options as possible. Numerous tools are available to help you track spending, reduce debt, and increase savings. However, the starting point is a budget and weekly cash-flow plan.

The goal is for you to value your time and efforts as much or more than your employer does.

Take some time to review the book's online resources. As your financial control stabilizes, your career options will open up.

Actions & Ideas

1. Using the spreadsheet from the *Building Your I.T. Career* website (www.ITCareerToolkit.com), create a simple budget (budget spreadsheet) today. Your budget doesn't have to be 100 percent accurate. As you gain additional information, add it to your budget.

2. Use the associated spending spreadsheet (Weekly Cash-Flow Planning spreadsheet). The website includes both of the forms in PDF format and as Excel spreadsheets.

3. Take a few moments to analyze your spending for the past week and the past month. What does your spending say about how you value your time and efforts?

EXPAND YOUR TOOLKIT

Remember to visit the book's website at http://www.ITCareerToolkit.com for supplemental and ongoing advice, tips, and data relevant to this chapter.

A Professional Blog

Blogging has been around almost as long as widespread adoption of the Internet. With the growth of social media as an avenue for publishing content, some believe that blogs have less value. The savvy professional understands that this is not the case.

Blogging can better position you as an expert, providing a publishing platform that has effectively grown many careers.

CHAPTER 26

A Professional Blog

I've been blogging professionally since 2003. It has and continues to be a strong platform for developing ideas and gaining new connections.

This chapter provides some insight into blogging as a career strategy, providing some insight into creating and publicizing content (and specifically, how to use WordPress, a powerful and free blogging and content management system).

What Is a Blog?

The word *blog* is an abbreviation of the term *web log*. Initially, web logs or online diaries were used by individuals for personal or professional expression. As the use of the Internet and web technologies grew, software companies maintained a log of software revision changes. These logs were used by power users and developers to stay up-to-date on software changes and bug fixes. This practice is still popular, but blogs have now become full-featured content management systems.

Really Simple Syndication and Notifications

To make it simpler for users to keep track of those changes, a technology software called RSS (popularly known as Really Simple Syndication) was added to blogs. RSS provides a time- and date-stamped record of entries added to the web log, allowing readers to subscribe to the blog and be notified of updates. Soon, the "we" was dropped, and web log was shortened to blog.

Developers ran special software that read those changes, letting them know when a given web log was updated. What made RSS especially appealing is that developers did not have to provide any personal information or an e-mail address to receive web blog update notifications. Instead, the software, an RSS reader, periodically checked the RSS file of one or more blogs, indicating which blogs had been updated.

RSS has now become commonplace. It is built in to most e-mail systems and web browsers. I use Google Reader as my primary blog or news reader. I like using Google Reader because it is tied to my Gmail/Google account, along with the many other Google productivity applications I use.

Later in this chapter, when we talk about writing your own blog entries and topic ideas, I discuss RSS in more detail.

How Do Blogs Work?

There are many blog platforms, but most share some common elements. The following list describes these common elements, but for a more complete treatment of the subject, including some instructional videos, visit this chapter's section at www.ITCareerToolkit.com:

- **Themes or layouts**—Most blogs contain a standard layout or framework. Themes or layouts often have one or two sidebars or columns with static information or other blog elements (a listing of post or a listing of categories). A larger column typically has the content—either blog posts or blog pages.

  Some blog platforms have complex themes that provide amazing layout flexibility. However, I recommend a more standard layout because with such your average reader will be able to find content more quickly. Also, it is much easier to change themes when you use a more basic layout.

- **Blog title**—Blogs always have a title. The title is available across the blog. It may be as simple as Matt's Blog or Mary's Technology Tips Blog. I've had my blog, Notes from the Toolshed, hosted at Toolbox.com for many years.

- **Posts**—Posts are the individual articles that make up the blog. This is the main content of your blog. Whereas a blog might be about a given technology (for example, programming in ASP.NET), the individual posts or articles might cover topics like "Connecting Your App to MySQL" or "An Introduction to Classes."

Posts are time- and date-stamped. In most cases, a blog's entries or posts show up in a list in reverse date order—the most recently posted article or entry first.

- **Pages**—Similar to a post but more static and less time driven or time-stamp sensitive, pages provide a way to use a blog as your company or personal website. You can have a traditional style menu on your blog with pages like About, My Resumé, My Interests, or anything else.

    Pages are usually not categorized and do not show up in the listing of content by date posted.

- **Categories**—Most blogs have multiple categories. You could place blog entries into one or more categories. That way, readers could find articles by similar topic. Categories are whatever you make them, so you can have categories that fall way off topic. For instance, you could have technical categories such as Networking, Cisco, PHP, MySQL, and SQL Server but also have personal interest categories like Cooking, Hiking, Music, Family Life, and so on.

- **Tags**—Tags are similar to categories. Not all blogs have them. They tend to be more freeform but are keywords you can add to your blog. You might have a category of Networking but then have tags like Router, Switches, Security, and Firewall.

- **Title**—Each blog post has a title. The title should be a short (60 or fewer characters) description of the content.

- **Body**—The body of the blog post is the article content itself. It can have images and hyperlinks. In addition, you can often embed multimedia such as video or audio files.

Why You Should Blog

For the I.T. professional, blogging provides an opportunity to showcase your knowledge. Whether through tutorials or case-study types of posts, you can create a platform that allows prospective employers or clients to see how you go about solving problems and demonstrate your knowledge/understanding of the technologies you use.

Sharing Expertise

By sharing expertise, you can become a go-to source for other I.T. professionals or for hiring managers and I.T. managers.

Some I.T. professionals believe that they protect their value by not sharing. They assume that if you give away the information, people will not need to contact you. Be careful of thinking this way; it will cost you. You might miss opportunities to show what you know and can do, and to attract interest from others, if you keep your skills and knowledge bottled up.

I subscribe more to a "give away the farm" mentality. The fact is, even if you shared how to solve a specific problem so that they can fix it on their own, you generate goodwill and bolster your image as an expert. You might soon find that you are receiving e-mails asking for assistance.

This is an extremely powerful way to network. Once they reach out to you, you are now in the role of a trusted advisor.

Search Engine Ranking

Blogs have a significant impact on natural search engine rankings. Google, Yahoo!, Bing, and other search engines all rely on new content to feed their search results. New content that is educational in nature ranks more highly than other types of content because it is deemed to be a greater value.

In addition, when you post to your blog, it sends a notification (a ping) to servers that specifically track and catalog blogs. The major search engines read this content regularly, and their software then "visits" the updated blogs, determines whether the content is of value (not spam), and adds it into their search catalog.

I use the Google Alerts feature to track key terms, specifically my blogs and blog topics. These alerts notifies me when those terms are cataloged by Google's search engine. I've received notification from Google Alerts about a new blog entry I've posted within an hour of posting it, which means that the new blog entry has already been cataloged by Google. In the recent past, Google's spiders (software that visits websites to determine changes) often went weeks without visiting a particular website.

Updated blog posts and the pages you link to on your blog are often added into Google's search catalog within hours of posting. This assumes, of course, that you are adding high-value and educational content.

Google and other search engines rank educational content much more highly that simply advertisement or promotion (sales-driven) content. Simply writing a self-promotional post that in effect says little more than "Here I am, hire me" is not nearly as effective as content that says "Here is information that you can use today." Share your knowledge!

Be Positioned As an Expert

The true power of blogging is that you can be positioned as an expert. You do not need thousands of blog readers to attain this. As you develop your career, you can send prospective employers to your blog as part of your job-search process.

If your blog content is of value, reasonably well-written, and clear, it can help an employer recognize your knowledge. It can also demonstrate your ability to document your work and think in an organized fashion.

Blogging Basics

This section covers some basic concepts to help you get started blogging, including schedule, topics, and the tone of your writing.

Most of these ideas are guidelines, not hard-and-fast rules. I share my opinion on these topics, but as you become familiar with more blogs and start blogging yourself, you will develop your own approach.

Schedule

One of the first questions I am asked about blogging is how frequently to post entries. I typically recommend that someone posts at least once a week, early on, but I also suggest posting 12 to 16 blog entries inside the first 2 months (if at all possible). That works out to two blog entries per week.

The reason for this is twofold. One, it provides multiple content points for Google to catalog. Two, it gives the appearance of a more established blog. When visitors read your blog, they will have several articles that they can read and review.

After that, almost any schedule that has you publishing regular content will work. I recommend you post more than once a month. Once a week is probably a good approach and would provide a significant library of content over the course of a year.

Quantity or Length

You might be intimidated by producing that much content. It is important that you realize that you do not need to publish 1,000- to 2,000-word articles. Your blog post can be much shorter. A quick tutorial or overview of a given technology that is 300 to 500 words is more than enough.

In fact, in the busy, highly distracted, content-rich world we live in, shorter is better. I break this rule often, but in most cases recommend that people post shorter articles more often.

Multipart Blog Post

Another way to help increase your posting frequency is to split longer topics into two or more parts. This serves two purposes. One, a single topic can effectively give you two weeks of blog updates. Two, your readers will have a reason to return to your blog. A multipart blog or series on a topic tends to encourage dialog as well. Readers commenting on your blog, and back and forth discussions on a topic, indicates that people are returning to your blog repeatedly. In addition, readers who are engaged in this type of dialogue are more likely to share your blog with their network of contacts.

What to Write About

The next step in planning and implementing a professional blog is determining what content to include. An adage in the writing world advises to "write what you know." This is great advice and works extremely well when you are writing a blog to accent your professional and technical knowledge.

Are you a programmer, project manager, network engineer, or I.T. manager? If so, that is the first place to start when it comes to content. Make a list of the technologies you work with and the tasks you perform daily at your job.

Go beyond just the technical. What about interactions with other staff? Running and planning meetings? Training? Documentation? All of these are potential topics to write about.

Make a list of topic ideas. I maintain a Google spreadsheet of content ideas. I also have a sheet where I plan when that content will be published. If you visit the website www.ITCareerToolkit.com, you can find a content-planning template that you can download and use. I also have other tools to help you plan and start blogging there.

Another great way to get content idea is through what others are writing about. Subscribe to some blogs that cover similar topics. An online search should turn up several. Read a few and see how they cover topics and emulate what you like.

Writing Style: Tone and Voice

If you are not a natural writer, there is no secret to improving beyond writing a lot. In addition, find a trusted source whose writing you enjoy and ask that source for feedback. Be willing to listen and try what is suggested.

As you become familiar with other blogs, you will discover the writing style of the individual blogger. Are they formal and serious? Do they write more humorous pieces? Do they write in a personal, day-in-the-life style?

All of these are examples of a writing style or tone you can adopt. Here are a few tips to help you write better and to find your style or voice:

- **Use shorter sentences**—Do not try to make your point in a single sentence.

- **Read what you've written out loud**—This is a great way to identify writing that sounds clumsy.

- **Break your writing up with spaces between paragraphs**—It makes your blog easier to read and will also help you identify sections that do not flow.

- **Do not edit as you write**—Get the idea written down and then edit the piece.

Over time, you will develop a flow and style. Do not worry if it does not come naturally at first. You need to let that part of your writing develop.

Blogging Multimedia

In addition to text blogging, you can also have a blog that features audio or video content. Referred to as a podcast (audio or video), multimedia is an excellent way to increase your blog's appeal.

Most blog platforms (see the section "Using WordPress" that follows) provide a way to embed audio or video directly into the blog.

Energy, Energy, Energy

I'm not covering podcast or video blogs (vlogs) in detail here. But I do offer this piece of advice: Audio and video content requires an extremely high energy level to make it engaging to the viewer. Speaking to the camera or microphone in a monotone or lifeless voice is certain to turn people off.

I am extremely high energy as a presenter, and even I struggled with this when I created my first podcast.

Using WordPress

WordPress is the blogging platform I use to run my websites. It is a powerful content management system and blogging platform. It benefits from a large and active community of developers who build third-party add-ons called plug-ins. In addition, its widespread use means that you can find many tutorials and community assistance online.

Content Management

WordPress is both blog software and content management. You can create pages, just like you would on any website software, and also run and manage your blog. All of your content runs through the same framework, which means that you do not have to have both a website *and* a separate blog.

Hosting Options

You can start a blog at WordPress.com for free or you can run WordPress on a self-hosted platform. The difference is important.

WordPress.com lets you set up a blog on their site. They manage all the software updates and have a number of useful features. One drawback is that you have file upload and space limitations. Furthermore, your site will be a subdomain of WordPress.com, which means the URL will be something like http://*blogname*.wordpress.com.

The other option is to register your own domain and either install a copy of WordPress on your hosted site or find a hosting company that has a WordPress auto-installer. I prefer the latter option.

Note While there is, in fact, a way to point your own registered domain (that is, yourcompany.com) to a Wordpress.com-hosted site, I do not recommend it. Many features, such as available plug-ins and file uploads, are greatly restricted.

For this reason, I use Bluehost.com as my hosting company. They have a WordPress install application that both installs WordPress and keeps it up-to-date. Many other hosting companies provide a similar service.

Domain Registration and Hosting

I have some tutorials online regarding domain registration and hosting WordPress. Visit www.ITCareerToolkit.com and look for the WordPress tutorial link.

When considering your own domain, as an individual, attempt to get a domain with your name. I was unable to get MatthewMoran.com or MattMoran.com, so I opted for MatthewMoranOnline.com and MattMoranOnline.com. For companies, the company name or abbreviations are fine. Although you can use a dash (-) in a domain name, you should avoid doing so. People looking for your site will often forget to add it. Plus, they are clumsy to say when giving someone your website's URL.

New domain suffixes continue to be introduced, allowing you the option of finding a domain with a .tv, .me, and other suffixes. I still prefer .com or .net, simply because they make up the greatest number of domain registrations. Anyone unsure of your domain suffix is likely to try .com or .net first.

Be aware, though, that your domain name will not be the most critical factor in your blog's popularity and success; your content will be. But once you have your domain name registered, hosted, and running, include your URL on everything you print or put online. You should also have it in your e-mail signature.

I mentioned earlier about hosting your blog at WordPress.com versus hosting it on your own hosting account. Hosting your own version of WordPress provides significant benefits. These include greater control over your layout, file uploads, and plug-ins or other extra software.

My hosting company, and many others, makes this a fairly simple process with a one-button install of WordPress. After that, setup of your WordPress site requires some technical knowledge. There are many tutorials and documents to guide you. WordPress.org has an active user community, as well. If you have specific questions, contact me at www.ITCareerToolkit.com or www.MatthewMoranOnline.com, and I will answer your question or direct you to a good resource.

Themes (Layouts)

Your WordPress design is controlled by the theme you use. You can change your theme from inside the WordPress admin console and see a preview of what your site might look like.

You can find thousands of free and low-cost themes online. Visit Wordpress.org to preview many of them.

Plug-Ins

Plug-ins are add-on software that adds functionality to your blog. As with themes, you can find thousands of free or low-cost plug-ins online. Plug-ins add functionality like photo/image galleries, music players, e-commerce features, search engine optimization, data capture forms, and many others.

Plug-ins you should consider for your blog include the following:

- **The All-in-One SEO Pack**—This plug-in adds key metadata fields to every page and blog entry on your site. It lets you customize your metadata for each page. The primary fields it adds are Title, Description, and Keywords. Filling these in for each entry is an important step in your site being highly ranked on search engines.

- **NextGen Image Gallery**—The NextGen Image Gallery plug-in lets you upload pictures and, using a simple and short code, include all of those uploaded pictures in a slideshow-style gallery.

- **Google Forms**—If you use Google Docs and have ever used Google Forms, you'll find this plug-in attractive. It enables you to embed a Google form into your WordPress blog. It also redirects visitors who fill out the form to a page of your choice.

- **JetPack by WordPress**—JetPack is actually several different plug-ins developed by the WordPress community. WordPress took all those plug-ins and wrapped them into JetPack. By installing JetPack, you have access to website stats, custom forms, share buttons for social media sites, and the ability to easily embed video and audio into your blog.

Sidebar Widgets

Most WordPress themes include one or more sidebars. These sidebars usually have links to blog entries, newsletter signup forms, and links to things like social media sites.

Widgets are small drag-and-drop components that enable you to determine what shows up in your sidebar. In the WordPress admin console, under Appearance, you will find dozens of widgets to enhance your blog's functionality.

Customizations

WordPress is built on PHP—a web-based scripting application language. From inside WordPress, you can get to many of the core PHP files for the theme you are using. If you are familiar with PHP and HTML, you can customize almost any part of your WordPress install.

Caution Make sure that you back up the files you are hacking before you start.

Getting Started with WordPress

You can find some instructional videos about getting started with WordPress and using Google Reader at ITCareerTookit.com. My recommendation is that you take some time and find some blogs you like. If you have an RSS reader, add the blogs to it. If not, consider getting a Gmail account and using Google Reader.

A professional blog is a great way to enhance your professional image and showcase your talent. It really does not take long to get started, and you might enjoy the process.

Actions & Ideas

1. Who do you consider an expert in the field, someone whom you look up to? Does that person have a blog?

2. Do a search on your topic of expertise and find three or four blogs that cover that topic. Add them to an RSS reader and also see what topics they cover. Note how long the blog entries are. Note the general tone of the blog entries.

3. What is your impression of the blog writers you discovered? Is their content valuable? Do you think it raises their professional reputation?

EXPAND YOUR TOOLKIT

Remember to visit the book's website at http://www.ITCareerToolkit.com for supplemental and ongoing advice, tips, and data relevant to this chapter.

How quickly can you make money as a consultant?

If you want to be a profitable consultant, sales and marketing must play a central role in what you do. The ability to craft a message that is credible and creates trust, and the ability to get that message out to your potential customer, will dictate how quickly you can become profitable.

CHAPTER 27

12 Weeks to Profitable Consulting

Chapter 19, "Consulting," provided an overview of how the IT professional can enter the consulting field. This chapter takes a more in-depth look at the topics of sales and marketing, the proposal process, tracking and billing for time, and winning new clients as quickly as possible.

About 12 Weeks

This chapter presents a step-by-step 12-week guide to launching a profitable consulting practice. Much of the information focuses on the independent consultant but is also applicable to the small firm and even contains some valuable information for large firm consultants.

However, I make this disclaimer: 12 weeks is a highly aggressive schedule involving best-case scenarios. On a personal note, when a startup client I was working for many years ago lost its funding, effectively making me unemployed overnight, these techniques were put into play. In addition, I've effectively used them in my coaching with other consultants and small consulting firms. They work!

A Week-by-Week Overview

At the end of the chapter, I cover a week-by-week overview with specific tasks that refer to information covered throughout the chapter. This becomes your map or guidebook to putting the chapter information to use as effectively as possible.

Your Starting Point

Each reader will be at a different starting point. Some of you may already be consulting and are simply looking for ways to grow the consulting practice or to make it more profitable. Others may be I.T. professionals currently employed at a company but intrigued by the idea and the "exciting" world of consulting.

Your starting point, your attitude, whether you are proactive by nature, and your existing professional network will all have an impact on how quickly and effectively you put these ideas into place. But wherever you are at, the adoption and execution of some of the ideas in this chapter will prove beneficial in creating a dynamic and profitable consulting business.

What Does *Profitable* Mean?

That is a fair question. Profitable consulting for the CIO looking to leave his corporate environment and become a high-price executive consultant is certainly different from that of a junior-level programmer who wants to take on some part-time projects. In addition, your lifestyle and current expenses will largely dictate what *profitable* means.

In my anecdote above, it took me nine weeks after losing my client to find enough clients to generate several thousand dollars per month. However, I'd been consulting and marketing consulting full time for nearly seven years. I had marketing material, I had been speaking professionally in the area, and I had a strong understanding of the talents I brought to the table.

This helped me ramp up my marketing activities much more quickly than those just starting to put together their consulting identity and materials.

The Profitable Consulting Toolkit

By the time we're done building our profitable consulting business, a number of critical pieces will be put into place. You may or may not adopt all of these pieces, and your success is not contingent upon doing so. But I do believe that each of these ideas adds to a stronger framework and therefore better supports a profitable consulting business.

What we will put in our toolkit:

- A website/blog
- Business cards

- A mailing list

- A strong message of value

- A case study

- A pitch

- A contact list

- A method for tracking time

- A method for invoicing

Some of these are more important than others, but in the end it is helpful to have as many of these things in place as possible. You may add other items to your toolkit, and that's okay. I'm not claiming to have everything in place that you'll ever need as a consultant; however, the items listed here are a great place to start.

In addition, I do not cover topics like business structure or how to manage your accounting or bookkeeping. I do believe there is a value to hiring people to take care of those areas for you, but the simplest way to get to a point where you can do that is to generate revenue. That is my focus.

A Website/Blog

This is an expected piece of your consulting puzzle. It is essential, as well. However, it might not be as important as you believe it is. One barrier to getting started for some of the consultants I coach is getting their website up and running.

In most cases, they want it to be much more developed than it needs to be. They are looking for the most professional-looking design, believing that a great design will be a primary factor in winning them business. They compare the designs readily available to them with multimillion (or billion) dollar firms. In doing so, they effectively freeze the launch of the consulting while they try to get a similar design.

Do not do this.

Take some time to go over Chapter 26, "A Professional Blog." It covers blogging, why it is effective, and some specifics on the WordPress blogging platform.

When it comes to starting your consulting business, your website is not necessarily there to win business. That might occur over time, as you develop content that intrigues visitors. In the beginning, it is more important that your website simply provide a short list of the services you provide. It is a reference point for your potential clients and possibly a way for clients to send your information to others.

It also needs to provide contact information.

You can simply have a page with your phone number, mailing address, and e-mail address; however, if you are concerned with spam, you have some other options. You can include that information in a graphic, making it less likely to be picked up through site scraping. Or you can include a contact form on your website. WordPress has several contact form plug-ins with CAPTCHA support to ensure that it is a person submitting the form and not a spambot.

What You Need on Your Website

I believe in starting simple. I recommend the following pages:

- Home
- Services
- About
- Contact

As you progress, your may subdivide services into specific major categories. In addition, if you are using WordPress to run your website, you might include menu items that point to specific blog categories. This helps your website visitors to quickly find the information important to them.

At the end of this section, I include a screenshot from my website with some notes about what I've included on the site.

Home

Your Home page should provide one or two short paragraphs about you and what you do. It is similar to your pitch or value proposition. You don't need much information. Remember, your visitors have likely already met you or were referred by another client. They have an interest in finding out about you and will likely delve deeper into the site.

Your Home page should not bog them down with details. It is better to provide shorter and more succinct pieces of information. That allows site visitors to determine what is important to them.

Services

You might have one or two sentences that describe your consulting focus. After that, I recommend, again, a short bulleted list. Avoid using terms that are confusing or are too much geared toward the I.T. industry insider; the person reviewing your site might not be the most technical.

Even a term like *integration* can be problematic. This is particularly true if your target audience or most of your clients are small to mid-sized businesses. They may view integration as expensive and more comprehensive than what their business needs. *Computer networking* is just as effective a term.

Another example is the term *ROI*. We know what it means, as do most of our clients, but it is rare that my clients truly speak in those terms. They have needs and want productivity and cost savings. ROI is, of course, assumed. They want their technology to help their business run smoothly and make more money.

I could see a potential client appreciating a statement as simple as "I make your computers run faster and help your business make more money." Below that, list technologies and services you make available.

About

What goes on the About page depends on whether you are primarily selling yourself as a consultant or selling the company (even if the company is you).

Initially, and if it is solely you doing the consulting, it is completely appropriate to sell the consulting as you. In fact, I recommend it. Why? Because that is what most of your clients are buying. They are buying their confidence in your ability to deliver solutions.

Later, you can transition to selling the company versus you.

However, even if you grow your consulting practice and have several staff consultants, each consultant will likely have a book of business that is there primarily because of them. This is true even with most of the largest consulting firms. In fact, a primary factor in hiring consultants from other firms is the strength and value of the business relationships that the consultant brings with him into the practice.

Transition from Selling You to Selling the Company

I address this concern briefly.

If you start your company and position your website as you but then start hiring others, use the following technique to transition to selling the company.

Extol the virtues and talents of the resource you are bringing into a client.

I had to go through this many years ago. My clients were comfortable with me. When there was a problem, they called me. As I hired people, they would voice skepticism or concerns that I was not on their project. They wanted me working on their systems. But I wanted to grow and take on more projects.

I learned that I needed to position my talent as less and my employee's talent as more. I would say something like this: "Oh, you need your Exchange Server looked at. I could do it, I have experience there, but you should really talk to David. He's the expert. I can't really match his expertise in that specific area. He's a better resource for this. Let me get him in here."

A couple things. Sometimes this was true, sometimes it was more about the role that person was taking with my client. I was never placing resources that could not do the work—and my employees all had areas where their skills surpassed mine.

But to start, I had to ensure that the client felt comfortable with a new person on their project.

It wasn't complicated, and soon my clients expected to see a variety of resources come into their offices to work on their projects. I was still available to them and maintained a hands-on role.

So, don't worry too much about how you might transition from a consulting practice and the About page on your website marketing you over the company. You can change that when it is appropriate to do so.

Contact

The Contact page should be sparse. It should contain your phone number, e-mail, and mailing address. You can also include a simple form for those who want to contact you.

Include your phone number and e-mail address on every page, as part of your header or footer information. Make it easy for clients and potential clients to get in touch with you.

Too many consultant websites I've seen make people dig through pages to find the best way to contact them. Some do not even provide a number or e-mail address, requiring me to fill in a form. I strongly recommend you do *not* do this. The simpler it is for them to contact you, the more likely they are to do so.

Other Web Content

After the basic web content above, you will want to turn to value-added content. For me, blog entries form the basis for high-value content. In Chapter 17, "Your Career and Social Media," and Chapter 26, I cover both strategy and techniques to help you grow your credibility online. A well-written blog with content that helps your client or potential client is a key element.

You should also have a page for media coverage and links to case studies. If you've been published anywhere, include links to the articles or do your own scanned version of the article if it was a print publication only. These are huge credibility boosters.

My Website: MatthewMoranOnline.com

My site is built on WordPress. It has most of the previously mentioned sections, with some variations, as shown in Figure 27-1.

Featured content slider. This section changes every few seconds, showcasing new or important blog posts.

The sidebar is a common element on Wordpress blogs. I use it to introduce myself and feature key products or events.

Figure 27-1 *MatthewMoranOnline.com*

Business Cards

This often proves to be a curious barrier to starting a consulting business. It often has something to do with some hang-up on logo or overall image. I caution you to be careful if you are heading in this direction. You might be passing on a lot of opportunities.

At its most basic, a business card needs little more than the following:

- Your name

- Your cell phone number

- Your e-mail address

- Your website URL

- A simple title or description.

A black-and-white card with the contact elements in each corner and a description in the center of the card is adequate to get started.

It isn't that I am against having a nice logo and the most attractive card possible, but I've yet to meet a successful and profitable consultant who attributes his success to his business card or logo.

If you've given someone your business card or a client gives one of your cards to an acquaintance, it was part of a conversation. The person getting your card is probably a warm lead or referral. At that point, the look of your card pales in importance to what the person who gave the card (either you or the source of the referral) said.

The other thing is that you may change your card a few times in the first year or two of consulting. In fact, I might recommend you simply get clean edge business cards from your local office supply and print them as needed. By doing this, you can play with the look and feel while you get your consulting going. After you've developed some working clients, you can ask them what they would like to see. You might be surprised what they say.

For instance, for me, I want a card that is plain paper, not glossy. I cannot stand it when I can't write on a card with a standard pen. I strongly recommend that you not use a glossy card and one with color across the card. At least make sure that the back is not glossy and can be used to write notes.

Mailing List/Newsletter

A consultant is sought after because of specialized or highly technical knowledge. One of the most powerful ways to convey that knowledge and position yourself as an expert is a newsletter.

There is a misconception that newsletters are no longer effective tools. People have begun putting all their content on and sharing their expertise purely through social networks like Facebook, LinkedIn, and Twitter. As discussed in Chapter 17 and Chapter 26, I believe that this is a mistake.

A newsletter provides one of the simplest ways to take your conversation directly to your clients and potential clients. Social media is busy and noisy, requiring a nearly constant influx of content. In addition, only a fraction of your social connections are likely to see any given post or update.

A newsletter also allows you to expand and develop your ideas more fully.

Don't Advertise, Teach

A mailing list should not be an advertisement for your services. Most of your readers will know what you do already, and those who receive your newsletter from a friend will find out what you do more because of what you taught them than because of what you sold them.

You earn the right to pitch your services by adding value to your readers. This cannot be overstated. In my coaching, whenever I find a consultant who is not seeing a benefit from a regular newsletter, it is invariably because he or she is using it as a sales tool without adding value.

What to Include

If you have started blogging, content is much easier to come by. I almost always use blog content to fill my newsletter. My approach is to write several blog entries over the course of a month and then reintroduce them in the newsletter.

These can be tutorials or news about products. If you consult to a specific industry, you can include developments in that industry that are related to the consulting you do. This presents you as an expert and someone willing to share knowledge across your network.

Newsletter Distribution

Use a professional newsletter service. It will help with spam compliance and provide tools to help you grow your list. You can also track how many people open your newsletter and click the links within it. This information is valuable. It lets you know what people find interesting, and you can then reach out to individuals specifically based on what they clicked.

I use mailchimp.com for my newsletter. It provides well-designed templates, suggestions on newsletter subjects, and great analytics so you know what content your readers are most interested in. Mailchimp.com also provides the technology to integrate your newsletter with your social media, your website, and your blog, whether you use WordPress or some other blog platform.

The following are some other services:

- ConstantContact.com
- AWeber.com
- MyNewsletterbuilder.com

If you are subscribed to any newsletters, you can probably find out what service they are using at the bottom of their newsletter.

Your Services

If you can do that effectively and consistently, you can take your greed or your good deeds wherever you want to.

Exercise 1: Why Do You Want to Be a Consultant?

Jot some notes. This isn't meant to be an essay. It isn't meant to be a value judgment. There isn't a right or wrong here. In fact, there are probably many reasons why. Your goal, however, should be honesty. For instance, *"I'm out of work and need to do something,"* might not be the best reason to become a consultant, but it might be a factor.

I've known consultants who started for just that reason, loved consulting, and never went back to a traditional job.

Some of my reasons are as follows:

- Pay
- Prestige
- Problems with authority
- Love problem solving (being the hero)
- Love having some freedom of schedule
- Like learning new things and tackling new problems

Exercise 2: What Can You/Should You Be Paid For?

Make a list. This is the first step in being a consultant: simple brainstorming. List every skill you have that is worth money to someone. It should contain broadly applied skills such as people skills, management, project development, technology, marketing, and so on, all the way to more specific skills, such as Cisco networking equipment, Microsoft Office, web design, CSS, JavaScript, .NET, PHP, and so forth.

Put a check box next to your strongest skills. Those are core moneymakers.

Sales and Marketing Basics

For some reason, people have an allergic reaction to the idea of selling their services. If you hope to build and maintain a profitable business of any kind, there will be some degree of involvement. I believe the aversion or fear of selling is based on a caricature of a stereotypical used-car salesman (the one with the big toothy grin). In addition, there's the fear of failure or of being rejected.

I want to paint a different picture of what selling consulting means. I want to challenge the perceptions and provide you, the consultant or aspiring consultant, a different way to view the selling you are going to have to do.

The first thing you need to understand is that we sell every day. In the same way that we consult, offering advice and opinion, we do the same with products and services that we find valuable. When we have a service provider, let's say a plumber, who does great work, we refer him to our friends. We have no qualms with doing this because we are confident in what he delivers. This same type of confidence (in the value you bring your clients) is critical to marketing and selling your consulting services.

If you knew you had a way to dramatically help the business function better and to save or make more money, would that business benefit from talking to you? That is the mindset you need to have when it comes to selling your consulting. Of course, it is important that you can back that up by providing great services and solutions to your clients.

If you are unable or unwilling to be a value-added part of the clients you serve (a contributing member to their team), consulting might not be for you.

The "I'm a High-Value Solution" Perspective

From this point going forward, you need to convey the message both in your subconscious and to existing and potential clients that you are, in fact, a high-value solution. As such, you can have confidence that you are not the previously mentioned used-car salesman. When you have a conversation with a new lead, in person or on the phone, know that you are offering something important: *You!*

Developing Your Pitch

To get your message of value and competence to the greatest number of people, create a succinct message that sounds natural and compelling. The first step in doing so is to create your elevator pitch, so called because it needs to be short enough (but with enough information) that you can state it in the time it takes to go down a couple floors on the elevator. It quickly answers the question "what do you do?"

Do not underestimate how difficult this can be. Not complicated, but not simple on either. Depending on the kind of work you do, it might be very simple.

A friend of mine and fellow consultant, Marc, says something like this: "You know that computer thing blinking in the corner. I make it work better." Sometimes he even refers to it as "the magic box." His consulting, which has been a successful and profitable practice for more than 20 years, generally focuses on small business computer technology. Most of his clients do not use terms like *integration*, *ROI*, *uptime*, and other terms germane to the computer business. He purposely avoids terms that imply complexity or simply are not understood.

As you create your elevator speech, make sure that it is understandable to the person who is going to hear it. In I.T. in general, we are often guilty of using confusing acronyms and terms that only we understand. This will kill a conversation and make selling your service almost impossible.

The online supplemental material for this chapter includes several elevator speeches or short explanations that I found interesting.

Your First Case Study

Much of this material comes from a workshop I teach called Solution Selling: A Case-Study Approach.

It is my contention that too many consultants and other professional service providers create brochures that tell us very little about what they do and how they do it. A one-page (and even half-page) summary of a project or client you've worked for is a much stronger piece of collateral.

The following sections explain some of the guidelines I use when creating case studies.

The Case Study Framework

Case studies are made up of the following seven components:

1. **A title**—The title is a couple words describing the primary technology or problems solved (for instance, "using WordPress for search engine optimization").

2. **A summary sentence**—The summary sentence encapsulates the entire case study. It could reference the type of client, the challenge, and the technology used to solve it.

3. **About the client**—If I have permission in this section, I reference my client by name. If the project is sensitive, I may just reference the primary industry of my client. When appropriate, I include a sentence or two about the client.

4. **The problem or challenge**—If I've referenced the client by name, I reference them again in this section. (For instance, "Company ABC came to Kreative Knowledge wanting a solution to their low page rank in Google's organic search.")

I also address some of the steps the client may have taken before my engagement to solve the problem. This demonstrates that previous attempts to solve the problem had not been successful and sets up the case study to show you how I solved this exact challenge.

5. **The solution**—This is the most important section of your case study and usually the longest. In this section, you not only talk about any technologies or services that you developed or helped implement but also showcase the thinking involved in creating the solution.

   In fact, the technologies put into place are not the most important part of the solution. You are! This is a chance for you to take center stage. But do so carefully.

   This solution section should clearly demonstrate your concern for the client and the challenge they faced. You also want to show that the solution involved you working with your client. I am fond of saying that no one likes technology done to them.

   Potential clients reading the solution should conclude that you have the right aptitude (the skills necessary) and attitude (the proper perspective) to solve their unique problem.

6. **Conclusion**—Conclude the solution with a statement that summarizes the benefit of the work you performed. If at all possible, include any metrics that demonstrates success.

7. **A call to action and contact information**—When I suggest a call to action, I mean simply asking them to contact you with any comments or questions. Finally, include your name, e-mail, and phone number.

How to Use Your Case Studies

Notice that I said case studies, plural. As soon as you are able, write up a few case studies, even including projects you've done for past employers; those are solutions you developed, as well. Here's why you want more than one.

Every case study that you write addresses a particular type of problem and solution and typically involves certain technologies. Each case study also addresses a specific type of client, whether by industry, size, geographic location, or any other factors.

In the process of your work and in marketing your consulting, you will run across many different types of businesses and many different types of challenges. The goal with your case studies is to be able to leave with, or send to, any potential client a case study that relates to them in some way.

You might work for a restaurant company, for instance, that is a looking for assistance with their network. You might have worked with a restaurant in the past, helping them with a database issue. You might have worked with another type of industry helping that company with a similar network challenge. In this case, you can leave the restaurant owner or management two different case studies. One shows that you understand their industry, and the other shows that you understand the challenge they are facing. The two together form a powerful statement that you are the right person for this job.

Online I've included in Microsoft Word template for a simple one-page case study.

Tools for Tracking Your Business

You need to track a number of pieces of information for your business to run successfully and profitably. Of those, the most important are leads, clients, time, invoices, and your activities.

Managing Your Time and Tasks

Benjamin Franklin once said, "Dost thou love life? Then do not squander time for it is the stuff life is made of" (*Poor Richard's Almanack*, June 1746).

This is one of the most critical concepts in growing and maintaining a profitable consulting business. Much of the time, you will be billing by the hour. In that sense, your income is directly tied to your time. Furthermore, your ability to quickly produce proposals, responses to questions, manage e-mail and other correspondence, and control interruptions will also impact profitability.

It Isn't the System But Being Diligent with a System

Many technologist I know want to find the perfect tool. This is a result of living in the I.T. world. We understand what technology can do and therefore are often dissatisfied when a given technology doesn't do it all.

However, whether you use a computer-based time management and calendar system, something online, or a traditional pen-and-paper planner is not the most important factor in his successful system. The most important factor is that you use the system in place.

This means setting aside time, usually at the start or the end of the day, to ensure that your calendar is up-to-date. It also means having the diligence to update the system as information is given to you, transferring any information on loose pieces of paper into the system as soon as possible.

Clarity and Reduced Mental Noise

Keeping appointments and not forgetting to perform tasks is an important part of calendar and task management. But I believe the most important thing that effective time and task management does is provide you with clarity for your day and reduce mental noise. Let me explain.

Without an effective system, keeping various papers around on your desk or in your computer bag leads to forgotten appointments and information. When we are structuring our timing information this way, we know it. This means we are constantly looking back over those papers to ensure that we have not forgotten something and living with the knowledge that we most certainly will forget something at some point. This produces mental noise and inhibits peak performance. Operating at peak performance is directly tied to profitability and being the best consultant possible.

It is impossible to keep a pile of papers in front of us with every task we are going to need to complete over the next several weeks and months. A well-maintained calendar and task system enables us to see the information we need when we need to see it. It also hides the information we don't need to see (while allowing us to have confidence that will see that information when necessary).

Let's assume, for instance, that you have an appointment three weeks from today and that you'll need two or three days to prepare for that appointment. You do not need the appointment or any associated tasks listed on the current week's calendar. Instead, you need to put the appointment on the date it is due and have a task or an appointment three days prior reminding you to prepare for that appointment.

If managed properly, you can put that appointment out of mind and thus reduce mental noise and instead focus on the tasks in front of you today.

Establish a Routine: Your Ideal Day/Your Ideal Week

Many week-to-week items (such as a daily preview, a daily review, a once-a-week calendar cleanup, invoicing clients, paperwork, and other repetitive tasks) can be scheduled as repeating appointments. In addition, schedule in time for other weekly or monthly items (for instance, updating your blog or writing and distributing your newsletter).

If you want to make sure that you get these important items completed, you must add them to your calendar.

I have a standard starting time for my day, as well. I wake up early and do some writing, but I also practice guitar and work out. I don't put all of those things on my calendar, but I do ensure that I have a starting time. At the start of my day, I must be showered, shaved, and dress for the day. All the activities mentioned earlier in this paragraph must take place prior to that.

I also recommend that you start your day with a preview of the day's events and tasks that need completion. This gives you an idea as to what the flow of your day will be. Similarly, I recommend that you end the day with a review of the day's events and ensure that any notes written in notebook or on paper are transferred to your calendar.

I also reserve a few minutes every Sunday evening to go over the past week, bring forward any incomplete tasks or appointments, and ensure that any appointments for the coming week have been entered. I find that doing a review on Sunday evening allows me to start my week more relaxed because I know what's coming up (and so, no surprises).

Using Google Calendar

I previously used Microsoft Outlook for calendaring but switched to Google Calendar several years ago. It does not have all the features of Outlook, but it has many features that are too convenient to pass up.

Figure 27-2 shows Google Calendar with Google Tasks integrated.

I have a repeated calendar item and changed the color to green for morning writing time.

Tasks are non-time-specific items for a given day. In Google Calendar, they show up above your time-specific calendar items.

My Sunday, prepare for the week calendar review.

Regular calendar items block out specific times on my calendar.

Tasks and appointments can be dragged between days to easily adjust your calendar.

Figure 27-2   Google Calendar integrated with Google Tasks

Pre 12-Week Kickoff: Getting You Ready

Poof! You are a consultant.

That was easy, right?

Reality check! Everyone consults. We do it all the time. We have experience and talents that others want. If you are great with computers, your friend and friends of friends will ask you for help. If you are good with cars or home repair, there will be a stream of people seeking advice. When you offer that advice, you are consulting.

But the trick is to be paid for it. Money matters (although not necessarily in some greedy I-want-it-all sort of way). Even non-profit-minded philanthropic individuals must earn enough to be able to do their good deeds. Even churches have budgets.

I'm going to talk a lot about time and activity management and specifically about using your calendar and tasks list effectively. The first task I want on your list is this:

Make money.

This is not because I am greedy. After all, even if you are a nonprofit, you must remain in the black through donations. The truth is, if you are in business, making money had better be a top-of-list item. It is how you can assess your time effectively: Is this paid time? Does it support paid time? Does it lead to paid time?

That isn't to say that you won't do unpaid time or pro bono work. You probably will. In fact, if you are a computer professional, you already do; your family and friends call you all the time, right?

By the way, that is a good place to start your marketing. Sure, you aren't likely to charge your mother for tech support, but reaching out to those people who understand your value enough to take your time seems like a fair trade. Let them be the first people to get you referral business.

Let's Hang a Shingle and Win a Client

Sounds simple, right? Simple? Yes. Easy? No.

Conventional wisdom is going to tell you that you need a business name, a logo, a website, brochures, and a presentation. Those are all good things. They are cool! You'll feel more official when you have all of that.

However, I know more than a few profitable consultants who have a black-and-white business card with their name, telephone number, e-mail address, and the words *consultant* or *computer consultant* printed on it.

I'm not saying you don't want a website (you do) and that you don't want a logo (you might) or a brochure and a presentation (maybe).

But all of those things can come in time. I know a successful consultant with more than 20 years in the business who does not use his website, rarely has business cards available, and does not have any brochures. He is consistently busy, though, often turning down work.

Why? How?

Because he started with a few small clients and makes sure that they are taken care of. When asked what he does, he does not use words like *integration* or *systems engineering*. Instead, he might say, "I work on computers" or "You know those magical and confusing computer things? I make them work for you."

You don't need the perfect marketing tool. You don't need the "right circumstance." You need consistent action over time. That is what the 12-week concept is all about: consistent action.

How to Use the 12 Weeks

This section lists some of the activities that you might undertake in a given week. Don't be consumed with each item being completed perfectly. Don't be discouraged if something gets pushed into the next week.

However, if nothing is getting done and everything is being pushed into the next week, you need to reassess or reestablish your commitment. Progress requires that goals be met reasonably consistently.

Move through the checklists in Table 27-1 and be sure to visit the 12 Weeks to Profitable Consulting resources online at www.ITCareerToolkit.com for additional tips.

Table 27-1   12-Week Checklist

Week	Tasks/Concerns
1	Make a list of your reasons why you want to consult.
	Make a list of what makes you a good consultant.
	Assess and list your personal network of contacts.
	List the 3 most valuable services you could provide immediately.
	Create a 1-page consulting resumé. Make sure to list and emphasize the above skills first.
2	Create a simple business card.
	Create an elevator speech or quick pitch.
	Draft an introductory e-mail to what you do.
3	Research and register a domain name.
	Host your website. (I provide some hosting information online.)
	Select 20 to 30 e-mail addresses from within your personal network and send them your introductory e-mail.
	Hint: Ask for their feedback, as well. Let them know that you are starting a consulting business and ask whether the e-mail was clear. You may discover a lot.

Week	Tasks/Concerns
4	Write content (or have it written) for a simple 4-page consulting website using the information in this chapter.
	Set up a tracking sheet for e-mail responses and how many e-mails went out.
	Send out 20 to 30 more e-mails from within your personal network.
	Select 3 to 6 individuals who responded to your e-mail to speak with directly.
5	Select 2 past projects for a case study.
	Outline and begin writing at least 1 case study.
	Publish your initial consulting website.
	Follow up with at least 10 e-mail recipients.
	Send out 20 to 30 more e-mails from within your personal network. (You should be modifying based on feedback; plus, your website can now be included.)
6	Outline second case studies, finish the first.
	Beat the street: Visit at least 1 networking group and visit a local business park. Your goal is to distribute 20 resumés and/or case studies and gather at least 14 business cards from those businesses.
	Send out 20 to 30 more e-mails from within your personal network.
	Follow up with 5 to 10 e-mail recipients via phone.
	Publish a blog entry introducing your consulting business to the world (and specifically to your city).
7	Open an e-mail newsletter account. (I use mailchimp.com, but you should visit www.ITCareerToolkit.com for more options.)
	Beat the street: Visit 20 more local businesses.
	Call at least 6 to 8 of the businesses you visited the week prior.
	Send introductory e-mails to any business cards from the prior week (even those you spoke to on the phone).
	Publish the first case study as a blog entry (or with a link to a PDF in a blog entry).

continued

Table 27-1 continued

Week	Tasks/Concerns
8	You should be seeing some traction by the end of 4 to 8 weeks (conversations and some questions coming your way). You may be surprised that between week 4 and week 8 that you have generated interest from 1 or 2 clients. If not, do not worry. Consistent activity is as important as results at this point. However, you should be modifying your e-mail and your phone conversations based on the feedback you are receiving. **Beat the street:** Visit 20 more local businesses and a networking group. Call at least 6 to 8 of the businesses you visited the week prior. Send introductory e-mails to any business cards from the prior week (even those you spoke to on the phone). Send an e-mail to all past e-mail recipients (those from your personal newsletter and those you have "beat the street" to find). Ask if you can add them to your e-mail newsletter.
9	**Beat the street:** Visit 20 more local businesses. Call at least 8 to 12 of the businesses you visited the week prior and past weeks. Send introductory e-mails to any business cards from the prior week (even those you spoke to on the phone). Write 3 newsletter article ideas (blog entries, case studies, services, perhaps tips).
10	**Beat the street:** Visit 20 more local businesses and a networking group. Call at least 8 to 12 of the businesses you visited the week prior and past weeks. Send introductory e-mails to any business cards from the prior week (even those you spoke to on the phone). Create your initial e-mail newsletter; send on Tuesday or Wednesday morning.
11	**Beat the street:** Visit 20 more local businesses. Call at least 8 to 12 of the businesses you visited the week prior and past weeks. Send introductory e-mails to any business cards from the prior week (even those you spoke to on the phone).

Week	Tasks/Concerns
12	**Beat the street:** Visit 20 more local businesses and a networking group.
	Call at least 8 to 12 of the businesses you visited the week prior and past weeks.
	Send introductory e-mails to any business cards from the prior week (even those you spoke to on the phone).

Review Constantly

Each week, you need to consider the feedback you get. Your materials should be modified for feedback that is consistent across your contacts, not necessarily based on one person's response.

At 12 weeks, you will have e-mailed 80 to 140 personal contacts. You will have approached 120+ local businesses and engaged in many follow-up calls and e-mails. You will have generated one newsletter at least and written several blog entries.

I have not begun any additional online presence in the form of social media, but that should be on your radar by now. Of course, read Chapter 17 and Chapter 26. Those activities correlate very well to the marketing of consulting.

Remember, however, that marketing with newsletters, blogging, and social media are much less about broadcasting your services and more about sharing your knowledge. This is the holy grail of marketing.

If you are able to engage readers with content that helps them, solves a problem for them at that moment, they will remain engaged, and you are then the top-of-mind expert.

In Chapter 12, "Building an Active Contact List," I wrote, "It's who knows you and knows what you know!" That idea is what embodies today's marketing strategy for the consultant. You are letting them know you and know what you know.

Actions & Ideas

1. Write down what you find interesting or exciting about consulting. What scares you?

2. If you have done sales of some type before, what bothers you about sales? What do you like about sales?

3. Does it change your attitude about sales when you consider the product or services as highly valuable (that is, your talent)?

4. List four projects you've worked on that you could turn into case studies.

5. Take a quick guess as to how many people you have in your personal and professional network. Take an hour or two and go through your phone, contact list online, work connections, family, and friends (and friends of those people). How many people do you have in that network?

EXPAND YOUR TOOLKIT

Remember to visit the book's website at http://www.ITCareerToolkit.com for supplemental and ongoing advice, tips, and data relevant to this chapter.

Good Times... Bad Times...

Dave Ramsey, the financial planner mentioned in Chapter 25, "Financial Controls," tells his audience that if you have a pulse, you will experience a financial setback at some point over the course of your life. I have stolen that idea and translated it to careers. If you have a pulse, you are guaranteed a negative career event at some point.

And even during the good times, you have the regular challenges that come with life and career. My goal in this chapter is to give you some words of encouragement and ideas that I try to live by.

CHAPTER 28

Be Proactive! Be Positive! Add Value! Share Opportunity!

It makes sense for me to title this chapter with the mantra that I try to put into play every day. I believe that every day is a blessing and something to be grateful for. I also believe that we have a responsibility to live by some type of positive code.

I started using this statement last year, but I've always maintained a positive and forward-thinking mindset. It actually came about during an online conversation— almost an impromptu coaching session. It felt as though everything I recommended for a given situation was met with a corresponding reason why it could not/would not work.

Eventually, I explained to him that I simply believed that to have ongoing success, one must be proactive, be positive, add value, and share opportunity. I don't need to find a special angle or learn some secret technique on how to speak to people. I don't need to learn how to manipulate situations. I simply need to follow this mandate: **Be proactive! Be positive! Add value! Share opportunity!**

In those simple phrases, you can remedy being stuck, deal with crises, improve your professional networking, learn new technologies, and take advantage of opportunities as they arise.

No Job Makes a Career, No Job Breaks a Career

Another important idea that I want to emphasize is that no job makes or breaks your career. I want to remove some of the pressure you might feel about that one job interview, a recent firing or layoff from that perfect job, or the current job that seems to provide no opportunity for growth.

Take some of the pressure off of yourself. There is no perfect job, and that one interview (although interesting and perhaps exciting) was not the turning point in your career.

It isn't that you shouldn't love your job; you should. It isn't that you shouldn't be excited about an upcoming interview; you should be. If we place too much importance on the job or some external factors, some (many) beyond our control, we are setting ourselves up for frustration and anxiety.

I am also not suggesting that disappointment is not normal when something does not go right (or worse, goes wrong) in your career. That is normal.

Adversity Happens

Adversity is normal, and I know that all too well. A few years ago, while en route to write this book and another book, I experienced several challenges in my professional and personal life. They included separation and divorce, a small fire in our home, and then two weeks later a massive flood that destroyed nearly everything that I owned, and an ensuing professional malaise that was financially and emotionally devastating.

I referred to these situations as "act of God" moments, a term that insurance companies often use in their policies. In fact, some friends referred to me as Job. To this day, I have pictures and some personal belongings that are water-damaged and mud-stained with flood residue. Having your home torn down without any flood insurance (we were not in a flood plain) is a sobering experience.

The process of rebuilding is ongoing. I tell you this because there are many who, whether personal tragedy or broad economic fallout, have experienced similar turmoil.

It is normal to be depressed or anxious or angry or frustrated in these situations. I won't minimize that. However, you are still required to take some next steps.

Overcoming Adversity

When we face challenges, whether caused by our own actions or due to circumstances beyond our control, we can do a few things to more quickly deal with and rebound from the adversity.

Talk to Someone

This seems to be something men struggle with more then women—although not always. I suppose under the guise of being "strong" some men do not feel comfortable reaching out. However, a positive-minded friend can help you get things off your chest and also point you toward actions you can take to get your life back on track.

Look at What You Can Be Grateful For

None of my family or animals were injured or killed in our flood. In fact, oddly, my daughter had made a comment a few days before the flood that we should simplify and get rid of things. It was an ongoing joke, and even at the time I reflected that it was nice to be able to laugh about some of the loss.

People (relationships) are the thing we can most often be grateful for. But it could be your health, your talent, or something as simple as a garden or hobby.

Set a Schedule

This can be a difficult one, which is why it is so important. During times of stress or anxiety, we often fail to set a schedule. This lack of a plan can further exacerbate feelings of futility and can, in fact, lead to more wasted time—making life corrections even more challenging.

To this day, I try to plan my week out ahead of time on Sundays and block my time in a pretty strict fashion. I find this a helpful exercise for me personally, and I am confident it can help you as well.

Find Someone You Can Be Accountable To

This might be the person you share with or it might be a mentor of sorts. I befriended a pastor soon after the flood, and he and I exchanged e-mails and short phone calls each week. In them, I asked him to keep me accountable to my goals.

Find an Easy Success

Success breeds success. This is a great way to start getting over an adverse situation. Find small successes. It could be nothing more than taking care of a nagging chore or a very small but overlooked project at work. Whatever it is, you want to be able to have a few of these successes to build from.

Try to make these things you can accomplish in less than a week (and possibly even in a single day).

Staying Engaged with Your Career

Over the course of your career, you might be working on the same project or performing the same type of task for a long time. This might be years of working on the same code. It is helpful to keep yourself engaged with your career, and the following tips can help you do that.

Always Have a Pet Project

Google has something like this, and other companies have adopted similar programs. Basically, some portion of an employee's time each week is allocated to a project of his or her choice. Google, for instance, sets aside 20 percent of an engineer's working time for a project of his or her choosing. It is the engineer's pet project, but in many cases these become future products/projects for the company.

This type of policy allows employees to stay fresh while learning new skills and putting them to use. A few hours each week spent on a pet project can actually increase your productivity at your regular work. In addition, you might add something valuable to the company in the years to come.

Surround Yourself with Positive People

This seems like a no-brainer, but it is easy to find yourself spending time with negative people. Positive people are generally more engaged with their career and see opportunity before they see challenges. If you find that you are spending time with people who constantly complain about their job or the company they work for, it is only a matter of time before you do the same.

Find people who are moving forward and who speak in terms of possibility.

Take a Leader to Lunch Once in Awhile

Get to know some of your department's or company's leadership. Don't be afraid to ask them to lunch or grab a coffee with them. Ask them how their career progressed. Try to discern any prevailing attitudes or ideas that you might want to adopt.

You serve a secondary purpose by doing so: They will see you as someone who is engaged with your career. It doesn't happen that often, and you will stand out (in a good way).

Spread a Little Bit of Passion or Excitement About Technology to Youth

Local schools are always looking for people to share career experience and advice with students. Even early on in your career, you can share how you got to where you currently are. You don't need to be well established to engender some excitement about technology (specifically) or careers (in general).

Beware, though: Kids have short attention spans. So, prepare a fast-paced delivery. Don't go into too much detail. (Refer to Chapter 7, "Communication Skills," for more information about communicating effectively.) Having a simple audio/visual demonstration or a handout of some type might also help.

In fact, some larger employers already have programs that send employees to speak at local schools. If your company does not have such a program, search for some established local organizations that provide this service.

The process of helping others become interested in technology is a great way to remind you of why you are in the technology field.

You Make a Difference

I.T. directly and noticeably impacts people's lives. You might hear about it more when it does not work, but just remember how much technology helps people get their jobs done. It is important that you understand the difference you make to individuals and to the company you serve.

But more important, you make a difference in people's lives. Unrelated to I.T. and the work you perform, your attitude and demeanor on any given day has an impact.

As a simple goal, I try to make one person laugh each day. This is something I've done from the very start of my career started and is a natural part of my personality. And remember, you never know the impact something like this can have on others. A few years ago, I began communicating again with a friend I knew through middle school and high school. We exchanged a few e-mails, and then she told me something very sobering. She had experienced abuse during this time that I knew her in school. At one point, she even contemplated suicide. She told me that one of the main reasons she did not go through with it was that I had promised to make her laugh every day. I remember the promise, but I don't remember why I made it; we just shared an interest in reading.

So, do not underestimate your power to change someone's life both with the work you do and beyond your work, in your everyday life.

Where Do You Go from Here?

You've now reached the end of this book, and I hope that you found it valuable. Because you are now here, in the last chapter, I trust that you did, in fact, find it valuable.

Now it is up to you.

What do you want to do with your career? What goals do you want to set for the next month, year, 5 years, and beyond?

I don't want to overstate and talk about pie-in-the-sky unlimited potential. The truth is, we all have limitations in talent and time. But within those limitations, we have almost unlimited opportunities.

I want to hear from you, either via e-mail or online at www.ITCareerToolkit.com. Let me know what you plan as your next step. Share with me your short-term and long-term goals. Sharing them publicly may encourage others to share theirs as well.

So, visit the website or e-mail me at goals@ITCareerToolkit.com.

Happy career building!

My Reading List

You will be the same person in five years as you are today except for the people you meet and the books you read.

—Charlie "Tremendous" Jones

The preceding statement resonates with me. My heroes have always been authors. Ideas conveyed through the written word can educate you, change your perspective, and help motivate you to take consistent action. It is not uncommon for me to have two or three books around at any given time. I may be reading one book cover to cover, while referring to a couple others as needed.

This appendix describes a few books related to specific topics in *Building Your I.T. Career*. Others are simply additional tomes I've found useful. I've also listed a few websites I visit often.

Be sure to reference www.ITCareerToolkit.com, where I will include additional books as I add them to my list. And feel free to let me know what material you find valuable.

Websites

Rapidly changing technology means that some information (and certainly, connections with other professionals) is best found on the Web:

- **Asp.net**—This has been the best resource I've found for answering questions with Microsoft ASP.NET programming.

- **Tek-tips.com**—One of the earlier technology forums. It has been less active the past couple of years, but it still has an active and responsive community.

Books

- *Mastering Microsoft Windows Server 2008 R2*, Mark Minasi. Sybex. I first read Mark Minasi's book on Windows NT 3.51. His discussion on Windows Server technologies is, to me, the clearest and most pragmatic. You would do well to find his other titles, as well.

- *The Back Channel*, Cliff Atkinson. New Riders. This was given to me when I spoke at an event for my publisher. As a public speaker and advocate and coach for online presence/social media, the discussion on how social media impacts live presentations is both interesting and important to me. This book provides tips on exerting some control, or at least engaging the "back channel."

Writing and Communication

- *The Elements of Style*, William Strunk and E. B. White. Longman. Likely the only book you need to help you become a better writer. I've purchased copies for many of my clients and friends who express an interest in improving their writing.

- *On Writing: A Memoir of the Craft*, Stephen King. Scribner. As you can see, I just stated that *The Elements of Style* is the only writing you book you need. Stephen King says the same in this book. However, I found *On Writing* to be one of the more inspired writing books I've ever read, so I am including it here.

- *Public Speaking and Presentations for Dummies*, Rob Yeung and Malcolm Kushner. Wiley. I recommend this book because public speaking holds so much fear for so many. It is accessible and does a good job of diffusing the anxiety surrounding public speaking. In my chapter on communication, I recommend that you consider joining Toastmasters or taking a class on public speaking. Whether you join a formal organization or not, this book will provide some great insight into becoming a better presenter.

- *Presentation Zen*, Garr Reynolds. New Riders. Several blogs and books warn you against using PowerPoint in your presentations. This, in my opinion, is the best. Garr Reynolds provides great insight into how to create a slide deck that adds to your presentation rather than simply parrot what you are saying.

Leadership and Business

- *ReWork*, Jason Fried and David Heinemeier Hansson. Crown Business. I rank this as one of the best and easiest-to-read business books I've ever read. The founders of the productivity software company 37 Signals provide some of the most effective advice about efficient business strategies and decision making. You will never look at meetings or business plans the same.

- *Escape from Cubicle Nation*, Pam Slim. Berkley Trade. I met Pam Slim at the Phoenix Social Media club. Her no-nonsense and fun-to-read blog with the same name as this book grew in popularity until she was approached by a publisher. Her book provides both motivation and strategies for moving from corporate life to entrepreneur.

- *The Art of Non-conformity*, Chris Guillebeau. Perigee Trade. If you want to learn how to go after anything, Chris is the guy to teach you how. This is one of my favorite reads of all time.

- *The Facebook Effect*, David Kirkpatrick. Simon & Schuster Paperbacks, 2010. My cousin bought this book for me. At first, I was hesitant to read it. However, it is an excellent discussion about the growth of Facebook and social media in general. Also, it provides some insight into business truths worth understanding—namely, business and situations are fluid and require rapid decision making.

- *The Business Playground*, Dave Stewart and Mark Simmons. New Riders. This was another book provided to me by my publisher. Besides the fact that I find Dave Stewart to be a musical genius, the book provides some fun background into the creative process. It includes some games, but those were less compelling to me than the overall book itself. Definitely worth taking a look at.

- *Free Agent Nation*, Daniel Park. Business Plus. One of the more interesting reads about trends in consulting or a free-agent-based workforce. The title is dated, but if you can pick it up, it is worth understanding the how and why of a free-agent (consulting) workforce.

- *7 Habits of Highly Effective People*, Stephen Covey. Free Press. Covey's first book is still his best. This book studies what makes people effective and helps you understand and adopt those strategies in your life. In my opinion, his other books don't really add much to the ideas from this first book. So, this one is a must-read.

- *The 21 Irrefutable Laws of Leadership*, John Maxwell and Zig Ziglar. Nelson Books. Anything by John Maxwell and Zig Ziglar is bound to be good. If you are interested in discovering what leadership looks like and how you can become a better leader, read this book.

Miscellaneous

- *The One-Minute Manager*, Kenneth Blanchard. William Morrow & Company.

- *Who Moved My Cheese? An Amazing Way to Deal with Change in Your Work and in Your Life*, Spencer Johnson. Putnam Pub Group.

- *The Tipping Point*, Malcolm Gladwell, Back Bay Books. I recommend this book more than any of Gladwell's others. He addresses the concept of how trends, ideas, and products gather momentum in small increments until they "tip" and become widely known across the culture or business landscape.

Consulting

- *Flawless Consulting*, Peter Block. Pfeiffer. This is a classic in the field of management consulting. However, much of the information is great for the technical consultant, too (in particular, Block's understanding of what makes a consultant and his discussions about the client/consultant relationship).

- *The Business of Consulting*: *The Basics and Beyond*, Elaine Beich. Pfeiffer. This book covers the nuts and bolts of many of the business aspects of consulting. From determining your rate to marketing tips, correspondence, contracts, and negotiations, Beich does an excellent job of providing tangible and pragmatic information.

- *The Entrepreneur Magazine Small Business Advisor*, Entrepreneur Media, Entrepreneur Press. This book covers what you need to know to start, develop, and run a small business. This extremely concise and well-organized book covers everything from business plans to financial analysis and selling your business. If you're serious about your business, you'll refer to this book often.

- *The Goal*, Eliyahu Goldratt. North River Press. This classic in business literature was (and might still be) required reading in Pepperdine University's MBA program. Written as a novel, this book covers the restructuring of a manufacturing company. As the story develops, you discover, along with the protagonist, much of what doesn't work and some of the most useful ideas in business.

Conclusion

I would love to hear from you. If you've read any of these titles and loved them or hated them, let me know. Plus, I'm always looking for something to read. Feel free to visit www.ITCareerToolkit.com. Go to the Reading List page and let me know what you are reading.

Index

mentors, 260-264
  characteristics, 262-263
  mentoring others, 264
  need for, 261
  qualifications, 264
micro-automation, 247
micromanagers, 175
Minasi, Mark, 340
mindsets
  process-driven mindset,
    246-247
  tool-driven mindset, 13-14
  value-driven mindset, 27-28
mission statements, 252
money. *See* financial control
motivator career coach style, 270
multipart blog posts, 296
multiple mentors, 263
myth of limitation, 256
myth of self-made man, 62-63

N

National Speaker's Association,
  74
need for I.T. toolkit, 6-7
negotiating salary
  creativity, 163-164
  employer's perspective, 162-163
  firmness, 164
  flexibility, 165
  salary requirements, identifying,
    162
  unsuccessful negotiations,
    164-165
  when to start, 161-162
networking, 119-120, 172-173
  developing areas of interest, 121
  developing personality, 120-121
  engaging in conversation, 122
  enjoying people, 120
  impact of social media on, 186
  sharing opportunity, 125-126
  social media, 126
  tracking and remembering
    contacts, 122-125
newsletters, 313-314
NextGen Image Gallery, 300
nonlinear nature of careers, 15

O

objectives, 244-245, 252
obsolescence, fear of, 80-81
offshoring, 26-27
omissions, 257
on-the-job promotions. *See*
  promotions, earning
*On Writing: A Memoir of the
  Craft* (King), 340
The One-Minute Manager
  (Blanchard), 342
online personae to avoid, 186
  Angry Individual, 187
  Conspiracy Theorist, 187
  Family Strife Poster, 189
  Party Animal, 187-188
  Unwanted Kisser, 188
  Used Car Salesman, 188
  Vulgar Vicky or Lewd Larry,
    188
online presence, 72
opportunities in I.T. careers, 22
  continuous learning
    opportunities, 24-25
  options, 22-23
  pay and perks, 25-26
  performance-based
    advancement, 23-24
  sharing, 125-126, 190
options
  creating with financial control,
    282
  in I.T. careers, 22-23
organizing presentations, 75
origins of COP (Concept Over
  Process), 245
out-of-town job searches, 142-143
outlines
  for job searches, 133-135
  for presentations, 76
outsourcing
  cost versus value, 27-28
  jobs that won't be outsourced,
    29
  local outsourcing, 27
  offshoring, 26-27
overcoming adversity, 333-334
ownership, attitude of, 61-62

P

paper-certified, 20
paragraph development, 71
Park, Daniel, 342
Party Animal (personality type),
  187-188
passion, 237-238
passive job searches, 136-138
pay
  considerations when choosing a
    career, 35-36
  for consultants, 211
  negotiating, 161
    creativity, 163-164
    *employer's perspective,
      162-163*
    firmness, 164
    flexibility, 165
    *salary requirements,
      identifying, 162*
    *unsuccessful negotiations,
      164-165*
    when to start, 161-162
  realistic salary expectations,
    25-26
peer knowledge network,
  creating, 235-236
perception, correcting, 108-109
performance-based advancement,
  23-24
perks of I.T. careers, 25-26, 167
personal use of social media,
  185-186
personal value, attitude of, 60-61
personality development, 120-121
personality styles of bosses,
  175-177
personality types to avoid online,
  186
  Angry Individual, 187
  Conspiracy Theorist, 187
  Family Strife Poster, 189
  Party Animal, 187-188
  Unwanted Kisser, 188
  Used Car Salesman, 188
  Vulgar Vicky or Lewd Larry,
    188

PEARSON

ALWAYS LEARNING

PEARSON IT CERTIFICATION

Browse by Exams ▼ | Browse by Technology ▼ | Browse by Format | Explore ▼ | I'm New Here – Help!

Store | Forums | Safari Books Online

Pearson IT Certification
THE LEADER IN IT CERTIFICATION LEARNING TOOLS

Visit **pearsonITcertification.com** today to find:

- IT CERTIFICATION EXAM information and guidance for

  CISCO CompTIA Microsoft vmware

  Pearson is the official publisher of Cisco Press, IBM Press, VMware Press and is a Platinum CompTIA Publishing Partner—CompTIA's highest partnership accreditation

- EXAM TIPS AND TRICKS from Pearson IT Certification's expert authors and industry experts, such as

  - *Mark Edward Soper* – CompTIA
  - *David Prowse* – CompTIA
  - *Wendell Odom* – Cisco
  - *Kevin Wallace* – Cisco and CompTIA
  - *Shon Harris* – Security
  - *Thomas Erl* – SOACP

- SPECIAL OFFERS – **pearsonITcertification.com/promotions**

- REGISTER your Pearson IT Certification products to access additional online material and receive a coupon to be used on your next purchase

Articles & Chapters

Blogs

Books

Cert Flash Cards Online

eBooks

Mobile Apps

Newsletters

Podcasts

Question of the Day

Rough Cuts

Short Cuts

Software Downloads

Videos

CONNECT WITH PEARSON IT CERTIFICATION

Be sure to create an account on **pearsonITcertification.com** and receive members-only offers and benefits